D0851941

The World of Wine

The World of Wine

David McCormack

Crescent Books

New York

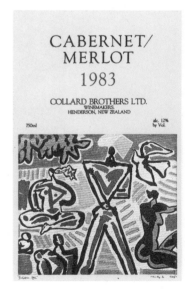

Contents

Morning mists cloak a valley in Rioja, producer of
some of Spain's best wines.

*J.E. Seppelt's liqueurs and bitters essence room at
Seppeltsfield, South Australia, established 1865.*

Preface

IT IS NOW almost a half century since Henri Soulé, self-appointed minister of French culinary culture, brought what was then the last word in fancy French cookery to New York's 1939 World's Fair. A couple of years later he opened his legendary restaurant Pavillon in the city itself, and some years after that its sister restaurant La Côte Basque — the only one of his enterprises that survives to this day. By Soulé's imperious lights, he was bringing to New York — and, by extension, to the western hemisphere — not only *haute cuisine*, but civilization itself. Were he to rise from his grave to dine at La Côte Basque today, and were he to send for the wine list, it is likely that there would be nothing civilized at all in his reactions to the current version of that document. True, it offers principally, as it always has, products that have been produced in France since long before living memory. But it incorporates as well wines from, of all places, California. Soulé would no more have served California wine than *sushi*.

Upon a time it was believed — and not only by the Henri Soulés of this world — that wine was a beverage made in France and imitated elsewhere. And so it continues to be believed, albeit somewhat less widely, to this day. In fact there is much truth to a slight restatement of the notion: *French* wine is made in France and imitated elsewhere. And wherever the imitation proceeds, a certain kind of failure, willy-nilly, follows. For wine, like art when it is well made, obeys only its own rules — which are implicit in the soil and climate in which the grapes are grown, in the individuality of the winemaker, and in the play of his style on the materials with which he works. Imitative wine is never what it might have been, but it will continue to be made as long as new wines are judged by old ones.

In time, one imagines hopefully, wines made in, say, Australia of Cabernet Sauvignon grapes will not be compared automatically to wines made in Bordeaux of the same fruit. In other words, a first-class Victoria will no more be judged a second-rate Médoc than a *quiche Lorraine* a misguided plate of bacon and eggs. (You will do well, however, not to look for the universal embrace of this broad-mindedness in the present century.) If that time ever comes, it will be when winemakers entertain dreams of their own, rather than the current one of outclassing "world-class" châteaux in blind taste competitions (events in which wines compete with one another in the manner of eggplants or bulls, and which serve only to perpetuate the evaluation of all wines by the ancient standards of a few).

Of course, the world really has not been saddled with a single set of wine styles ever since the time that grape juice was first fermented. There is nothing French about the wines of France's neighbors — Italy, Spain and Germany. In fact, the wines of those countries express with striking clarity the regions in which they are produced. And despite this evidence — that superior wines are distinctly characteristic of their regions, and never at all of regions across the border — most winemakers in new locales, including those in North America, are trying to squeeze Old World wine from New World land. Excellent wine is made in Europe, and much may be learned from how it is done and how it is not done, but the most important lesson is that no one in Bordeaux, for example, is struggling to turn out a first-class Riesling or Rioja — or, for that matter, Burgundy.

It is the especial merit of this volume that, though it duly acknowledges European achievements, it treats the continents of the rest of the globe not as inferior siblings, but only as (viniculturally) younger ones. As David McCormack notes, wine is now produced in most of the states and provinces of the United States and Canada, as well as in most of the countries to the south. And though, of the myriad winemakers in the business, most are simply in business, there are those who make wine not only to sell it, but also study their results in the way that — as Mr. McCormack points out in his Introduction — the early European monks did, with an eye to determining the secrets of the properties they work. Since these producers are only infrequently monks, most of their study is aimed at determining answers to questions about cost efficiency, marketability and profitability. But there are those — many of them operators of the so-called "boutique vineyards," small, intensely managed properties — whose first purpose is to turn out excellent wine. In the effort, some of these pioneers have created a number of bizarre bottlings, but even that unavoidable judgment is the product, in part, of prejudices based on old standards. However, many vineyards established in recent decades — particularly in California, but also in other parts of North America and in the other viniculturally youthful continents — have created wines that are undeniably of the first water. This has to be accounted very rapid progress for, in making wine, a lesson is often not learned until years after the decisions, right or wrong, have been made — when the mature wine itself hands down the final verdict.

The making of good wine will become a commonplace when each region is studied for its own potential. *The World of Wine*, happily, is a view of *all* the winegrowing regions of the world — the old ones, the young ones, even the future ones.

Seymour Britchky
New York

Opposite: *Winter sunshine glints past mountains onto a California vineyard.*

Introduction

No ONE KNOWS when or where wine was first made, or by whom. Noah is sometimes given the honor because of the reference to his planting a vineyard on leaving the Ark, but, to my mind, the fact that he had knowledge of viticulture prior to entering the Ark may indicate that winemaking was already an established pursuit in the antediluvian era.

My personal theory is that the whole thing was an accident. I surmise that a neglected bunch of grapes, left in some kind of an open vessel, went about its natural business of fermenting. In time, some tidy-minded individual decided to clean the vessel, got some of the fermented juice on a finger, idly licked the juice, and the wine industry was born.

Given the way the roles of the sexes have developed over the centuries, it is probable, according to my theory, that the world's first wine maker was a woman. I also like to think that it was while sipping some wine that inspiration came to the inventor of the wheel. Whimsy aside, it is almost certain the cultivation of the vine began somewhere in the lands of the eastern Mediterranean.

The Egyptians were familiar with wine, and there are many references and illustrations about wine in the pyramids. It was, however, the period of the Greek Empire that saw the beginning of the expansion of viticulture that was to spawn the vineyards of Europe as we know them today.

There can be no doubt that the conquering Roman Legions, and their subsequent lengthy occupations of much of Europe, resulted in significant growth of vine plantings, particularly in France and Germany.

By the fifth century, when the Romans either went home or remained to assimilate into the societies they had built, many of what are now the world's finest vineyards were already planted with vines. Even England and Wales had thriving wine industries.

The fall of Rome plunged Europe into a darkness that lasted for almost five hundred years. During that time, the power of the church grew, and many new monasteries were established. The monks became the custodians of wine evolution by virtue of developing new vineyards and adding to their vineyard holdings through bequests.

One other major contribution of the monks was that they were methodical. They took note of which vines responded most generously, what caused the vines to yield the best grapes, and what fermentation and cellaring procedures resulted in the best wines.

Among the results of their meticulous methods was the recognition that certain varieties were better suited to specific locations than others. It was they who began to concentrate on the propagation of Pinot Noir for the red wines of the Côte d'Or and Chardonnay for the whites. They also observed that in the more southerly district of Beaujolais conditions were ideal for the Gamay.

In Bordeaux, a larger number of vines were found to be particularly suitable. Of these, the Cabernet Sauvignon and Merlot were most important for reds, while the Sémillon and Sauvignon Blanc emerged as the best for whites. Moving north into Germany, the monks there concluded that the Riesling yielded the most regal wines, while the Sylvaner was identified as a solid performer for the production of very sound, if not outstanding wines.

This pattern of selecting particular vines for specific areas continued throughout Europe, but all of the vines chosen had one thing in common: over and above being of the genus *Vitis*, they were all of the species *vinifera*. The full significance of this family relationship between all of the European wine-producing grape varieties did not become

Opposite: Wine casks overlook the sea in Banyuls, in the south of France.

fully apparent until the settlement of the Eastern United States and Eastern Canada, where native grapes of the *Vitis labrusca, riparia* and *rotundifolia* were found to produce wines of inferior quality.

The magnitude of the monks' contribution can be appreciated, to some degree, when it is realized that while there are some 8,000 grape varieties cultivated today, there are still only a few dozen that are recognized as being capable of providing genuinely superior wines, and only about the same small number that can be relied upon to consistently produce good, pleasant wines.

To a very large extent, the monks laid the foundation of techniques upon which the wines we know today are based.

A major discovery that changed several things in the wine trade was that of the cork. This happened late in the seventeenth century, and it gradually became apparent that wine stored in bottles with a tight-fitting cork kept better than a wine kept in casks which had a tendency to sour after the level of wine in the barrel fell.

Early bottles, however, were dumpy in form, and did not lie down easily. This led to the development of bottles that lay flat and could be conveniently stacked in cellars or racks. This in turn, and over time, revealed that wines kept in this manner matured differently, and often acquired an attractive bouquet and greater complexity and depth of flavor.

Coincidentally with the introduction of the cork, the corkscrew was invented, but no one knows to whom credit should be given for that ingenious tool.

Even in Europe, the wine industry has been, and

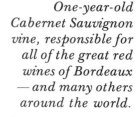

One-year-old Cabernet Sauvignon vine, responsible for all of the great red wines of Bordeaux — and many others around the world.

still is, in a constant state of evolution. One of the most important developments occurred in 1863 when Napoleon III, a man who obviously took his wines seriously, appointed Louis Pasteur to investigate all of the things that could cause a change in the nature of a wine. Pasteur fortunately took this assignment to heart, and can justifiably be regarded as the father of modern oenology.

He set out to document the precise nature of the alcoholic fermentation that turns grape juice into wine. He then went on to examine the diseases of wine and sought methods for their treatment. After only two years of intensive research he presented the Emperor with his monumental work, "Studies on wine, its diseases and the causes which provoke it; new and old ways of keeping it."

One of Pasteur's most far-reaching discoveries was of the effect of air, or more accurately oxygen, on wine. He correctly determined that excessive exposure to air would cause the development of vinegar bacteria in wine. Likewise, however, he identified the fact that very small amounts of air were beneficial to wine and, in fact, concluded that the influence of air was what caused wine to change for the better as it matured. He even proved that there was enough air dissolved in a bottle of wine to cause it gradually to age over a long period of time.

The way he proved the accuracy of his conclusions was by sealing wines in test tubes. Some of the test tubes were full, while others were sealed half-full. The wines in the half-full test tubes, exposed to much more air, changed so rapidly that in a few weeks, they had thrown a deposit such as would not normally develop in a bottle of wine until many years had elapsed. In this experiment he also showed that the air caused the color to fade in red wines, and that it turned white wines brown.

Pasteur showed that wines in barrels, while they picked up such desirable characteristics as extra tannin, are also exposed to greater amounts of air than is the case once they are bottled. He also proved that extra exposure to air occurs when wines are being racked, changed from one barrel to another, and that even the nature of the barrel could alter the condition and speed of aging of the wine. He illustrated this point by citing a cask at Clos de Vougeot which had been painted. The wine in the painted cask invariably tasted about

*Left and below:
Vintage season in
the mountainous
Douro region of
Portugal*

*Overleaf Brazil is
the third largest
wine producer in
South America, with
vineyards covering
nearly 120,000 acres.*

two years younger than the wines stored in unpainted casks.

These observations about barrels finally led him to the conclusion that, while a certain amount of aging in cask was beneficial, excessive time in barrels would finally cause the wine to deteriorate.

The process for which Pasteur is best remembered, pasteurization, required the wine to be heated to about 60° C (140° F). While this process kills the bacteria in the wine and is an effective cure for the ills that can be caused by acetic and lactic bacteria, it also eliminates any possibility of the wine developing. In practice, pasteurization of wine is carried out by heating the bottles in hot water prior to their being filled with wine, but as this has the side effect of neutralizing the elements that cause the wine to improve with age, it is used only for ordinary table wines.

Pasteur's work was invaluable in making the vignerons (wine-growers) of the world understand, and, subsequently, control fermentation and the storage and handling of wines prior to bottling. His pasteurization process actually proved more practical in making milk safe to drink and in beer making.

Tragically, at the same time that Pasteur was experimenting and investigating, the most devastating predator of the vine was about to make its presence known.

Phylloxera vastatrix, an aphid native to Eastern North America, was brought to France on vines that were imported from North America for experimental purposes. Aptly named the ravager, phylloxera was first observed at Gard in 1864 and in less than twenty years it had devastated almost every vineyard in Europe. The anguish of the vignerons is not hard to imagine. Accustomed to coping with frost, hail, and other vagaries of the weather, not to mention such vine diseases as mildew, they were faced with a foe against which they had no weapons. In fact, if tears had been an effective solution, all the vignerons would have had to do to turn the tide would have been to walk in their vineyards.

The tiny predator, however, was not to be moved by tears. But water was tried as an answer when it was observed that the aphid hibernated in the root system of the vines. A method known as submersion was tried, but it was only partially successful, and then only in low-lying vineyards. Even to this

day, there are some submerged vineyards to be found near the Mediterranean coast. Other methods were attempted, including injecting the soil with carbon bisulphide, but all such efforts were to no avail in halting the relentless invasion of the pervasive phylloxera.

Finally, however, it was noted that phylloxera caused no damage to its North American host vine. It was a short step from this observation to the conclusion that European vines grafted to American root stock would probably share the same immunity to predation.

Fortunately, this proved to be the case, and the vines that had introduced the curse also transpired to provide the solution. By the beginning of this century almost all productive vines in Europe had been re-established by grafting to American root stocks. Initially, there were reservations that this marriage of two species of vines would result in inferior wines. As the rejuvenated vineyards came of age for wine making, it soon became apparent that the grafted vinifera vines had absolutely no trace of the undesirable characteristics of the labrusca wines.

With tragedy thus averted, the vignerons got back to the business of making wine. The cost of replanting the vineyards fell entirely upon the vignerons and other members of the wine trade. In France alone, the cost was somewhere in the order of 1,800 million francs. Considering that a tonneau containing 225 litres (59 gallons) of even the finest Bordeaux wines was selling for 4,000 francs, and considerably less for lower growths, the cost of recovering from the phylloxera devastation was enormous.

Some old vineyard areas, in fact, were never replanted and simply disappeared from the world of wine. For those who continued in business, however, the phylloxera disaster was little more than a bad memory by the turn of the century.

During this century, there have been two major influences. One is the pursuit of naturalness, and the other is technical development. The latter has given winemakers far greater control over what they produce. Much of the chance element in producing a good wine has been eliminated to the point where a truly badly made wine is now rarely found.

Viewed in the most basic way, wine is made from grape juice by the entirely natural chain of events known as fermentation, which is the chemical reaction that turns sugar into alcohol and carbon dioxide gas. The catalyst that causes this process to begin is the yeasts that are found on grape skins. As about one-third of the pulp of grape is sugar, all it takes for the yeasts to go to work is for the skin of the grape to be broken. Nature will then go about the business of making wine.

In practice, however, Mother Nature is not one of the world's most reliable wine makers, and it takes the intelligent interference of man, and in increasing numbers woman, to exercise controls to ensure that the end result is the best wine that can possibly be made.

It is many years, for example, since natural yeasts were permitted to live, far less act upon the juice to commence fermentation. Natural yeasts were found to be unreliable. One year they would carry out their task to perfection, but the next year they might prove lethargic and loath to start work. Not only vignerons, but also consumers, would be unhappy if such a situation had been allowed to continue. After literally hundreds of experiments, reliable, energetic, ambitious strains of yeast were developed. Different yeasts were found that acted best in specific areas. One strain of yeast is predominantly used in Burgundy, while a completely different strain was created for Champagne, and strains specially suitable for vinification in Germany were isolated. This process has been carried out in every part of the wine-making world, so that every wine maker now has a completely reliable catalyst for fermentation at his disposal.

Just as wild yeasts have been replaced with

Red wines age in imported wood at Hardy's Tintara Winery, McLaren Vale, South Australia.

When the buds begin to flower, the vines need warm, sunny weather to promote pollenation.

While much vine-tending is still done by hand, harvesting has become increasingly mechanized in many countries.

Vines must be sprayed regularly to guard against such pests as red spiders, phylloxera, and mildew.

cultured yeasts, so too has the romantic picture of peasants treading grapes with their feet disappeared.

In modern wine making, white grapes are usually first put through a stemmer crusher that removes the stems and crushes the grapes, which are then pumped into a press. There are two main types of horizontal presses used in making white wines. One is a screw press, which brings two steel plates together to press the grapes. The other is a bladder press, which operates when a bladder running the length of the press is inflated to give a gentle crush to the grapes. In each case, the juice is pumped directly from the press to fermentation tanks.

Although some fermentation is still done in wooden vats or casks, it is now much more common to use stainless steel fermenters. These steel fermenters are often jacketed to accommodate coils of pipes through which cold water can be pumped to allow the wine maker to control the temperature of the fermentation. This is particularly beneficial in the making of white wines where a slow fermentation is frequently desirable.

In making red wines, the grapes are put through a crusher and the juice, pulp and skins are pumped directly into a fermenter. This allows the juice to take color from the skins. The length of time the wine is left on the skins varies according to the amount of color the wine maker wants the wine to acquire.

Once the wine maker decides that it is time to remove the wine from the skins, the "free-run" wine is drawn off to another fermenter. The skins and pulp are then pumped into a vertical press which has a steel plate that is brought down on top of the grapes to press out the remaining wine. This "press-wine" is then usually added to the "free-run" wine, and the fermentation continues.

Once fermentation is complete, it is up to the individual wine maker to decide whether the wine will then be aged in small barrels and for how long. Barrel aging adds many elements to the wine, particularly reds which pick up extra tannin and other esters from the wood.

Even the type of wood used makes a considerable difference to the characteristics imparted to the wines. The French oak casks made with Navarre and Limousin oak are amongst the most highly regarded, but many other woods are used, including Yugoslavian and American oak and chestnut.

Although some wine makers produce unfined and unfiltered wines, the vast majority of wines are both fined and filtered. Traditional fining agents such as egg whites, blood and bentonite clay have been largely replaced by centrifuges and filtering machines. The result is that it is comparatively rare to see a wine that is not impeccably clear and appears brilliant to the eye.

One unnecessary process that has been introduced in recent years is equipment that is based on refrigeration and will cause the tartaric crystals, usually referred to as wine diamonds, to be precipitated from the wine. In saying that this is an unnecessary step, I mean that tartaric crystals, rather than being a flaw in a wine, indicated that it was a well-made, healthy wine. The problem, however, is that the vast majority of new wine consumers perceive wine diamonds as unclean. Consequently, as it is impossible for the wine producers to explain the facts to each individual, the easiest approach was to devise a method of removing the crystal from the wine prior to bottling.

During 1985, a series of disturbing discoveries were made regarding the fitness of some wines for consumption. A few wine makers in Austria were found to have added diethylene glycol, a

Above: *Once the vines flower, the vineyard workers can cut out any unwanted buds to encourage higher quality in the remaining buds.* Below: *Treading of grapes has long since given way to the use of machinery to extract juice.*

Stainless steel fermentation tanks in a Brazilian winery.

component of anti-freeze, to their wines. Two Canadian wineries in Ontario were later discovered to be following the same practice. At the same time one Italian wine producer was also found to have added anti-freeze to his wines. A second concern emerged with the discovery of excessive amounts of Mesurol, a chemical bird repellant, in wines from New Zealand and California and Washington in the United States.

Although it is completely unacceptable from the point of view of human health, the presence of excessive amounts of Mesurol in some wines is understandable. It is a comparatively new chemical and farmers, bent only on protecting their crops from predation, may have used more than was necessary. Likewise, the wineries may have been unaware of the presence of excessive amounts of the chemical. This is a problem caused by progress, and it can be resolved either by reducing the dosage in the vineyards, or by extending the time prior to harvesting when the chemical can be applied. Alternately, the wineries can introduce ways of treating the grapes to eliminate the chemical prior to crushing.

Previous page: Autumn descends on a vineyard in British Columbia, Canada.

The presence of diethylene glycol, however, is another matter entirely, because it was deliberately added during the wine making process. There can be absolutely no acceptable explanation for any such practice. There have always been, and, in all probability, there always will be unscrupulous wine producers who will resort to any methods to enhance an inferior product, and they will unashamedly foist their wines on an unsuspecting public until such time as they are caught.

In the wake of such scandals the saddest consequence is that suspicion falls upon every wine maker. People whose families have produced honest wines for generations are suddenly subjected to questions about the authenticity of their wines. Likewise, relative newcomers in the same area as the culprits find themselves disbelieved when they deny using such practices on their own wines.

Only time and perseverance will finally dispel the cloud as people begin to accept the fact that there was never any question of their wines being of sound quality.

Such scandals apart, and in the world of wine

Wines may be stored and aged in wooden casks or in bottles, as in this Portugese wine cellar.

they are fortunately very rare, the study of wines is an exciting, ever-changing subject.

For example, the spread of the vine to the New World has added considerably to the variety of wines that are available. South Africa, Australia, New Zealand, Canada, the United States and South America all produce wines of various qualities. Some of those are of such high quality that they rival, and in some cases surpass, all but the very best of Old World wines.

The New World provides a continuing sense of excitement as established areas gradually improve their quality and range of wines and new areas are opened up to the cultivation of the vine. In the United States, for example, California has long enjoyed a particularly good reputation for its best wines, but now such states as Washington, Oregon and many others are rapidly developing vineyards and producing very attractive wines.

Not that the New World has exclusivity on innovation. The vine has returned in considerable strength to England and Wales, and their wines are gaining a reputation for soundness.

The endless fascination of wine owes much to its infinite variety. The range of grapes used to make wine presents an almost infinite range of tastes. Added to this, the same grape grown in different soil and in a different climate will yield yet another individual wine experience.

Wines made with the Cabernet Sauvignon grape under the hot Australian sun, for example, will have a depth of color and character that does not occur in the cooler conditions found in Bordeaux where, nevertheless, it can be reasonably argued that the finest wines made from the Cabernet Sauvignon are produced.

Similar differences are apparent with other grape varieties. Just as Bordeaux is held to be the producer of the finest Cabernet Sauvignon wines, so too Burgundy sets the standard by which Pinot Noir and Chardonnay wines are judged, and the Rheingau, Nahe and Mosel-Saar-Ruwer in Germany make the wines from the Riesling grape that are considered the pinnacle for wines made with that variety.

For the wine lover, one of the joys that the expansion of the wine world provides is the possibility of bringing together the wines made from the

same grape in various parts of the world for a comparative tasting to learn what the different soil and climatic conditions contribute to the style of wine that can be made.

Each vintage offers a new point of reference. A poor year gives an experience that adds to the appreciation of better years, while the occasional perfect year yields wines of such monumental character that they will live in the memory forever.

Too much, however, can be made of vintages. Granted, it is almost impossible to over-rate such vintages as 1961 in Burgundy, Bordeaux or Côtes du Rhône; however, it is unwise to be too hasty in condemning an apparently poor year.

Just as 1961 has been exalted as the best French vintage since either 1945 or 1929, so 1954 has been vilified as an indifferent vintage. True, no one could claim it as a great year, but I recall being served a Clos de Vougeot of that vintage in 1979. Time had been kind to this ugly duckling. It was light, to be sure, but it had an elegance and charm that made it a perfect selection with an equally light and elegant luncheon.

Just as assembling wines from around the world made from one grape variety can be instructive, so too can a great appreciation of vintage variations be learned by conducting a vertical tasting of a single wine. In such a tasting, the outstanding vintages will become clearly apparent, but perhaps the greatest surprise will come from the realization that the wines from so-called poor vintages, far from tasting bad, are usually perfectly pleasant wines that lack only the character to age as long as the sturdier wines of favored years.

In fact, vintages that are described as poor or fair are well worth watching as they are usually sound wines that were deprived of greatness be-cause of the vagaries of the weather during their growing season. These lesser wines have a unique attraction in that they are generally sold at significantly lower prices than the wines of the finest years. A prime example of this occurred with the 1972 vintage in Bordeaux. It was apparent right from the start that this was not going to be a great vintage; some went so far as to condemn it as the worst vintage of the century. I, and many other open-minded wine lovers, will be eternally grateful to these vociferous critics. The effect of their words was that the 1972 wines sold at rock-bottom prices and provided some excellent drinking that did not break the budget. These young-drinking wines also served the purpose of reducing the temptation to broach bottles from superior vintages resting in the cellar!

Unquestionably, the most important thing in exploring the world of wine is an open mind. By all means be guided by the observations of those with extensive experience, but finally, it is up to each individual to determine his or her own preferences.

Almost everyone starting to explore the world of wines will find the sweeter wines such as the white wines of Germany or the rosés of Anjou in the Loire Valley an enjoyable starting point. The palate, however, will gradually develop, first to the point where dry white wines become appreciated. At about this point, such light red wines as Beaujolais are found to be pleasant and, finally, an appreciation of dry red wines develops.

This development should not be construed to mean that at each step the wines you previously enjoyed will become unenjoyable. Rather it means that, with the passage of time, an appreciation of a greater and greater range of wines become possible.

The vineyards of Alsace run like a ribbon less than a mile wide along the slopes of the Vosges.

France

FRANCE AND WINE are so inexorably linked, they are virtually synonymous. This is not because the country is one gigantic vineyard; rather, it is because centuries of diligent dedication have resulted in vineyards being planted on the most favorable sites, with the result that an incredible array of fine wines is produced.

The French wine producers have devoted themselves, with an unstinting singleness of mind, to determining the best grape varieties for each region, and thereafter developing viticultural and vinicultural techniques to yield the best wines possible.

At their best, the wines of France's wine-growing regions set the world standard against which wines from other parts of the world are judged. Whether this is fair, or even warranted, is questionable, but it is a fact.

It should be borne in mind, however, that France also produces a lot of wine that can most kindly be described as *très ordinaire*. They are usually labelled simply as *vin de table*.

In all probability, the wines of France centuries ago were not of the quality that they are today. In part, this is due to improvements in technology and, if you will, clearly illustrates the truth of the old aphorism that practice makes perfect.

One factor in French wine production that is responsible for the quality of the wines we know today is the *appellation contrôlée* regulations which were introduced only about fifty years ago.

These regulations can be applied to individual vineyards or to specified regions or villages. The appellation laws control almost everything that can be done in the vineyard and with the grapes once they are harvested, right up to the point where the wine is bottled.

In the vineyard, the variety and number of vines per hectare are controlled, as are the number of buds that can be left on the vine each year. The yield is controlled, both in the weight of grapes that it is permitted to harvest and in the quantity of wine that can be made from those grapes. These regulations vary from region to region, reflecting the maximum yields according to climatic conditions and grape variety.

The appellation contrôlée regulations in some regions, notably Burgundy, permit *chaptalisation*, the addition of sugar to the grape juice prior to fermentation, which is strictly controlled.

While there are occasional scandals about fraudulent wines being produced by unscrupulous individuals, the majority of wine producers and merchants adhere to the appellation laws as they recognize that these laws protect their own names and, in turn, generate consumer confidence.

In the various regions of France, certain individual vineyards have come to be recognized over time as producing the finest wines. This is particularly true in Bordeaux and Burgundy, which have developed classification systems ranking the wines of their best vineyards at various levels. The most famous, and easily understood, is the classification of Médoc in Bordeaux which was carried out in 1855 and has stood the test of time with few changes.

Below the appellation contrôlée wines are a level of wines designated as Vins Délimités de Qualité Supérieure (VDQS). These are sound wines that are as strictly regulated as appellation contrôlée wines, but are not expected to attain the same stature as the finest wines. Nevertheless, some VDQS wines can attain very high quality and have the added attraction of being reasonably priced.

No one can explain why France, more than any other country, has the capability of producing such a wide variety of truly great wines. The simple truth is that it does and, rather than try to analyze why, the wine lover is better advised to go on in blissful ignorance, giving thanks that there is such a bountiful supply of great wines to be appreciated.

Opposite:
Chaumont-sur-Loire, France.

BURGUNDY

Now, who would dare to say what is the wine of Burgundy? All that it is, all that it means to us, all that it gives by its subtle aroma, all that testifies to its harshness, its firm flesh or sensual caress . . . all that it takes to spell out from the moment that it starts its Dionysiac life gently bubbling in the vats . . . all that it perfects in the ritual stillness of the underground cellars; such is the beautiful Adonis of the Greeks, the living emanation begot from a soil which has accumulated offerings and legacies, the noble earth, the earth whose patrician veins know how to bleed in the sun!

GASTON ROUPNEL

THE REPUTATION of the wines of Burgundy is so great that its diminutive vineyard area comes as a complete surprise to most visitors. The Côte-d'Or which yields the most noble of the region's wines is a mere 30 miles of vineyards stretching, in a narrow band, from Dijon in the north to Chagny in the south. To the south of the Côte-d'Or are the Mercurey and Mâconnais districts which lead to the threshhold of Beaujolais, Burgundy's largest wine-producing district. Finally, some 45 miles north west of Dijon, and quite remote from the rest of Burgundy, lies the town of Chablis whose name has become almost too famous.

Burgundies are expensive and some people would say over-priced. In fact, because of the small quantity produced, the high price is set by the fundamental rules of supply and demand.

Steeped in history, and with a wine reputation pre-dating the Christian era, Burgundy has retained a charming rustic simplicity which belies her centuries of fame and fortune. The present stature of Burgundian wines can be traced back to the sixth century when a number of monasteries were established throughout the region. The monks, whatever the success of their other endeavors, were extremely accomplished vineyardists and wine makers. Wars and other social upheaval caused many disruptions in the cultivation of the vine, but in the twelfth century, the monks finally established the vineyards upon which Burgundy's fame rests today. Later, the Dukes of Burgundy became willing ambassadors for the wine of their duchy and were so successful in the promotion of their region's wines that they came to the attention of Louis XIV, who drank the wines of the Côte-d'Or on the recommendation of his doctor.

Unlike Bordeaux, with its great estates and imposing mansions, Burgundy is the most fragmented important wine-growing district in France, and grand houses are a rarity. The fragmentation of Burgundy causes a degree of unpredictability in the wines and also makes it one of the most difficult wine regions to get to know well. Entire vineyards with a single owner are exceptions. It is more usual for a vineyard to be owned by several growers each of whom makes his own wine. The Clos de Vougeot, for example, has over 60 growers on its 124 acres. Consequently, even when a vineyard has been identified, the wine could have been produced by any one of a number of growers.

This very fragmented situation has led to the emergence of the *négociant*, or shipper. The first of these wine merchants established their businesses in Beaune at the beginning of the eighteenth century. As most growers produce only a few casks of wine, the négociant buys wine in cask from several growers and blends the wines to create a marketable quantity. Once the wine is blended it becomes the wine of its district of origin, rather than the product of one grower. The wine can be from a single vineyard if that is how it has been blended, but it can also be a marriage of several wines from the same district, in which case it would most likely carry a commune, or village, name on its label.

As a result, it becomes important to learn to distinguish between a vineyard and a village. Several villages, such as Puligny-Montrachet, Aloxe-Corton and Gevrey-Chambertin, have hyphenated their names to include the name of their district's most illustrious vineyard. A label, therefore, which bears the name of Chambertin alone is the product of that Grand Cru vineyard, but a wine bearing the name Gevrey-Chambertin can be drawn from any number of vineyards within that commune.

Prior to this century, there was very little legislation regarding wine. The ravages of the

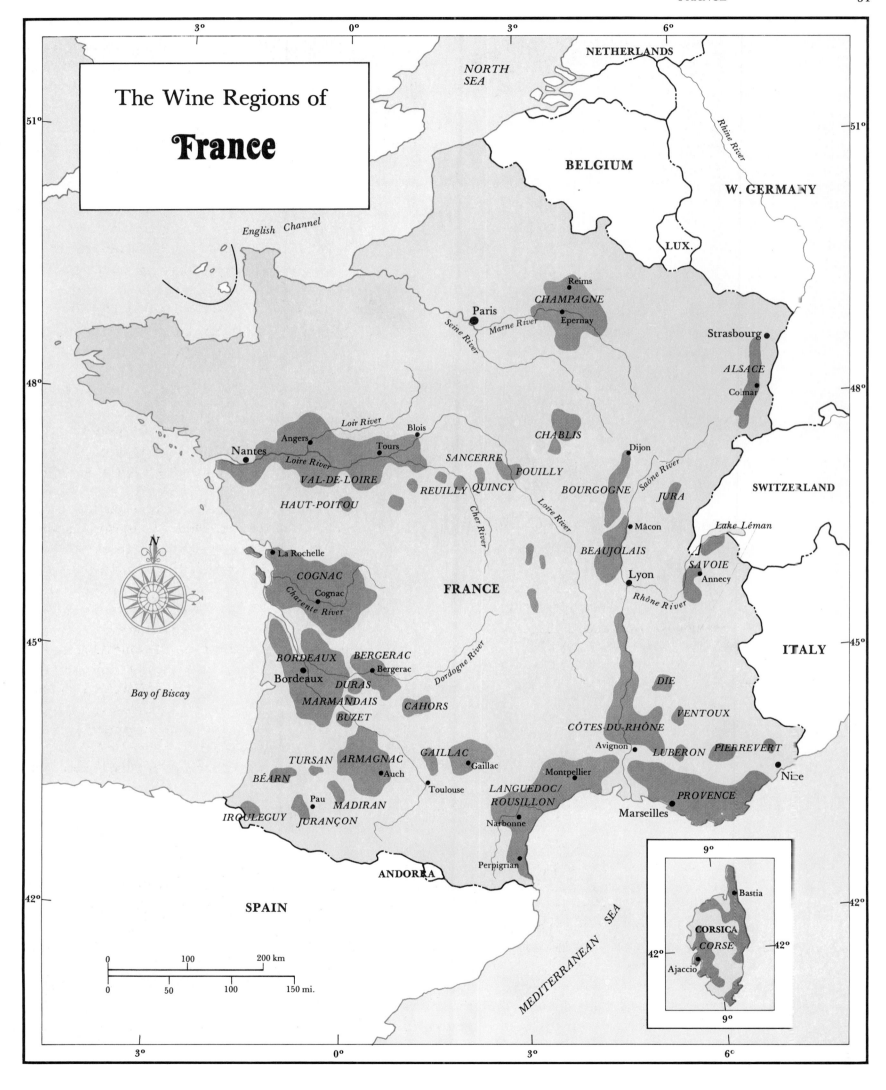

The Wine Regions of
France

Pinot Noir *grapes are small, ellipsoidal, and blue-black. The cluster is small and cylindrical. Dating back to the first century* A.D., *this variety has brought fame to Burgundy and Champagne, producing wines of great flavor, aroma and soft finish.*

American root louse, Phylloxera vastatrix, which decimated the vineyards at the end of the nineteenth century, caused a wine shortage that resulted in an unprecedented number of fraudulent wines reaching this thirsty market. A law was introduced in August 1905 in an effort to stop these deceitful practices. Following the First World War, the demand for wine increased considerably, and this gave the unscrupulous a fresh opportunity to abuse an unsuspecting public. As a result, a new law was put into effect in May 1919 which defined the appellations of origin, stated the rules and enforced them. During the Depression, between 1930 and 1934, it became apparent that the law of 1919, although it solved some problems, had opened the door to other abuses, especially in the vineyards. This led to the introduction, in July 1935, of the decree that now controls the appellations of origin. These regulations defined the area of production, the type of vine, the maximum yield per hectare and the minimum alcoholic strength for each denomination. Since 1974, it has been possible to classify quantities of wine beyond the maximum permitted yield up to a limit which is usually set at 20 per cent in Burgundy. This classification is granted only after the wine has been tasted and approved at the property. If it is not approved, the wine is consigned for distillation or vinegar-making. European Economic Community regulations and French legislation, also enacted in 1974, aimed at guaranteeing the quality of wine, demanded that official tasting must be carried out at the property. Since that time, the vintage of each producer with the right to an appellation contrôlée has been tasted, at least once every three years, by the Institut National des Appellations d'Origine.

The fine red wines of Burgundy are produced from the Pinot Noir grapes, while the fine whites are made from the Chardonnay. In Beaujolais, the Gamay Noir à Jus Blanc is king and some, generally unspectacular, white wine is made with the Aligoté.

In Burgundy, a village, parish, or area producing wine is known as a *finage*, and individual vineyards within each finage are referred to as a *climat*. The finest wines from the best climats are known as either Grand Cru, or Tête de Cuvée; those in the next classification are called Premiers Crus, and they are followed by the

Deuxièmes and Troisièmes Crus. In the case of the Grands Crus, their names alone become their appellation. Those climats entitled to the designation Premier Cru can add the name of the vineyard to the name of the village to indicate the exact origin of the wine. For example, in the case of Clos-des-Mouches in Beaune, the label can read either Beaune Clos-des-Mouches; Beaune Clos-des-Mouches Premier Cru; or Beaune Premier Cru. All three descriptions must be followed by the words appellation contrôlée. A number of Burgundy villages legally give their name to wines produced in their designated area. Examples of this are: Brouilly, Mâcon, Santenay, Meursault, Beaune, Nuits-Saint-Georges and Chablis. Finally, there are lesser appellations which can be applied to lesser or, in some cases, reclassified wines. The

Chardonnay *grapes are small spherical, amber, and translucent in color when matured. The leaf is slightly lobed. As this variety begins its growth early, it is vulnerable to injury by spring frosts.*

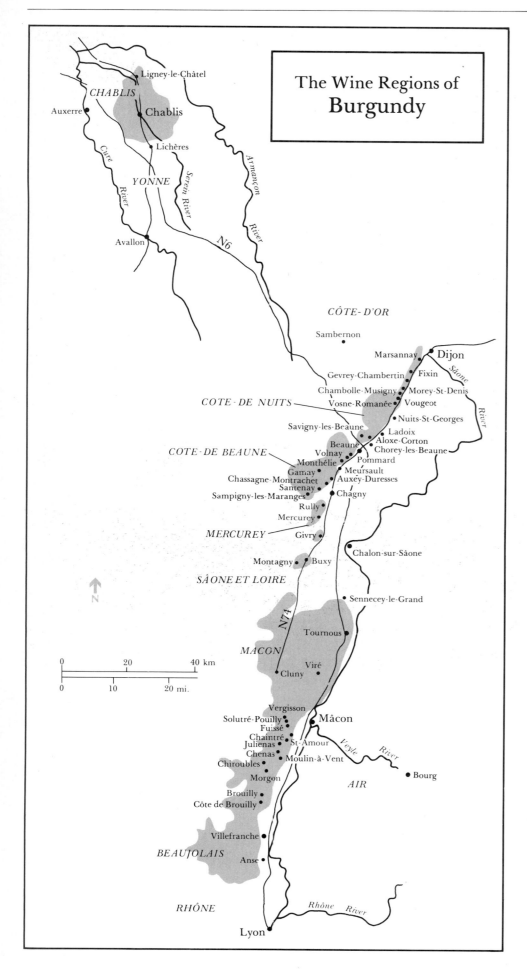

The Wine Regions of **Burgundy**

wines entitled to it can be simply labeled as Bourgogne or Bourgogne Grand Ordinaire. Two appellations rarely seen outside of the region are: Bourgogne Hautes-Côtes de Beaune and Bourgogne Hautes-Côtes de Nuits both of which include the less favored vineyards in the Côte-d'Or. Wines made with the Aligoté must carry the designation Bourgogne Aligoté or Mâcon Aligoté. Red and rosé wines made with Gamay and at least one-third Pinot Noir carry the description Bourgogne-Passe-tout-Grains.

Côte de Nuits

The Côte de Nuits begins just south of Dijon at the northern boundary of the commune of Fixin and then through Gevrey-Chambertin, Morey-Saint-Denis, Chambolle-Musigny, Vougeot, Vosne-Romanée and Nuits-Saint-Georges. At the southern end of the Côte, the village of Prémeaux produces wines that are sold under the name of Nuits-Saint-Georges.

The vineyards of the Côte de Nuits cover a mere 3,000 acres in a stretch of about 12 miles. Rarely wider than 875 yards, it narrows in places to between 220 and 320 yards. The east-facing slope of the Côte is broken by several steep-sided valleys, and the hill is frequently topped by rugged, rocky outcroppings which give those places a barren appearance. In fact, there are places where quarrying displaces the vine. Comblanchien, at the southern end of the Côte de Nuits, is famous for its marble quarries which break the viticultural scene between the Côte de Nuits and the Côte de Beaune.

FIXIN makes only red wines which are from fair to fine in quality. The climats classified as Premier Cru are: Les Meix-Bas, Le Clos-du-Chapitre, Aux Cheusots, Clos de la Perrière, Les Arvelets and Les Hervelets. The wines, at one time reputed to be as fine as Chambertin, are of fine color and they have an intense bouquet that develops with time. They tend to be long-lived and the climats of Clos-de-la-Perrière and Les Hervelets are currently considered to be Fixin's greatest.

GEVREY-CHAMBERTIN produces some of the finest and longest-living red wines in the Côte de Nuits. The first historical reference to the village of Gevrey was made in the year 895 at which time it was given to the Abbey of Saint-Benigne. In 1847, the village hyphenated its name to incorporate that of its most famous vineyard. Chambertin is a mere 32 acres which were planted during the 13th century, while the adjacent, and perhaps even more prestigious, 37 acre Clos-de-Bèze was established in the year 630 by the monks of the Abbey de Bèze. The wines from these two Grand Cru vineyards can be named simply Chambertin, but the wines of Chambertin cannot be labeled as Clos-de-Bèze. Chambertin was Napoleon's favorite wine, and it is alleged that on the eve of Waterloo, the wagon containing the wine was lost. Perhaps it was an omen Bonaparte should have heeded!

The commune of Gevrey-Chambertin is blessed with an incredible acreage of good vineyards. The fertile land extends further out from the hill than in any other part of the Côte and there are Premiers Crus on both sides of the main road. Clustered around Chambertin and Clos-de-Bèze are the Premiers Crus vineyards of Charmes-Chambertin, Mazoyères-Chambertin, Chapelle-Chambertin, Griotte-Chambertin, Latricières-Chambertin, Mazis-Chambertin and Ruchottes-Chambertin. Other classified climats in this cluster are Aux Combottes, Bel-Air, Les Corbeaux, Cherbaudes, La Perrière, Clos-Prieur, Le Fonteny, Champonnets and Petite-Chapelle. The commune has a second slope; the two most notable vineyards on that slope are Les Véroilles and Clos-Saint-Jacques. Other vineyards in that area with good reputations are Lavaux, Cazetiers, Combeaux-Moines, Etournelles, Poissenot, Champeaux, and Les Goulots.

The wines of Chambertin are equalled, but rarely surpassed, by other wines on the Côte de Nuits. It should be borne in mind, however, that a wine bearing the name Gevrey-Chambertin is one of the plain wines of the commune that is unlikely to contain any Chambertin whatsoever. The noble wines of the commune will always display their birthright, the name of their vineyard, on the label.

MOREY-SAINT-DENIS is a tiny village that traces its origins back to the Gallo-Roman period. It was

Château Clos-de-Vougeot, built in 1551 by the 48th abbot of Cîteaux. The monks began developing the property early in the twelfth century.

*Underground wine cellars in Burgundy protect the wine
by keeping it at a constant temperature.*

only as recently as 1927 that the village added the name of one of its smallest vineyards, Clos-Saint-Denis, to its own. The other Grands Crus of Morey are Close-de-la-Roche, Clos-de-Tart and Bonnes-Mares. In the case of Bonnes-Mares, only a small part of the vineyard is in Morey; the remainder lies within the boundaries of Chambolle-Musigny. Clos-de-Tart, which is solely owned by Mommessin, and its neighbor Clos-des-Lambrays (Premier Cru), owned by a M. Larrets, are two of the rare monopolies to be found in Burgundy.

As well as Clos-des-Lambrays, the other Premiers Crus of Morey are Les Ruchots, Les Sorbés, Le Clos-Sorbés, Les Millandes, Le Clos-des-Ormes, Meix-Rentiers, Monts-Luisants, Les Bouchots, Clos-Bussières, Aux Charmes, Les Charrières, Côte Rôtie, Calouères, Maison-Brûlée, Chabiots, Les Mauchamps, Les Froichots, Les Fremières, Les Genevrières, Les Chaffots, Les Chénevery, La Riotte, Le Clos-Baulet, Les Gruenchers, Les Façonnières.

Although a little white wine is made in Morey, it is the reds that have earned it its reputation. At their best, they are remarkable wines that, although quite light, have a full bouquet and a marvellous delicacy of flavor and texture which makes them very attractive drinking when they are quite young, although they will develop well with moderate aging.

CHAMBOLLE-MUSIGNY. Once the site of a Roman camp, the village of Chambolle adopted the name of its most notable vineyard in 1875. The two most highly regarded vineyards are Bonnes-Mares, in the north, which spills over into Morey-Saint-Denis, and Les Musigny, in the south, which lies on the higher part of the slope above Clos-de-Vougeot. Although a little white wine is made at Les Musigny, it is best known for its reds, which are full-bodied, delicate of bouquet and flavor, and were probably best described by Gaston Roupnel who said, "The Musigny, the silk and lace; wherein its supreme delicacy ignores all violence and can conceal its strength." Bonnes-Mares, at the other end of the commune, produces a wine that is slightly harder when young, but slowly develops a similar strength and delicate charm.

The Premiers Crus of Chambolle-Musigny are Les Amoureuses, Les Charmes, Les Cras, Les Borniques, Les Baudes, Les Plantes, Les Hautes-Doix, Les Châtelots, Les Gruenchers, Les Groseilles, Les Fuées, Les Lavrottes, Derrière-la-Grange, Les Noirots, Les Sentiers, Les Fousselottes, Aux Beaux-Bruns, Les Combottes and Aux Combottes. Les Amoureuses and Les Charmes are considered by many to be amongst the best Premiers Crus in Burgundy, but, largely because the vineyards are shared by only a few owners, any Musigny wine will likely be found to be very good.

VOUGEOT is a tiny village that was originally named Gilly. Later it added the name of its most famous vineyard, Clos-de-Vougeot, but today the Gilly has fallen out of use and the village is most often referred to simply as Vougeot. The vineyards of Clos-de-Vougeot were planted centuries ago by monks and its 125 acres are still largely enclosed by the high stone wall they built around it. Sadly, the ownership of the vineyard is so fractured that, although the climat is a Grand Cru, its name on a label is not a reliable guide to quality. At its best, however, it ranks, along with Romanée, Chambertin and a few others, as one of the finest wines of the Côte-d'Or.

The other vineyards of Vougeot, which are all Premiers Crus, are Le Clos-Blanc de Vougeot, Les Petits-Vougeots, Les Cras and Clos-de-la-Perrière. Les Clos-Blanc de Vougeot is a 5-acre site planted entirely with Chardonnay grapes which produce the commune's only white wine. Clos-de-la-Perrière lies just below the vineyards of Musigny, and, given a good vintage, it can yield a wine as great as that of Musigny.

VOSNE-ROMANÉE is a tiny knot of stone houses that give no hint that they are surrounded by the vineyards that produce the world's most expensive wines. Various decrees have included certain climats in this commune, although they are actually in the commune of Flagey-Échézeaux.

La Romanée-Conti was one of the last vineyards that was able to preserve ungrafted French root stock. The unavailability of carbon sulphide during the Second World War, however, resulted in the vineyard being destroyed by phylloxera. The vineyard was replanted with grafted stock and the first wine from these new vines was made in 1952.

Romanée-Conti is generally regarded as the finest of the Romanées, but its immediate neigh-

bors, Richebourg, Romanée, La Tâche and Romanée-Saint-Vivant all bear a strong family resemblance. The wines have a delicate, spicy sweetness in their bouquet that conjures up images of the orient, and their velvety smoothness on the palate gives them a finesse of extraordinary completeness.

Échézeaux and Grands Échézeaux, although actually in Flagey, are permitted to use the Vosne-Romanée appellation. Échézeaux is a massive 79 acres, while Grands Échézeaux occupies around 23 acres. Their wines have a lingering intensity that ensures them of their place amongst the great Burgundies.

The Premiers Crus of Vosne-Romanée are Aux Malconsorts, Les Beaux-Monts, Les Suchots, La Grand Rue, Les Gaudichots, Aux Brûlées, Les Chaumes, Les Reignots, Le Clos-des-Réas and Les Petits-Monts. All of them produce wines of

remarkable quality which prompted Courtépée to comment, somewhat tersely, "No ordinary wines are to be found in Vosne." Not, perhaps, the most effusive praise for the wines of this remarkable, reddish slope of earth, but nevertheless, it is accurate.

NUITS-SAINT-GEORGES is a bustling little market town that is the main shopping center of the Côte de Nuits. In 1892, the town of Nuits added to its own name that of its best vineyard, Saint-Georges. The reputation of the Saint-Georges vineyard can be traced back to 1023 at which time it was presented to the Canons of Saint-Denis. The appellation Nuits-Saint-Georges is also used for the wines of the commune of Prémeaux which lies further to the south.

There are no Grands Crus at Nuits-Saint-Georges, but the wines of Les Saint-Georges, Les

The tiny village of Vosne-Romanée boasts no fewer than seven Grands Crus — and some of the world's most costly wines.

Vaucrains and Les Cailles are held in the highest regard. All the red wines of Nuits-Saint-Georges are of consistently high quality. They are full-bodied, strong wines that age well, and, at their best, attain a quality similar to that of Chambertin.

The other vineyards at Nuits are Les Porets, Les Pruliers, Les Hauts-Pruliers, Aux Murgers, La Richemonne, Les Chaboeufs, La Perrière, La Roncière, Les Procès, Rue-de-Chaux, Aux Boudots, Aux Cras, Aux Chailettes, Aux Crots, Les Vallerots, Aux Champs-Perdrix, Perrière-Noblet, Aux Damodes, Les Argillats, En La Châine-Carteau, Aux Argillats.

At Prémeaux, the vineyards are Clos-de-la-Maréchale, Clos-Arlots, Clos-des-Argillières, Clos-des-Grandes-Vignes, Clos-des-Corvées, Clos-des-Forêts, Les Didiers, Aux Perdrix, Les Corvées-Paget, Le Clos-Saint-Marc.

The greatest strength of the wines of the Côte de Nuits is that they are of dependably good quality, and, consequently, consistently satisfying.

COTE DE NUITS-VILLAGES is an appellation under which various communes of the Côte de Nuits sell a part of their wine. The right to use this appellation must be claimed at the time of the declaration of the harvest. The communes entitled to this designation are Fixin, Brochon, Prissey, Comblanchien and Corgoloin. It is not permitted for any other communes of the Côte de Nuits to sell any of their wines under the appellation Côtes de Nuits-Villages. Although these wines are of good quality and are pleasant drinking, they are never great wines.

Côte de Beaune

The Côte de Beaune starts at the northern edge of the commune of Ladoix-Serrigny and runs south to the Saône and the Loire. Côte de Beaune is wider and longer than the Côte de Nuits, and has more than twice the vineyard area with almost 7,000 acres under vines. The hillsides generally face east, but where the many valleys indent the slope, the vineyards have a southeast exposure that shelters them from the north winds and frosts. The scenery is softer than in the Côte de Nuits, and

the hills are rounded, with gentle, well-balanced slopes. The vines grow almost to the summits which are covered with box trees and junipers.

The city of Beaune has sprawled beyond the ancient walls that still surround parts of the old town, but within those old ramparts lies a picturesque town with narrow streets, lined with quaint buildings, which form a cobweb-like tracery around a few central squares such as Place Carnot. Dating from the Roman era, the city sprang to prominence under the Dukes of Burgundy who located their palace there. The jewel of the city, however, is Les Hospices de Beaune, which has been alleviating the predicament of the poor for over 500 years. Built in 1443 by Nicolas Rolin, the hospital, which is an exquisitely beautiful building, is unique in that since the death of its founder, its ever-increasing financial needs have been met by wine produced from vineyards bequeathed to the hospital, first by Nicolas Rolin and his widow, Guigone de Salins, and ever since by other benefactors. Vineyards owned by Les Hospices de Beaune are dotted all along the Côte de Beaune from Aloxe-Corton to Meursault. Les Trois Glorieuses is a festival that centers around the public auction of the Hospices wines, an event that takes place on the third Sunday of November each year. The wines, sold under the names of different cuvées, mostly bear the names of the donors of the vineyards that now belong to the Hospices.

ALOXE-CORTON, standing at the north end of the Côte de Beaune, is the only isolated hill in the district. The crown of the hill is densely wooded, but the broad band of vineyards on its east, south and west slopes produce the only red Grand Cru wines in the Côte de Beaune. The white wines of Corton and Corton-Charlemagne are also of Grand Cru status. Certain decrees have included some of the vineyards in the communes of Ladoix-Serrigny and Pernand-Vergelesses in the Corton appellations. This makes Corton a confusing appellation to understand, but is in no way reflected in the wines, which are all of exceptional quality. It was only in 1862 that the tiny village of Aloxe, with its narrow streets winding between picturesque stone houses, added the name of its most prestigious vineyard to its own. The Grands Crus are Corton, Corton-Charlemagne and Charlemagne. Corton produces both red and white wines, while

the vineyard now known as Corton-Charlemagne makes a white wine from Chardonnay grapes planted on the upper part of the slope and red wines from the lower part of the vineyard. The appellation Charlemagne can be applied only to white wines. Other individual vineyards entitled to market their wines under the Grand Cru designation are: Les Chaumes, Vigne-au-Saint, les Meix Lallemand, La Voirosse, Les Pougets, Les Fiètres, Les Perrières, Les Languettes, Le Clos-du-Roi, Les Renardes, Les Grèves, Les Bressandes, Les Vergennes, Le Rognet-Corton and the upper part of Les Meix.

The Premiers Crus of Aloxe-Corton are: Les Valozières, Les Chaillots, Les Fournières, les Maréchaudes, En Pauland, Les Vercots, Les Guérets and the lower part of Les Meix.

In Ladoix-Serringy, the Premiers Crus are: La Maréchaude, La Toppe-au-Vert, La Coutière, Les Grandes-Lolières, Les Petites-Lolières and Basses-Mourettes.

Pernand-Vergelesses vineyards entitled to a Premier Cru designation are: Les Basses-Vergelesses, Creux-de-la-Net, Les Fichots, En Caradeux.

SAVIGNY-LES-BEAUNE is a sprawling village that is divided by the small River Rau. It produces red wines that have a richly scented bouquet and are soft and fresh. A little white wine is also made, but it is rarely found outside of the area. The best vineyards are those to the north, directly adjacent to those of Pernand, and those to the south where they border Beaune.

The most highly rated vineyards of Savigny are: Aux Vergelesses (sometimes referred to as Bataillière), Les Marconnets, La Dominode and Les Jarrons. Other noteworthy vineyards are: Basses-Vergelesses, Les Lavières, Aux Gravains, Les Peuillets, Aux Guettes, Les Talmettes, Les Charnières, Aux Fourneaux, Aux Clous, Aux Serpentières, Les Narbantons, Les Hauts-

Marconnets, Les Hauts-Jarrons, Redrescuts, Les Rouvrettes, Aux Grands-Liards, Aux Petits-Liards and Petits-Godeaux.

CHOREY-LES-BEAUNE is tiny commune, on the plain to the west of Aloxe-Corton, that produces both red and white wines. These can be sold either under their own appellation, or under the designation Côte de Beaune-Villages, Bourgogne, or Bourgogne Grand Ordinaire for the reds, while the whites can be marketed under the commune name or only as either Bourgogne or Bourgogne Grand Ordinaire. There are no individual vineyards of note in this commune.

BEAUNE has no Grands Crus vineyards; however, many of them were known by name long before most other French vineyards. The earliest records go back to 1220 when ownership of Clos-de-la-Mousse was bestowed upon the Chapter of Notre-Dame of Beaune. Les Marconnely, Les Cras, Les Grèves and Les Fèves were all names in records prior to the fifteenth century. For many centuries, the largest vineyard owners were the Carthusians, Benedictines and Knights of Malta. Today, in common with the rest of Burgundy, the vineyards have been divided amongst several owners. This situation has given rise to the Burgundian saying, "There are no great wines, only great bottles of wine." There is an element of truth to the saying, which reflects the fact that it is more important to know the grower than the vineyard in Burgundy. Les Grèves, for example, which with 80 acres is the largest vineyard in Beaune, has several owners who produce very fine wines, but it is generally agreed that the wines coming from the top corner of the vineyard are the finest. This particular plot was owned by the Carmelites until 1789, but is now the property of Bouchard Père et Fils. The Carmelites named their corner of Les Grèves La Vigne de l'Enfant-Jésus, and that is the name under which it is sold to this day. Likewise, the portion of Clos-des-Mouches owned by Joseph Drouhin produces an excellent red wine and an exceptional white wine.

Of the Premiers Crus, Les Marconnets, Les Fèves, Les Bressandes, Les Grèves and Les Teurons are held in the highest regard, but the others with the same classification all produce fine wines with a light, delicate style. They are: Le Clos-des-Mouches, Champs-Pimont, Clos-du-Roi, Aux Coucherias, En l'Orme, Les Perrières, À l'Écu, Les Cent-Vignes, Les Toussaints, Sur-les-Grèves, Aux Cras, Le Clos-de-la-Mousse, Les Chouacheux, Les Boucherottes, Les Vignes-Franches, Les Aigrots, Pertuisots, Tielandry or Clos Landry, Les Sisies, Les Avaux, Les Reversées, Les Bas-des-Teurons, Les Seurey, La Mignotte, Montée-Rouge, Les Montrevenots, Les Blanches-Fleurs and Les Épenottes.

POMMARD enjoys a worldwide popularity and reputation that, strictly speaking, are of greater stature than the wines themselves. Bounded on the north by Beaune and on the south by Volnay, Pommard produces only red wines, which are rather stout, well-colored, and will take considerable aging well. Nevertheless, they are no match for the finer wines of Beaune and Volnay.

The most highly regarded vineyards of Pommard are Les Rugiens-Bas, Les Rugiens-Hauts and Les Epenots. The Hospices de Beaune wine sold under the name Dames de la Charité is a blend of Les Rugiens-Bas and Les Epenots. The other vineyards of Pommard are: Les Petits-Epenots, Clos-de-la-Commaraine, Clos-Blanc, Les Arvelets, Les-Charmots, Les Argillières, Les Pézerolles, Les Boucherottes, Les Sausilles, Les Croix-Noires, Les Chaponnières, Les Fremiers, Les Bertins, Les Jarollières, Les Poutures, Le Clos-Micot, La Refène, Clos-du-Verger, Derrière-Saint-Jean, La Platière, Les Chanlins-Bas, Les Combes-Dessus and La Chanière.

VOLNAY is a small commune to the south of Pommard, but its vineyards are situated on higher ground than its northerly neighbor. Only red wines are produced, and they are of a lighter color than those of either Beaune or Pommard, but they achieve an elegance and delicacy of flavor that gives them great charm.

The most highly regarded vineyards are En Caillerets, Caillerets-Dessus, En Champans and En Chevret. The other notable vineyards of the commune are: Fremiets, Bousse-d'Or, La Barre (also known as Clos-de-la-Barre), Le Clos-des-Chênes, Les Angles, Pointe-d'Angles, Les Mitans, En L'Ormeau, Taille-Pieds, En Verseuil, Carelle-sous-la-Chapelle, Ronceret, Carelle-Dessous, Robardelle, Les Lurets, Les Aussy, Les

Corton-Grancey,
Côte de Beaune.

Brouillards, Les Clos-des-Ducs, Les Pitures-Dessus, Chanlin, Les Santenots and Les Petures. It should be noted that wines sold under the name of Volnay-Santenots are from the commune of Meursault.

MONTHELIE sits on the last tableland of the Côte de Beaune, on the edge of a ravine that separates it from the Côte de Meursault which, although known by that name locally, is more generally regarded as being the southern part of the Côte de Beaune. The vast majority of Monthelie wines are red, and the quality is usually excellent. However, they are not very well known, which is a pity, as they deserve more attention.

The vineyards of greatest note are: Les Vignes-Rondes, Sur Lavelle, Clos des Champs-Fulliot, Le Clos-Gauthey, Le Cas-Rougeot and La Taupine. The other vineyards of the commune include: Le Meix-Bataille, Les Riottes, Le Château-Gaillard and Duresse.

AUXEY-DURESSES is a small commune and one of the oldest in the Côte de Beaune. The village of Auxey added the name of its most highly regarded vineyard, Duresses, to its own only in July 1924. The commune clings to a rocky spur on the left bank of the Meursault River. In common with Monthelie, the wines of Auxey-Duresses are not

very well known. Prior to the introduction of the appellation laws, the wines of Duresses were often sold as either Volnay or Pommard and were never considered to cause harm to the reputations of either of these great wines.

Apart from Les Duresses, Les Bas-des-Duresses, Les Grands-Champs, and Reugne (also known as La Chapelle) are regarded as the finest vineyards. Others of note are: Climat-du-Val, (known as Clos-du-Val), Les Ecusseaux, Les Bretterins (also known as La Chapelle).

SAINT-ROMAIN is a tiny village that lies at the foot of the cliffs that girdle the valley of Auxey-Duresses. Its houses climb the slope like a giant staircase, and its vineyard area, a mere 358 acres, produces both red and white wines of which 80 per cent is red. A comparatively unknown commune, it has no named vineyards, and the only tribute to its wines seems to have been made by Roland Thévenin, a poet, who also happened to be mayor of the village. He wrote, "O Saint-Romain, bold, robust and so fruity, We like your freshness as much as your finesse."

MEURSAULT is the thriving center of a large commune whose vineyards stretch uninterrupted from Volnay in the north to Puligny-Montrachet in the south. Although best known for its white wines, there are red wines made in the northern part of the commune where it abuts Volnay. The finest of these vineyards is Les Santenots-du-Milieu which, along with Les Santenots-Dessous and Les Petures, has sold its wine under the name Volnay-Santenots for more than 200 years.

It is, however, on its white wines that the reputation of Meursault rests. Greenish-gold in color, they are unusual in that they are both dry and mellow with a hint of nuttiness in their flavor. The vineyard considered to produce the finest wines is Les Perrières. However, the wines of Les Charmes-Dessus and Les Charmes-Dessous, which lie below Les Perrières, and Les Genevrières Dessus and Les Genevrières Dessous, which border its northern edge, can all be depended upon to produce very reliable wines.

Other notable vineyards are: Le Poruzot-Dessus, Le Poruzot, Les Bouchères, Les Santenots-Blancs, Les Caillerets, Les Cras and La Goutte-d'Or. The wine of La Goutte-d'Or has gained a worldwide reputation of such proportions that it is impossible for the vineyard ever to meet the demand because of the small amount of wine it can produce.

The village of Blagny lies within the commune of Meursault and its finest vineyards are: La Jennelotte, La Pièce-sous-le-Bois and Sous-le-dos-d'Ane. Red wines made in this hamlet are sold under the name of Blagny, while the white wines are sold either under the name of Meursault or Puligny-Montrachet.

PULIGNY and CHASSAGNE are two communes that may best be viewed together, as there is considerable overlapping of their finest vineyards, which are the source of Burgundy's only Grands Crus white wines. Both communes attached the name of the famous Montrachet vineyards to their own in 1879. In colloquial Burgundian, *rachet* means bald. Hence, Mont-Rachet meant "the hill without a tree."

The five vineyards that constitute the Grands Crus are: Le Montrachet (in both Puligny and Chassagne), Chevalier-Montrachet (entirely in Puligny), Bâtard-Montrachet (in both Puligny and Chassagne), Bienvenues-Bâtard-Montrachet (entirely in Puligny) and Criots-Bâtard-Montrachet (entirely in Chassagne).

There has been considerable speculation about the naming of these vineyards, and, whether fact

Statue of Nicolas Rollin, founder of the Hospices de Beaune, on the grounds of the Hospices.

or fancy, the most popular account relates that while the son of the governor of the castle at Montrachet was at the crusades, his father, yielding to temptation from the devil, not to mention the apparently tempting local maidens, begat an illegitimate son. Reportedly, the Duke of Burgundy was not amused by this turn of events, but the decree he issued may indicate that he had a more highly developed sense of humor than he is given credit for. He ordered that the old lord was to be known as Montrachet the Elder, the Crusader as the Chevalier, and the child as the Bâtard Montrachet. Subsequently, when the Chevalier was killed in battle, the bastard became the old man's heir and was welcomed to the castle with shouts of, "Welcome to the bastard of Montrachet." The baby's crying disturbed Montrachet the Elder so much that he was moved to complain in dialect, "A croi l'Bâtard" (the bastard is crying). In time, the castle was razed, and the vineyards were named in memory of this Montrachet trio and the two events attributed to the bastard's life at the castle.

Meursault produces mainly Chardonnay grapes, which yield golden-green white wines that are dry and mellow.

Irrespective of the authenticity of this tale, there is no question that the wines of Le Montrachet are the finest white wines of Burgundy and amongst the finest anywhere in the world. The wines of the other four Grands Crus, although not quite so fine, are of outstanding quality and distinction.

The other notable vineyards of Puligny-Montrachet are: Le Cailleret, Les Combettes, Les Pucelles, Les Folatières, Clavoillons, Le Champ-Canet, Les Chalumeaux, Les Referts, Sous-le-Puits, La Garenne and Hameau-de-Blagny.

In Chassagne-Montrachet, the other principal vineyards are: Clos-Saint-Jean, Abbaye-de-Morgeot, La Boudriotte, La Maltroie, Les Chenevottes, Les Champs-Gain, Grandes-Ruchottes, La Romanée, Les Brussolles, Les Vergers, Les Macherelles, and En Cailleret.

SAINT-AUBIN is a tiny village situated behind Chassagne-Montrachet. There are only about 300 acres under vine and these include the vineyards of the hamlet of Gamay, where the grape of the same name was first grown.

The vineyards regarded as "first growths" are: La Chatenière, Les Murgers-des-Dents-de-Chien, En Remilly, Les Frionnes, Sur-le-Sentier-de-Clou, Sur Gamay, Les Combes and Champlot.

SANTENAY traces its history back to the Neolithic and Iron Ages, and the caves that penetrate the Côte at this point still bear reminders of these ancient inhabitants. The town also has a mineral water spa, but the locals tend to avoid using it. The vast majority of Santenay wines are red. They are firm yet mellow, and always reward those with the patience to age them.

Les Gravières, of which Clos-de-Tavannes is part, and La Comme are the most highly regarded vineyards, but others worthy of note are Beauregard, Le Passe-Temps, Beaurepaire and La Maladière.

CHEILLY, DEZIZE and SAMPIGNY-LES-MARANGES between them form the tail end of the Côte de Beaune. Although almost equal quantities of red and white wines are produced, the reds are best and are usually sold under the Côte de Beaune-Villages appellation.

The primary vineyards of Cheilly are Les Maranges, Les Plantes-de-Maranges and La Boutière. In Dezize the top vineyard is Les Maranges, and in Sampigny, Les Maranges and Le Clos-des-Rois are most noteworthy.

CÔTE DE BEAUNE-VILLAGES is an appellation that is used extensively, particularly by the lesser-known villages that are entitled to sell their red wines under this designation.

The villages authorized to use the Côte de Beaune-Villages appellation are: Auxey-Duresess, Blagny, Chassagne-Montrachet, Cheilly-Les-Maranges, Chorey-les-Beaune, Dezize-les-Maranges, Ladoix, Meursault, Monthélie, Pernand-Vergelesses, Puligny-Montrachet, Saint-Aubin, Saint-Romain, Sampigny-les-Maranges, Santenay and Savigny.

The Mercurey Region

The vineyards of Mercurey extend some 15 miles from Chagny in the north to Saint-Vallerin in the south. The region is sometimes called the Côte Châlonnaise after the town of Châlon-sur-Saône which was once an important wine center and has now become completely industrialized. Known to relatively few people until recent years, the wines of the Mercurey region, which have always been of excellent value, have been "discovered" by those seeking refuge from the soaring prices of better-known Burgundies.

Today, the main vineyards of the area are clustered around the four communes of Rully, Mercurey, Givry and Montagny. Unlike the continuous slope of the Côte de Beaune, Mercurey's vineyards are planted on a chain of hillocks which are surrounded by crop fields and orchards.

Rully in the north and Montagny in the south both concentrate on producing white wines. Rully's wines are light and fruity and are used as the base for an excellent sparkling Burgundy. Montagny, on the other hand, produces a more powerful wine with a pronounced bouquet and style that makes it resemble some Pouilly-Fuissé wines.

Mercurey and Givry are responsible for mostly red wines, which are of a quality equal to those of the Côte de Beaune. In a way this is not surprising as the climate and soil are very similar to that of the Côte de Beaune, and the vignerons of the area use the same cultivation and vinification techniques as their neighbors in Beaune.

The appellation of Mercurey actually includes two other communes, Saint-Martin-sous-Montaigu and Bourgneuf-Val-d'Or. The vineyards of Mercurey entitled to Premier Cru classification are: Clos-du-Roi, Clos-Voyens, Clos-Marcilly, Clos-des-Fourneaux and Clos-des-Montaigus.

Rully's First Growth vineyards are: Margottey, Grésigny, Vauvry, Sous Mont-Palais, Meix-Caillet, Les Pierres, La Bressande, Champ-Clou, La Renarde, Pillot, Cloux, Raclot, Rabourcey, Écloseaux, Marissou, La Fosse, Chapitre, Préau and Moulesne.

Neither Givry nor Montagny have any classified vineyard sites. The Montagny appellation also includes wines from the neighboring communes of Buxy, Saint-Vallerin and Jully-les-Buxy.

Mâcon

The Mâcon region is immense by Burgundian standards, as it covers an area some 25 miles in length and 9 miles in width. This area, however, is far from entirely devoted to vineyards. Unlike the Côte-d'Or with its uninterrupted ribbons of vines, the Mâconnais is composed of a series of pockets of vineyards dotted amongst fields of crops and grazing meadows.

The town of Mâcon, from which the region takes its name, was an important center as early as Roman times. In the past, the town was considered to be the gateway between northern and southern France. This position also made it the gateway for invaders, most notably the Barbarians in the fifth

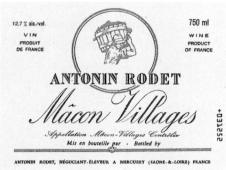

century and the Saracens in the eighth century. Both of these armies laid the town to waste.

The Mâconnais is not a source of great wines; rather, it produces wines of sound quality that are reliable, enjoyable and decently priced.

At its northern end, the Mâconnais begins as a series of gently rolling hills that gradually grow in elevation until they suddenly erupt into massive, jagged, tooth-like rock formations. It is on the slopes below these rocky outcroppings that Mâcon's most famous wine, Pouilly-Fuissé, is grown.

Pouilly-Fuissé is an appellation that designates the wines of the five communes of Fuissé, Solutré, Pouilly, Vergisson and Chaintré. Made with the Chardonnay grape, Pouilly-Fuissé is a white wine with all the style one expects from a white Burgundy. A delicate wine, it has a haunting bouquet, a golden color with a hint of emerald, and a gentle presence on the palate.

Contrary to the common perception, at least in North America, Pouilly-Fuissé is not a great wine. It is certainly a very good wine, but it has been put in a very curious position which was articulated most eloquently by the late Jean Mommessin upon serving a Pouilly-Fuissé as the opening wine to a meal at his home. He observed that as North Americans had learned to pronounce the name and felt comfortable ordering it, consequently, the laws of supply and demand prevailing, the price went beyond reality.

As M. Mommessin put it, "No one can afford this wine anymore; we are just drinking it ourselves."

Pouilly-Vinzelles and Pouilly-Loché, two communes to the south of Pouilly-Fuissé, have their own appellation and are very similar in style to their better-known neighbors. They are generally also less pricey.

Saint-Véran is an appellation that can be used for white wines made with the Chardonnay grape, from the communes of Chânes, Chasselas, Davayé, Leynes, Prissé, Saint-Amour, Saint-Vérand and in Solutré. These villages all lie to the north and south of Pouilly-Fuissé, to which they bear a marked resemblance.

Elsewhere in the Mâconnais, a large quantity of red wine of a pleasant nature is produced. Likewise there are many simple white wines that are at their best when drunk while they have all of their freshness.

Most of these wines are entitled to use the designations Mâcon Supérieur, Mâcon or Mâcon-Villages. The first two of these designations can be applied to red, white and rosé wines, but Mâcon-Villages can be applied only to a white wine. Finally, white wines made from Pinot Blanc or Chardonnay grapes may use the appellation Pinot-Chardonnay-Mâcon.

Beaujolais

Few wines are better known, or more readily accepted than Beaujolais, yet it was not until the latter part of the last century that the name was introduced. Prior to the name change, the wines were sold as Vins de Mâcon. The source of the name, however, is ancient. It is taken from the château of Beaujeu which was built in the middle of the ninth century. At that time, and, for several centuries to come, Beaujeu was the administrative center of the region, a position of influence now held by Villefranche.

Since adopting its pretty name, Beaujolais has grown in popularity to the point of embarrassment, with world demand far outstripping the supply. A light, fruity, uncomplicated and easy-drinking wine, which is ready to drink within a year to eighteen months of its birth, its ready acceptance is hardly suprising.

A large area, Beaujolais is some 45 miles long and ten miles wide, and the Gamay grape reigns supreme in these vineyards which climb right to the summits of the hills. Between them, Beaujolais and Mâcon produce more wine than the rest of Burgundy combined. Unlike the other Burgundy wine-producing regions, with their clearly defined boundaries, the transition from Mâcon to Beaujolais is somewhat blurred. Two of the Beaujolais

La Roche de Solutré, whose vineyards stretch as far as Mâcon and the Beaujolais.

Overleaf:
Mont Brouilly in Beaujolais, surrounded by six communes, is topped by a nineteenth-century chapel to which wine-lovers from all over the world have journeyed.

Gamay grapes grow in large, compact clusters that are conical and heavy-shouldered. The vine which takes its name from a Côte de Beaune village is the grape responsible for the wines of Beaujolais.

Grands Crus, St.-Amour and Moulin-à-Vent are actually in Mâcon, while the other seven, Juliénas, Chénas, Fleurie, Chiroubles, Morgon, Brouilly, and Côte de Brouilly, are in Beaujolais. The nine Grands Crus each display an individual style and more weight than other Beaujolais, and, with the exception of Brouilly, it is permissible for the name of an individual vineyard to be added to the commune name.

The next highest classification is Beaujolais-Villages. Wines bearing this appellation can either be reclassified Grands Crus or come from the communes of Jullié, Émerignes, Lancié, Villié-Morgon, Lantignié, Beaujeu, Régnié, Durette, Cercié, Quincié, Saint-Lager, Odenas, Charentay, Saint-Étienne-la-Varenne, Vaux, Le Perréon, Saint-Étienne-des-Ouillères, Blacé, Arbuissonnas, Marchampt and Vauxrenard in Beaujolais and Leynes, Saint-Amour-Bellevue, La Chapelle-de-Guinchay, Romanèche, Pruzilly, Chânes, Saint-Vérand and Saint-Symphorien-d'Ancelles in Mâcon.

The other classifications of Beaujolais Supérieur or simply Beaujolais can be used, through re-classification, by the Grands Crus and Beaujolais-Villages, but most wines labeled in this way come from the Lower Beaujolais, south of Villefranche.

Some of Beaujolais' oldest, and most devoted customers are the Lyonnais, a fact that has given rise to the adage that Lyon has three rivers, the Rhône, the Saône and the Beaujolais!

One phenomenon that has caught on in recent years in North America is Beaujolais Nouveau, which has been all the rage in Paris and London for many years. Usually released on November 15 amidst much fanfare, the wine is more of an occasion than anything else.

Made by carbonic maceration, a method by which the grapes are loaded uncrushed into the fermentation tanks so that their own weight causes a form of crushing and subsequent fermentation, the wine is bottled about six weeks after the harvest.

In truth, the result is usually a purplish wine with a very earthy bouquet and extremely high acidity. Looked at as an event, the wine is lots of fun and a great excuse for a party, but there can be no doubt that this frothy young wine is vastly over-priced.

Only one tower remains of the ancient windmill from which Moulin-à-Vent derives its name. Its wine is among the best known of the Beaujolais.

The hills and dales of Beaujolais descend from west to east, offering its vineyards great variety in their exposure to the sun.

The vineyards of Beaujolais cover 42 miles in length and nearly 10 miles in width, with over 37,000 acres planted for viniculture.

Vineyards of the Morgon region, Beaujolais.

Sadly, almost sixty per cent of the wine made in Beaujolais is now processed as nouveau. While this may well keep the bankers in the region happy, it does somewhat limit the supply of fully matured Beaujolais.

Chablis

Isolated from the rest of Burgundy, Chablis, located northwest of Dijon and almost halfway to Paris, is a modest-sized wine-producing island which has an international reputation far exceeding its size. More wine is sold each day under the name of "Chablis" than can be produced in the region in an entire year! Those who masquerade in Chablis' borrowed plumes, however, never come close to duplicating the unique character of genuine Chablis.

Winemaking in Chablis, which is in Yonne département, can be traced back to the Roman era. The industry was originally centered on the town of Auxerre, and its wines were sold under that name until the eighteenth century. Most Auxerre wines were red, but white wines were grown around Chablis by the twelfth century.

Wine production continued to spread in Auxerre, and by the nineteenth century, it was the largest vineyard region of Burgundy. This expansion of the vineyards was due largely to the Serein River, which is a tributary of the Yonne, which in turn flows into the Seine. This allowed the wines of Auxerre and Chablis to be sent to Paris by boat, thus avoiding the perils of the roads which were infested by bands of brigands. Thus, with a safe and reliable transportation system, the wines from Auxerre, which were finer than those grown on the Ile-de-France, were very much in demand in the French capital.

The golden age continued for Auxerre and Chablis until the close of the nineteenth century when phylloxera invaded and destroyed the vineyards. Almost simultaneously, the development of the railroads enabled wines from the south of France to be readily transported to Paris, and, even with the cost of transportation, they could be sold at lower prices than the wines of Auxerre. The main reason for this was that the vignerons of the south could rely on the weather each year; the growers in Auxerre had to contend with frost and a shorter growing season, and, consequently, had to price their wines to compensate for any shortages in a vintage due to such adverse conditions.

Confronted with this competition, the growers of Auxerre did not think it was worth going to the expense of restocking their vineyards. Chablis, in fact, was the only place in Yonne where the vineyards were restocked.

The Chardonnay is the only grape permitted in the production of Chablis, but because of microclimates there is a considerable variation in the quality of the region's wines. By far the finest are the Chablis Grands Crus which are produced from seven vineyards with a total of only 112 acres. Located on a slope on the right bank of the Serein River facing the town, the Grands Crus are: Blanchot, Les Clos, Valmur, Grenouille, Vaudésir, Les Preuses and Bougros. These wines owe their strength and character to the combination of a southern exposure of the slope and a chalky soil. One drawback faced by the growers is that heavy rains wash the soil down to

The remaining Saracen tower at the Château des Tours (Brouilly-Beaujolais).

*Robert Drouhin,
head of the Beaune
négociant house of
Joseph Drouhin, in
a Chablis vineyard.*

*Vaudésir, which
produces one of
the Grands Crus
of Chablis.*

the foot of the steep slope, and every now and again it has to be carried back to the top and distributed amongst the vines. As one grower put it, "It used to be a back-breaking job carrying the soil up the slope, but it's much easier today, thanks to the tractor."

After the Grands Crus, the next classification is the Premiers Crus: Mont de Milieu, Montée de Tonnerre, Fourchaume, Vaillons, Montmains, Mélinots, Côte de Léchet, Beauroy, Vaucoupin, Vosgros, Vaulorent and Les Fourneaux. These wines are permitted to contain at least half a degree of alcohol less than the Grands Crus and can be relied on to be very good wines.

Wines bearing the name Chablis, but without a vineyard name will again be lighter than the Premiers Crus. They are generally wines made with grapes grown in less favored locations.

Finally, there is Petit-Chablis, which is produced from vineyards on the fringes of the region. Until recently these wines were rarely bottled or exported, but they are now available in many countries. They tend to be rather weak wines with a pronounced acidity.

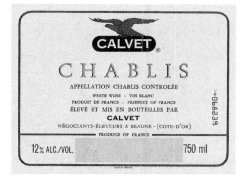

BORDEAUX

THE ASSOCIATION of Bordeaux with wine predates the Christian era. Although the records are vague, it is suspected that in those early days the city was a trader in wines, rather than a producer. By the first century, however, vineyards had been planted outside the city, which was then known as Burdigala, and the wines drew praise from the Roman writer Columella. Later, in the fourth century, the Roman poet Ausonius sang of the charms and vir-

tues of Burdigala wines. According to tradition, Château Ausone in Saint-Emilion was named in memory of the poet whose villa is thought to have occupied the same site.

After the departure of the Romans, historical records about the development of the vineyards are vague. In the fifth century, the Visigoths invaded the region, wreaking their usual devastation. They were followed by the Franks; Charlemagne passed through on his way to Spain. Later, Norman longboats penetrated the Garrone and Dordogne rivers, and set about pillaging the countryside. During this period, it is thought that the vineyard area was gradually expanded, but it was not until

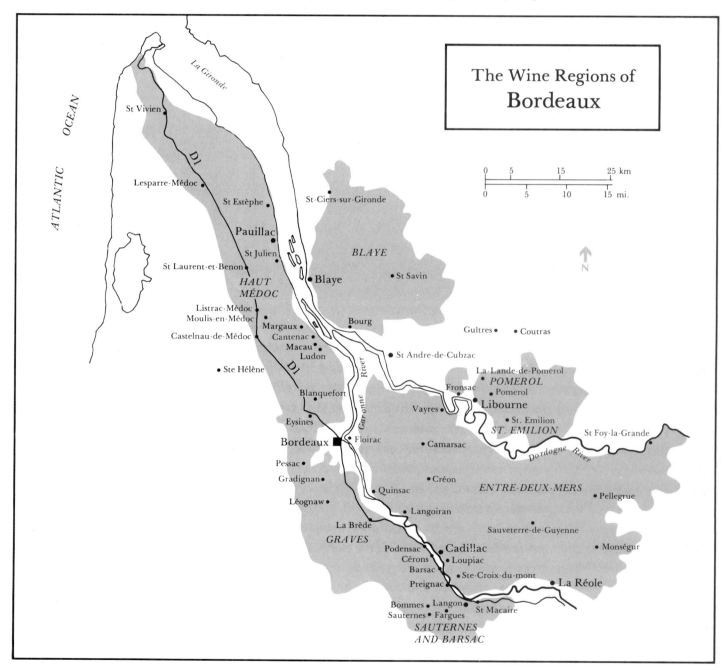

The Wine Regions of
Bordeaux

after the arrival of the English in the twelfth century that documentation of the wine trade was again established.

In 1152, Henry of Anjou married Eleanor of Aquitaine in Poitiers. Between them they held title to most of the western part of France up to Normandy. Poitou, Gascony, Auvergne Limousin, Périgord and parts of Touraine and Berry were Eleanor's, while Henry brought the rest of Touraine, Anjou, Maine and Normandy to the marriage. Two years later, on the death of King Stephen, Henry and Eleanor became King and Queen of England with extensive lands in France. In 1156, Henry II paid his first visit to Bordeaux, which at the time was part of Gascony. That visit was the beginning of a three-hundred-year era during which Bordeaux would remain under the rule of the English monarchy until they were finally expelled in 1453.

Although the French kings resented the English presence, most likely because of lost tax revenues rather than patriotic zeal, it did have a very positive effect on Bordeaux. The English quickly became the best customers for Bordeaux's red wines, which they called Claret. Even today, Britain is the biggest purchaser of Bordeaux wines. The English appreciation of Claret almost certainly contributed to the demise of their own wine industry, which did not experience a serious revival for over 800 years.

The establishment of the Bordeaux estates as we know them today occurred slowly over a period of almost 300 years. As Graves is the oldest vineyard area of Bordeaux, it is not surprising that Château Haut-Brion, situated on the doorstep of the city, was already known by the mid-seventeenth century. The planting of vines continued to spread in the Médoc throughout the sixteenth and seventeenth centuries, when the marshes of the Médoc were drained. By the late 1700s the vineyards of Bordeaux were very similar to what they are today, although Saint-Emilion and Pomerol were not then developed as extensively as they are now.

One of the most controversial aspects of the Bordeaux wine trade is the 1855 classification of the Médoc. The origins of Médoc classification are unclear, but there was some form of ranking in existence at least one hundred years prior to 1855. One theory which makes sense is that the classifications came into existence as a matter of conve-

nience for the trade. The establishment of classes (initially there were only four) made it easier to determine prices for the fifty or sixty vineyards that were considered to be the top growths. The 1855 ranking was compiled by the Syndicate of Brokers and endorsed by the Bordeaux Chamber of Commerce which shrewdly alluded to the fact that the classifications were based on "experience extending back more than a century." Although the ranking was essentially of the Gironde, the white wines of Sauternes and Barsac were also classified. Because the classification of the red wines was, with the sole exception of Château Haut-Brion in Graves, entirely those of the Médoc, it became known as a Médoc classification.

There are those who contend that the classification is irrelevant or out-of-date. The fact that it remains controversial and that the Graves and Saint-Emilion first adopted similar classification in 1959 and 1954 respectively would indicate that a classification system has some merit.

Harvesting the grapes, Bordeaux. Here viticulture dates back to Roman times, when the region was known as Burdigala.

Harvest cellar in Bordeaux

The 1855 Classification of Médoc
Revised 1973

FIRST GROWTHS

Ch. Lafite-Rothschild	Pauillac
Ch. Latour	Pauillac
Ch. Margaux	Margaux
Ch. Mouton-Rothschild	Pauillac
Ch. Haut-Brion	Pessac

SECOND GROWTHS

Ch. Rausan-Ségla	Margaux
Ch. Rauzan-Gassies	Margaux
Ch. Léoville-Las-Cases	Saint-Julien
Ch. Léoville-Poyferré	Saint-Julien
Ch. Léoville-Barton	Saint-Julien
Ch. Durfort-Vivens	Margaux
Ch. Gruaud-Laroze	Saint-Julien
Ch. Lascombes	Margaux
Ch. Brane-Cantenac	Cantenac-Margaux
Ch. Pichon-Longueville-Lalande	Pauillac
Ch. Pichon-Longueville	Pauillac
Ch. Ducru-Beaucaillou	Saint-Julien
Ch. Cos-d'Estournel	Saint-Estèphe
Ch. Montrose	Saint-Estèphe

THIRD GROWTHS

Ch. Kirwan	Cantenac-Margaux
Ch. d'Issan	Cantenac-Margaux
Ch. Lagrange	Saint-Julien
Ch. Langoa-Barton	Saint-Julien
Ch. Giscours	Labarde
Ch. Malescot-Saint-Exupéry	Margaux
Ch. Boyd-Cantenac	Margaux
Ch. Cantenac-Brown	Cantenac
Ch. Palmer	Cantenac
Ch. La Lagune	Ludon
Ch. Desmirail	Margaux
Ch. Calon-Ségur	Saint-Estèphe
Ch. Ferrière	Margaux
Ch. Marquis-d'Alesme-Becker	Margaux

FOURTH GROWTHS

Ch. Saint-Pierre	Saint-Julien
Ch. Talbot	Saint-Julien
Ch. Branaire-Ducru	Saint-Julien
Ch. Duhart-Milon	Pauillac
Ch. Pouget	Cantenac-Margaux
Ch. La Tour-Carnet	Saint-Laurent-Haut-Médoc
Ch. Lafon-Rochet	Saint-Estèphe
Ch. Beychevelle	Saint Julien
Ch. Prieuré-Lichine	Cantenac-Margaux
Ch. Marquis-de-Terme	Margaux

FIFTH GROWTHS

Ch. Pontet-Canet	Pauillac
Ch. Batailley	Pauillac
Ch. Haut-Batailley	Pauillac
Ch. Grand-Puy-Lacoste	Pauillac
Ch. Grand-Puy-Ducasse	Pauillac
Ch. Lynch-Bages	Pauillac
Ch. Lynch-Moussas	Pauillac
Ch. Dauzac	Labarde
Ch. Mouton-Baronne-Philippe	Pauillac
Ch. du Tertre	Arsac-Margaux
Ch. Haut-Bages-Libéral	Pauillac
Ch. Pédesclaux	Pauillac
Ch. Belgrave	Saint-Laurent-Haut-Médoc
Ch. Camensac	Saint-Laurent-Haut-Médoc
Ch. Cos-Labory	Saint-Estèphe
Ch. Clerc-Milon-Rothschild	Pauillac
Ch. Croizet-Bages	Pauillac
Ch. Cantemerle	Macau-Haut-Médoc

THE 1855 CLASSIFICATION OF SAUTERNES AND BARSAC

SUPERIOR FIRST GROWTH

Ch. d'Yquem	Sauternes

FIRST GROWTHS

Ch. La Tour-Blanche	Bommes
Ch. Lafaurie-Peyraguey	Bommes
Clos-Haut-Peyraguey	Bommes
Ch. Rayne-Vigneau	Bommes
Ch. Rabaud-Sigalas	Bommes
Ch. Rabaud-Promis	Bommes
Ch. de Suduiraut	Preignac
Ch. Coutet	Barsac
Ch. Climens	Barsac
Ch. Guiraud	Sauternes
Ch. Rieussec	Fargues

SECOND GROWTHS

Ch. de Myrat	Barsac
Ch. Doisy-Daëne	Barsac
Ch. Doisy-Védrines	Barsac
Ch. Doisy-Dubroca	Barsac
Ch. d'Arche	Sauternes
Ch. Filhot	Sauternes
Ch. Broustet	Barsac
Ch. Caillou	Barsac
Ch. Suau	Barsac
Ch. de Malle	Preignac
Ch. Romer	Preignac
Ch. Lamothe	Sauternes
Ch. Nairac	Barsac

THE 1959 CLASSIFICATION OF GRAVES

RED WINES

Ch. Haut-Brion	Pressac
Ch. Bouscaut	Cadaujac
Ch. Carbonnieux	Léognan
Domaine de Chevalier	Léognan
Ch. de Fieuzal	Léognan
Ch. Haut-Bailly	Léognan
Ch. La Mission Haut-Brion	Pessac
Ch. La Tour-Haut-Brion	Talence
Ch. La-Tour Martillac	Martillac
Ch. Malartic-Lagravière	Léognan
Ch. Olivier	Léognan
Ch. Pape-Clément	Pessac
Ch. Smith-Haut-Laffite	Martillac

WHITE WINES

Ch. Bouscaut	Cadaujac
Ch. Carbonnieux	Léognan
Domaine de Chevalier	Léognan
Ch. Couhins	Villenave-d'Ornon
Ch. La Tour-Martillac	Martillac
Ch. Laville-Haut-Brion	Talence
Ch. Malartic-Lagravière	Léognan
Ch. Olivier	Léognan

The vineyards of the Médoc stretch along the Gironde River, its eastern perimeter.

Médoc and Haut Médoc

The Médoc is a 45-mile-long triangle that is only three to six miles wide. The long eastern leg of the triangle is bounded by the Gironde River, while the western border consists of the sand dunes and firs that lie between the fertile lands of Médoc and the Atlantic. The city of Bordeaux lies on the short southern base of the triangle.

The land is generally flat, with a few sloping areas that never exceed a height of 150 feet above sea level. It is on these slopes, which descend gradually to the estuary of the Gironde, that the finest wines of the Médoc are grown.

The soil of the Médoc is surprisingly poor. The sub-soil ranges from chalk and clay to iron and sand, while the top soil varies considerably in both its depth and composition, which is generally of a gravelly and sandy nature. These variations in soil undoubtedly influence the character of wines and account for some of the noticeable differences that occur in wines made from vines grown in neighboring plots. It must be borne in mind, however, that a considerable part of these variations are due to the proportions of the grape varieties that a proprietor chooses as his blend. The main red wine grape variety is the Cabernet Sauvignon; the Merlot is the second most important variety. Cabernet Franc, Malbec and Petit Verdot are also grown. A wine made with a high proportion of Cabernet Sauvignon will have a far firmer style than a wine that contains more of the softer Merlot. The combination of agricultural conditions and blending styles, however, produces some of the finest red wines in

the world and an almost endless variation in styles that has made the wines of Médoc amongst the most fascinating for any wine lover.

The Médoc is composed of two parts. The southern part, the Haut Médoc, begins about five miles north of Bordeaux and ends just north of the village of Saint Seurin-de-Cadourne. From there north to Soulac is the Médoc which was formerly known as Bas Médoc. During the Second World War, the growers requested that the "Bas" be dropped and that their appellation become simply Médoc. The finer wines of the Médoc are all produced in Haut Médoc.

The four most important wine-producing communes of the Haut Médoc are Saint-Estèphe, Pauillac, Saint-Julien and Margaux.

SAINT-ESTÈPHE is the most northerly of the four leading communes and is divided from Pauillac

by a small *jalle*, the Médoc word for a stream. Because much less gravel has been washed this far downriver by the Gironde, the soil of Saint-Estèphe is heavy with clay and drains more slowly compared to its neighbor to the immediate south, Pauillac.

The heaviness of the soil is reflected in the sturdy character of the wines which have an earthy bouquet and, although full-flavored, are rather high in acid when young. Those who give them time to mature, however, will be rewarded with wines that are at once mellow and vigorous.

The commune boasts two Second Growths, Château Cos-d'Estournel and Montrose; one Third Growth, Château Calon-Ségur; one Fourth Growth, Château Lafon-Rochet; and one Fifth Growth, Château Cos-Labory.

Châteaux Cos-d'Estournel and Montrose are responsible for the commune's most outstanding

Harvesting at the Château Loudenne, Bordeaux.

Lush vineyards surround Château Latour in the Médoc.

Château Cos D'Estournel, Saint Estèphe of the Haut Médoc. The château produces outstanding wines that are noted for their dark color, strong flavor and longevity.

wines which are dark-colored, strong wines that live for a long, long time.

The commune is particularly noted for its plethora of Crus Bourgeois. Three that have built sound reputations and are worth seeking out are: Châteaux Meyney, Haut-Marbuzet and Phélan-Ségur.

PAUILLAC. This richly endowed commune is in many ways the wine capital of Haut Médoc. It is the headquarters of the Commanderie du Bontemps du Médoc et des Graves, a wine fraternity whose two main ceremonies of the year are the Fête de la Fleur in June and the Ban de Vendages in September.

Pauillac boasts three of Médoc's First Growths, two Second Growths, one Fourth Growth and twelve Fifth Growths. As if this were not enough, the commune is additionally blessed with twenty Crus Bourgeois Supérieurs.

The two longest established First Growths, Château Latour and Château Lafite-Rothschild stand at opposite ends of the commune. Lafite is at the northern gateway adjacent to Saint-Estèphe, while Latour is at the southern boundary hard by Saint-Julien. Peculiarly, the wines of Lafite are soft and graceful in a style similar to that of Saint-Julien, while Latour's wines are big and robust and more reminiscent of Saint-Estèphe.

In the 1855 classification, Château Mouton-Rothschild was ranked at the top of the Second Growths and it was not until 1973 that it was elevated to the status of a First Growth. The Second Growth classification caused Baron Nathaniel Rothschild to say, "Premier ne puis, Second ne daigne, Mouton suis." While the elevation prompted the present Baron, Philippe, to observe, "Premier je suis, Second je fus, Mouton ne change."

Anyone who has had the good fortune to drink a mature Mouton will readily understand why classification as a Second Growth rankled the Rothschilds. Individual in style, the wine is dark red, powerfully constituted and very long-lived. Much of the wine's strength, as with that of Latour, is due in large measure to the proportion of Cabernet Sauvignon grapes which can be as high as 90 per cent.

The case of Château Mouton-Rothschild, and its owners' 118-year wait for the ultimate recognition, clearly illustrates why the 1855 classification has become a cause for controversy. Although the vineyards of Mouton-Rothschild have remained in the same diligent family throughout that time, some of the châteaux which were being well cared for in 1855 have passed through less caring hands in the meantime, and have not always measured up to the mark set for them in 1855.

The two Second Growths, Châteaux Pichon-Longueville and Pichon-Longueville-Lalande, are located just north of Saint-Julien to the west of Latour. The larger of the two estates, which were originally one, Lalande generally produces the better wine.

Next in the 1855 rankings comes Château Duhart-Milon which is a Fourth Growth. The château adjoins both Lafite and Mouton, and, like them, is the property of the Rothschilds, whose expertise is evident in the quality of this property's wines.

Pauillac dominates the Fifth Growths with twelve out of the eighteen châteaux in this classification. Quality in this group is rather uneven, with the most notable being Châteaux Pontet-Canet, Grand-Puy-Lacoste, Grand-Puy-Ducasse, Clerc-Milon, Lynch-Bages and Croizet-Bages.

SAINT-JULIEN. This small commune is, internationally, the best known of the Médoc's big four. Proportionate to its size, it has a higher number of classed growths than any other commune.

The land of Saint-Julien is ideal for vineyards, and, when mature, the wines develop a unique delicacy and softness as well as an attractive, flowery bouquet.

Five of the commune's châteaux are Second Growths. The crowning glory of Saint-Julien is the massive Léoville vineyards which are divided in three as Châteaux Léoville-Las-Cases, Léoville-Poyferré and Léoville-Barton. The latter is considered the finest and is owned by the Bartons of Barton & Guestier which, in turn, is owned by Joseph E. Seagram & Sons of Montreal, Canada.

The other Second Growths are Château Gruaud-Laroze and Château Ducru-Beaucaillou. Gruaud-Laroze produces a wine that is exemplary of the smooth Saint-Julien style, while Ducru-

Pavilions and gables make Château d'Issan, Haut Médoc, Bordeaux, especially picturesque.

Guests gather at Château Dauzac for the spring celebration of the Commanderie du Bontemps de Médoc et des Graves, the Fête de la Fleur, 1983.

Beaucaillou is responsible for a drier wine with an incredible depth of character.

Of the two Third Growths, Château Langoa-Barton is under the same ownership as its neighbor, Léoville-Barton, in whose cellars the wine is now aged. The wines of Léoville are generally ranked higher than those of Langoa, but the latter still produces an extremely fine Saint-Julien. Château Lagrange, on the other hand, lies far back from the river, and, although it once enjoyed a reputation for its fine, robust wines, would probably not be considered for classification in any revision taking place today.

Château Lafite-Rothschild and vineyards in fall. The wine of the same name produced here is considered to be one of the finest in all Bordeaux.

Château Talbot, like Gruaud-Laroze, yields a wine with the fine, smooth style that is the hallmark of a Saint-Julien. The other Fourth Growths are Châteaux Saint-Pierre, Beychevelle and Branaire-Ducru. Château Saint-Pierre is now linked with two other estates, Bontemps and Sevaistre, and is owned by a Belgian wine merchant who reserves the majority of these wines for that market. Beychevelle, while one of the best-known wines of the region, does well in good vintages, but can be disappointing in even the most slightly adverse season. Its less well-known neighbor, Branaire-Ducru, has shown itself more reliable in recent years.

MARGAUX. The closest of the big four communes to the city of Bordeaux, Margaux is peculiar in that, instead of its vineyards being dotted evenly across the commune, they form a tight knot around the village of Margaux, almost to the point of overlapping each other in some cases.

The soil of Margaux is the shallowest in the Médoc and has the highest gravel content. Although this soil offers little nutrition to the vines, it does drain well, and, in rainy years, that is a great advantage.

The jewel of the commune is unquestionably Château Margaux itself, which is its only First Growth. The château enjoys an international reputation for its extraordinarily fine wines which are, with justification, regarded by many as the epitome of everything a fine Claret should be. Although its fame is based upon its red wine, the château also produces a white wine, which is sold as Pavillon-Blanc du Château Margaux. The grapes for this white wine are grown on a small area of the estate where the soil is particularly chalky.

For many years now, the neighboring communes of Cantenac, Labarde, Soussans and Arsac have been allowed to sell their wines under the Margaux appellation.

Consequently, the leading Second Growth of Margaux is Château Brane-Cantenac which produces a more powerful, if less fragrant wine than Margaux. The other Second Growths of the appellation are all in Margaux. They are: Châteaux Durfort-Vivens, Lascombes, Rausan-Ségla and Rauzan-Gassies.

The appellation's Third Growths are dominated by the Cantenac estates Châteaux Kirwan, Cantenac-Brown, Boyd-Cantenac, d'Issan and Palmer. Of these five Palmer is generally held in the highest regard. Kirwan's wines have been of uneven quality recently, but extensive replanting has been done in recent years and by 1990, the wines should regain their former stature. The other Third Growths are: Châteaux Ferrière, Malescot-Saint-Exupéry and Mârquis-d'Alesme-Becker in Margaux and Château Giscours in Labarde. In the classification of 1855, Château Desmirail, in Margaux, was ranked as a Third Growth, but it has now essentially disappeared to become a subsidiary of Château Palmer.

The commune's Fourth Growths are: Châteaux Prieuré-Lichine and Marquis-de-Terme in Margaux and Château Pouget in Cantenac, while the Fifth Growths are: Château Dauzac in Labarde and Château Mouton-Baron-Philippe in Arsac. A great deal of replanting and upgrading of the winery facilities has taken place at Dauzac over the last several years, and this is another château that can be expected to regain its former glory in the next few years.

Although it is not in the classification, Château d'Angludet in Cantenac can be relied upon to produce excellent wines that have a high percentage of Cabernet Sauvignon grapes.

Besides the galaxy of classified growths, there are over two hundred châteaux, usually referred to as Crus Bourgeois, in Haut Médoc. Many of these châteaux produce very decent wines of considerable style. Although they do not measure up against the top growths, they also do not command the high price of these wines, and are generally good value.

MÉDOC. To the north of Haut Médoc lies a twelve-mile-long strip of vineyards that is four to five miles wide. There are no classified growths in this area, whose wines are entitled to the simple appellation Médoc.

The area used to be known as Bas Médoc, but during the Second World War the growers of the area demanded that the appellation be changed to Médoc. Apparently, they felt that the Bas (lower), referring to their location on the lower estuary of the Gironde, was derogatory and carried the implication that their wines were of lower quality.

The fact is that there are no classified wines in Médoc, and, while there are many wines of very satisfactory quality, there are no outstanding wines produced in the Médoc.

Graves

To the south of the city of Bordeaux lies the region of Graves which is in every sense the birthplace of the Bordeaux wine industry. It was here that the first vineyards were established outside of the ancient city walls. When the vine was first planted is uncertain; suffice to say that wine has been produced in Graves as long as history has been recorded.

At one time, vineyards surrounded the city on all sides except the east where the Gironde flows. Indeed, in the middle ages, the vine grew within the city.

Today, the expansion of the city has seen a diminishing of the vineyards. The wines that were once produced to the north and west of Bordeaux disappeared many years ago, and, in more recent years, the continuing expansion of the city has virtually eliminated vineyards from the commune of Mérignac, although Château Picque-Caillou continues to produce a red wine that is remarkably fine.

The châteaux of Graves tend to be isolated from each other as they are generally little more than clearings in the heavily forested land. Because of the forests, the region is prone to damage from late frosts which have caused many vineyards to be abandoned and placed an extra burden, or challenge, on those who remain.

*Château La Tour-
Martillac, Graves-
Bordeaux.*

*Rolland Kressman
in the vineyards at
Château La Tour-
Martillac, Graves-
Bordeaux.*

There is a commonly held belief that Graves produces mainly white wines. Actually, while it is true that a great deal of white wine is made, it is rarely of more than average quality. The red wines produced on this gravelly, sandy soil, from which the district takes its name, are often outstanding and, in some cases, can rival the wines of Haut Médoc.

The true situation becomes quite clear in the classification of the region that was established by decree on February 16, 1959. It shows clearly that more red wines were considered worthy of classification than whites which, with two exceptions, are produced on estates that also have classified reds. The classified estates are:

RED WINES

Château Haut-Brion
Château Bouscaut
Château Carbonnieux
Domaine de Chevalier
Château de Fieuzal
Château Haut-Bailly
Château La Mission-Haut-Brion
Château La Tour-Haut-Brion
Château La Tour-Martillac
Château Malartic-Lagravière
Château Olivier
Château Pape-Clément
Château Smith-Haut-Lafitte

WHITE WINES

Château Bouscaut
Château Carbonnieux
Domaine de Chevalier
Château Couhins
Château La Tour-Martillac
Château Laville-Haut-Brion
Château Malartic-Lagravière
Château Olivier

The châteaux, in this classification, are presented in alphabetical order, rather than rank, with the exception of Château Haut-Brion which is placed first in recognition of its having been given First Growth status in the 1855 classification of the Médoc.

Château Haut-Brion, in the commune of Pessac, is now literally on the southern doorstep of the City of Bordeaux as are Châteaux La Mission-Haut-Brion, La Tour Haut-Brion and Laville-Haut-Brion in the commune of Talence.

The only other classed growth in the northern part of Graves is Château Pape-Clément, in Pessac, which is one the region's oldest vineyards that continues to produce an excellent red wine.

There is a gap of several miles to the south of Pessac in which very few vineyards have survived. In the commune of Léognan, however, there are six of the classed growths. The most northerly is Château Olivier which makes both red and white wines, but tends now to concentrate more on the white.

Château Haut-Bailly is the odd-man-out in Léognan as it makes only red wines that are deservedly held in high regard. In the west of the commune lies Château Carbonnieux which enjoys the reputation of producing the finest white Graves.

In the south of the commune are Châteaux Malartic-Lagravière, de Fieuzal and Domaine de Chevalier. All three produce both red and white wines of which the best are currently being made by Domaine de Chevalier.

The other four classed growths are strung down the western edge of the region.

Château Couhins, in Villenave-d'Ornon, vints both red and white wines, but again it is its white that is most worthy of remark. Château Bouscaut, in Cadaujac, is justly renowned for both its red and white wines which have won recognition in the form of medals and awards in the United States and Belgium as well as France.

Finally, in Martillac are Château Smith-Haut-Lafitte which specializes in red wines and Château La Tour-Martillac where both red and white wines are produced. This estate is owned by Jean Kressmann, and the white wine is sometimes sold in Britain and the United States as Château Kressman-La-Tour.

To the south of Martillac, the Graves narrows to a narrow strip in the west that curves south before swinging north to form a crook around the communes of Cérons, Sauternes and Barsac.

Château La Mission Haut-Brion, south of the city of Bordeaux.

Cabernet Sauvignon,
*the grape responsible
for the great red
wines of Bordeaux.
The fruit is small
and spherical, black
with a whitish bloom
and thick skin. It
falls in long, conical
clusters, with a lacy
leaf. Red wines
produced from it are
highly colored, with
a characteristic
violet bouquet, and
age well.*

Merlot grapes are medium-sized, spherical, and reddish-black to black. The rich varietal featured in St Emilion and Pomerol, Merlot is used extensively for blending with Cabernet Sauvignon to add lush flavor, softness, and complexity.

Cérons

Wedged between Graves and Barsac, this region comprises the three communes of Cérons, Podensac and Illats. It is something of an ambiguous region in that it produces dry red and white wines that are entitled to carry the Graves appellation. The whites, in particular, do indeed rival even the finest white Graves.

On the other hand, wines carrying the Cérons appellation are made in the same manner as Sauternes. The Sémillon grapes, the most widely planted white variety for sweet white wines, are allowed to over-ripen and develop *pourriture noble*, or noble rot, which is the result of the grapes being attacked by the fungus *Botrytis cinerea*. The grapes affected in this way are gathered in successive pickings, and the result is a sweet white wine similar in style to a Sauternes, except that it is lighter in weight.

A few châteaux produce wines of distinction, although they do not enjoy wide distribution. Those worth seeking out include: Château de Cérons et de Calvimont, Grand enclos du Château de Cérons, Château Mayne-Binet, Lalannette-Pardiac, des Bessanes, le Bon-Dieu-des-Vignes, d'Anice, des Mauves, Chantegrive, Ferbos and Domaine de la Courrège.

Sauternes and Barsac

This region, which also includes the communes of Bommes, Preignac and Fargues, produces one of the greatest sweet white wines in the world.

The principal grapes are the Sémillion, Sauvignon, with some Muscadelle and Ugni-Blanc also being grown.

It is, however, the method used in making this wine that transforms it into a golden nectar which, at its best, has an intensity of flavor, sweetness and complexity.

Even fully ripe grapes are inadequate in this region, where the growers patiently wait until their grapes have noble rot before they begin picking. At this point, the *Botrytis cinerea* has done its work of reducing the water content of the grape and concentrating the sugars and other flavor elements.

Even then, it is not a matter of harvesting the whole vineyard. Only those grapes that are fully infected are gathered, and the grower may have to harvest seven or eight times before the work is completed.

The first harvest can be as early as September and it can continue into December. The risks of losing much of the crop to inclement weather and killing frosts are phenomenal, but there are no options if the Sauternes style of wine is to be made.

All too often, weather conditions are not ideal, causing the wines to be thinner than they should be, and, although still pleasant enough, they lack the body and breeding that are achieved in good years.

Just as the Haut Médoc was classified in 1855, so too was Sauternes in the following manner:

SUPERIOR FIRST GROWTH

| Ch. d'Yquem | Sauternes |

FIRST GROWTHS

Ch. La Tour-Blanche	Bommes
Ch. Lafaurie-Peyraguey	Bommes
Clos-Haut-Peyraguey	Bommes
Ch. Rayne-Vigneau	Bommes
Ch. Rabaud-Sigalas	Bommes
Ch. Rabaud-Promis	Bommes
Ch. de Suduiraut	Preignac
Ch. Coutet	Barsac
Ch. Climens	Barsac
Ch. Guiraud	Sauternes
Ch. Rieussec	Fargues

SECOND GROWTHS

Ch. de Myrat	Barsac
Ch. Doisy-Daëne	Barsac
Ch. Doisy-Védrines	Barsac
Ch. Doisy-Dubroca	Barsac
Ch. d'Arche	Sauternes
Ch. Filhot	Sauternes
Ch. Broustet	Barsac
Ch. Caillou	Barsac
Ch. Suau	Barsac
Ch. de Malle	Preignac
Ch. Romer	Preignac
Ch. Lamothe	Sauternes
Ch. Nairac	Barsac

Pourriture noble,
the "noble rot" that
helps to produce the
sweet white wines of
Sauternes, Barsac,
Bommes, Fargues,
Preignac and
Cérons.

Château d'Yquem's unique location favors the ripening of its grapes and the development of pourriture noble.

The placing of Château d'Yquem in an exalted position of its own is fully justified. No other wine in the region can measure up to the quality of the wines from this estate. The reason they are superior is the location of the vineyards.

Château d'Yquem stands on the top of a hill, with all of the other châteaux spread out below it. The micro-climate created by this unique location favors the ripening of the grapes and the development of noble rot. Even with these advantages, however, it is not always a good year at d'Yquem. If the grapes are not judged good enough to bear the name of Château d'Yquem, then such wine as can be made will be labeled and sold as Château "Y".

The First Growths of the region, however, all make excellent wines that take second place only to d'Yquem, but to no other sweet wines in the world.

Except in the worst years, the Second Growths can also be relied upon to produce wines of outstanding quality.

Wines that bear such labels as Sauternes, Barsac, have no official standing and are blends of wines taken from the unclassified vineyards of the region. They are never outstanding, but they can be pleasant drinking nevertheless.

Saint-Emilion

On the right bank of the Dordogne, and a few miles east of Libourne, Saint-Emilion is the largest of Bordeaux's important wine-producing regions.

The ancient and picturesque town of Saint-Emilion is Roman in origin, perched on a corner of an escarpment, and is surrounded by vines that sweep down the slope and then on to a plateau that stretches into Pomerol behind it and down on to the plain in the other direction.

Saint-Emilion is comprised of two completely different areas. The larger part is the Côtes Saint-Emilion located on the escarpment around the town, while the other is Graves-Saint-Emilion which occupies the plateau. This latter area is not to be confused with the Graves region on the left bank south of Bordeaux city.

The wines from the Graves grow in a gravelly, sandy soil and tend to be more fruity than the Côtes wines. Nevertheless, the best of the Côtes wines are amongst the finest in Bordeaux.

Generally, Saint-Emilion wines mature more quickly than those of the Médoc and Graves, and, consequently, are more readily appreciated for their forthright, earthy flavor by many people before they can learn to enjoy the dryness and complexity of a Médoc.

One of the reasons for the character of Saint-Emilion's wines is that they have a higher proportion of Merlot and Malbec grapes than Cabernet Sauvignon which is the principal variety in both the Médoc and Graves blends.

For one reason or another, the Saint-Emilion wines were completely ignored in the 1855 classification of the Médoc which made one exception to include Château Haut-Brion in Graves. It is speculated that Saint-Emilion was excluded because of politics or envy, or, perhaps, because the wines were not of the quality we know today.

In any event, under the aegis of the National Committee of the Institut National des Appellations d'Origine, a classification of Saint-Emilion was undertaken and has been established since 1955.

On January 11, 1984, however, the INAO concluded that a revision of the classification was appropriate. Subsequently, on February 16 of the same year, a panel of nine, referred to by the French press as "les neuf sages," was appointed to that task.

Muraille de Saint-Emilion, Bordeaux. A good Saint-Emilion wine has a dark, brilliant color and a pleasant hint of bitterness.

Their deliberations were concluded during 1985 and the following, which is likely to be adopted in its entirety, is their proposed re-classification to take effect with the 1986 vintage:

PREMIERS GRANDS CRUS CLASSÉS

A. Ch. Ausone
    Ch. Cheval-Blanc

B. Ch. Beauséjour (Duffau-Lagarrosse)
    Ch. Belair
    Ch. Canon
    Ch. Clos Fourtet
    Ch. Figeac
    Ch. La Gaffelière
    Ch. Magdelaine
    Ch. Pavie
    Ch. Trottevieille

GRANDS CRUS CLASSÉS

Ch. L'Angélus
Ch. L'Arrosée
Ch. Balestard-la-Tonnelle
Ch. Beauséjour (Bécot)
Ch. Bellevue
Ch. Bergat
Ch. Berliquet
Ch. Cadet-Piola
Ch. Canon-la-Gaffelière
Ch. Cap-de-Mourlin
Ch. Le Châtelet
Ch. Chauvin
Clos des Jacobins
Clos La Madeleine
Clos de L'Oratoire
Clos Saint-Martin
Ch. La Clotte
Ch. Corbin
Ch. Corbin-Michotte
Ch. La Clusière
Couvent-des-Jacobins
Ch. Croque-Michotte
Ch. Curé-Bon-la-Madeleine
Ch. Dassault
Ch. La Dominique
Ch. Faurie-de-Souchard
Ch. Fonplégade
Ch. Fonroque
Ch. Franc-Mayne
Ch. Grand-Barrail-Lamarzelle-Figeac
Ch. Grand-Corbin-Despagne

Ch. Grand-Corbin
Ch. Grand-Mayne
Ch. Grand-Pontet
Ch. Gaudet-Saint-Julien
Ch. Haut-Corbin
Ch. Haut-Sarpe
Ch. Laniotte
Ch. Larcis-Ducasse
Ch. La Marzelle
Ch. Larmande
Ch. Laroze
Ch. Matras
Ch. Mauvezin
Ch. Moulin-du-Cadet
Ch. Pavie-Decesse
Ch. Pavie-Macquin
Ch. Pavillon-Cadet
Ch. Petit-Faurie-de-Soutard
Ch. le Prieuré
Ch. Ripeau
Ch. Sansonnet
Ch. Saint-Georges-Côtes-Pavie
Ch. La Serre
Ch. Soutard
Ch. Tertre-Daugay
Ch. La Tour-du-Pin-Figeac (Giraud)
Ch. La Tour-du-Pin Figeac (Moueix)
Ch. La Tour-Figeac
Ch. Trimoulet
Ch. Troplong-Mondot
Ch. Villemaurine
Ch. Yon-Figeac

The continuation of Château Ausone and Cheval-Blanc in the highest category will surprise no one familiar with these excellent wines. Perhaps the biggest surprise is the demotion of Château Beauséjour (Bécot) from Premier Grand Cru to Grand Cru.

Likewise, the number of Grands Crus Classés is reduced from 72 to 63, although all of the old stalwarts, such as Château Figeac, La Tour-du-Pin-Figeac in the Graves and Château Pavie, Magdelaine, Trottevieille and La Gaffelière-Nandes have retained their positions in the (B) category as Grands Crus Classés.

To the north, east and south of Saint-Emilion proper are several communes that are entitled to the Saint-Emilion appellation. They are: Saint-Christophe-des-Bardes, Saint-Etienne-de-

Lisse, Saint-Laurent-des-Combes, Saint-Hippolyte, Saint-Pey-d'Armens, Saint-Sulpice-de-Faleyrens, Vignonet, Montagne, Saint-Georges, Parsac, Lussac, and Puisseguin.

Of these communes the most important are the four closest to Saint-Emilion — Saint-Christophe, Saint-Étienne, Saint-Laurent and Saint-Hippolyte.

Among them they have twelve Grands Crus: Château Fombrauge, Haut-Sarpe, Lapelletrie, Puy-Blanquet and Tour-Saint-Christophe in Saint-Christophe, Château Larcis-Ducasse in Saint-Laurent and Château Capet-Guillier, Haut-Plantey, Maurens and Clos des Sarazins in Saint-Hippolyte.

Pomerol

Located on a sandy-gravelly plateau, Pomerol is a confusing commune in several ways. To begin with, there is no village of Pomerol, and even the church stands in isolation, as do the majority of houses, divided by a sea of vines in this compact area of some 1,550 acres.

Also there is no official classification. There is an unofficial classification, which appears to be more concerned with not causing offence to anyone, rather than making a genuine attempt to present a quality evaluation.

Although the vine has been grown in Pomerol since Roman times, it is only in the last hundred years that it has developed its own identity. Up until then the wines were sold as Saint-Emilions. In fact, it is only in the last thirty or forty years that Pomerol has received any serious recognition as an important individual region.

Equally, despite the lack of an official classification, some châteaux have earned reputations which are built on the quality they produce and the consensus of the wine trade around the world.

The best châteaux are those that border the Graves-Saint-Emilion. Château Pétrus is accepted as the finest wine of Pomerol and is set apart from the others in the same way as Châteaux Ausone and Cheval-Blanc in Saint-Emilion.

The twelve held in the highest regard, in alphabetical order are: Châteaux Gazin, La Conseillante, Lafleur, La Fleur-Pétrus, Le Gay, Clos l'Eglise, Châteaux l'Eglise-Clinet, L'Evangile, Nenin, Petit-Village, Trotanoy and Vieux Château Certan.

At least another twenty châteaux produce wines of considerable style and quality, and there are many people who have "discovered" their own personal favorites in that group.

As in Saint-Emilion, the wines of Pomerol owe their bigness of fruit and flavor to the Merlot grape which is often responsible for as much as 70 or 80 per cent of the blend.

Pomerol is surrounded by the communes of Lalonde-de-Pomerol, Néac and Fronsac. All three communes produce wines in the Saint-Emilion/Pomerol style and can often equal the quality of the lesser châteaux of these appellations.

Until 1954, Néac was entitled to sell its wines under its own appellation, but since that time its wines have been sold under the appellation of Lalonde-de-Pomerol.

Entre-Deux-Mers

This region is an enormous triangle set between the rivers Garonne and Dordogne. The apex of the triangle is in the north, and the area widens, as the rivers diverge, until its base is formed some fifty miles to the south.

The region is composed of several districts. In the northwest is Carbon-Blanc and coming south from there on the west side are the districts of Créon, Targon, Sauveterre, Monségur, La Réole and Haut-Benauge. In the north, beside the Dordogne, are the districts of Branne and Pujols.

To complicate matters further, there are areas within the region that are entitled to their own appellations. In the northeast, on the left bank of the Dordogne opposite Libourne, is the tiny appellation of Graves de Vayres which produces a white wine under that designation.

Upstream, at the other end of the Dordogne valley, is the fairly large area of Sainte-Foy-la-Grande which presents its wines under the appellation Sainte-Foy-Bordeaux.

On the western boundary of the region, stretching for thirty miles along the right bank of the Garonne, is a narrow strip of the Premières Côtes

Three generations of the House of Mau. Left to right: grandfather Yvon, Jean François, Michel in the vineyards of Château Lavison, once a hunting lodge of the Black Prince. (Bordeaux-Entre-Deux-Mers)

de Bordeaux, at the southern end of which is the Côtes de Bordeaux-Saint-Macaire.

The best reds of this appellation come from Camblanes, Quinsac and Cambes, while the best whites originate in Monprimblanc and Gabarnac. Only the white wines of the Côtes de Bordeaux-Saint-Macaire are entitled to use that appellation.

Within the vast area of Entre-Deux-Mers, the majority of the wines produced are white and are made from the Sémillion, Sauvignon and Muscadelle, while the red grape varieties used are the Cabernet Sauvignon, Malbec and Merlot.

Only white wines may be sold under the appellation of Entre-Deux-Mers, while the reds must be sold either as Bordeaux AC or Bordeaux Supérieur.

Although many sound wines, both red and white, are produced in the region, there are no truly outstanding wines. Having said that, however, while a Chablis may be the wine of choice with oysters, a good Entre-Deux-Mers has always seemed more appropriate to me when enjoying the glorious oysters at Arcachon.

Bourg, Blaye and Bergerac

Regarded for many decades as having been born on the wrong side of the tracks, or in this case, the wrong side of the river, the communes of Bourg and Blaye were well established and reputable wine exporters before the Médoc was even planted!

Overshadowed and outclassed by the newcomers on the left bank, these communes languished in obscurity for many decades.

Changing economic conditions have rekindled interest in these wines, which can never hope to command the prices of even the lesser wines of Haut Médoc, far less the Grands Crus.

Nevertheless, the Côte de Bourg, in particular, produces red wines of very respectable quality and whites that offer enough depth to demand more than a cursory examination.

Overleaf: Château de Montbazillac. When its wines are aged, they turn deep gold, with a full, rich character.

The Côtes de Blaye is a considerably larger area, but the quality of its wines tends to be lower than those of Bourg.

It is easy to dismiss these two regions glibly, but it should be remembered that they are, in every sense, Bordeaux wines, albeit generally for everyday consumption; but there are the odd gems that will reward those with the patience to age them in the same way as any sound Claret.

Bergerac, occupying the hinterland to the southeast of Bourg and Blaye, is a beautiful region that produces red wines of acceptable, but not outstanding quality, and white wines that range from dry to sweet. In fact, if its whites have a fault, it is that sometimes they are neither exactly sweet nor dry.

Ironically, perhaps, the restaurants of Périgord are of international renown, and typically, along with their array of imaginative and delicious foods, traditionally incorporating truffles and foie gras, they feature local wines.

CÔTES DU RHÔNE

THE ALREADY MIGHTY River Rhône is augmented at Lyon by the substantial waters of the River Saône, and at this point turns south to set course for the Mediterranean. On its way to the sea, it fathers some of the finest wines of France.

Directly south of Burgundy, the Côtes du Rhône stretches for 125 miles from just south of Lyon to Avignon. In general, the finest wines come from the northern part of the region, but there are also wine gems to the south.

The Côtes du Rhône is an ancient home of the vine which, it is claimed, has grown there since 300 A.D. It was certainly from this region that the vine spread north into Burgundy and east to Savoie where the great wall of the Alps prevented any further conquest.

Côte-Rôtie

Some twenty miles south of Lyon, around the village of Ampuis on the right bank of the river, the steep twin slopes of Côte-Rôtie rise as a dramatic beginning to the vineyards of the Côtes du Rhône.

The stony slope of the northern côte, which forms a spectacular backdrop to the village, is known as the Côte Brune. Immediately to its south is the Côte Blonde, which has a lighter-colored soil because it has more lime than its neighboring côte.

The grapes of Côte-Rôtie are the Syrah, known locally as the Sérine, and the Voignier. The vines are pruned in an unusual manner in which three plants are tied to three poles to form a pyramid.

The resulting red wine is one of the Rhône's finest and, with age, develops a marvellous delicacy while retaining a powerful bouquet and full, fruit flavor.

The vines of the Côte Rôtie are traditionally pruned in this distinctive manner.

Viticulture in the Côtes du Rhône has flourished for 1,700 years.

Condrieu

Travelling south on the right bank, the next appellation is Condrieu which includes the villages of Vérin, Saint-Michel and Condrieu.

The only grape variety permitted is the Voignier which yields a delicate, golden wine with a flowery nose and considerable charm.

Between Vérin and Saint-Michel is the heart of Condrieu, Château Grillet which, with only 4 acres of vines, is the smallest appellation in France. The Voignier is planted in the granite soil on terraces that are often so narrow they can carry only one row of vines.

Only about twelve barrels of wine are produced each year, and they can be left to wait for as long as two years in the cellars below the château before being bottled.

The result of this patience is a wine with a boldness of bouquet and an individual, but completely confident, personality.

Hermitage and Crozes-Hermitage

About twenty miles south of Condrieu, on the left bank of the Rhône, is the village of Tain-l'Hermitage which is the center of two appellations, Hermitage and Crozes.

The imposing slope of Hermitage looms suddenly out of the plain to its north. Its name is derived from the crusader knight Stérimberg who obtained land from Blanche of Castille to serve as a retreat where he could live as a hermit.

Only the Syrah is grown for red wines, while the Roussanne and Marsanne are used to produce white wines.

The reds are solid, balanced wines of incredible longevity. I recall being in the cellars of the reputable grower Jaboulet in 1983 when Gérard Jaboulet presented me with a bottle of 1961 Hermitage La Chapelle. Remarkably, at twenty-two years of age, the wine exhibited no sign of weariness, but rather held a promise of even better things to come.

The white wines, although sound and attractive, do not require extensive aging and can be enjoyed from their first year.

Crozes-Hermitage, composed of the villages of Crozes, Tain, Beaumont-Ventoux, Erôme,

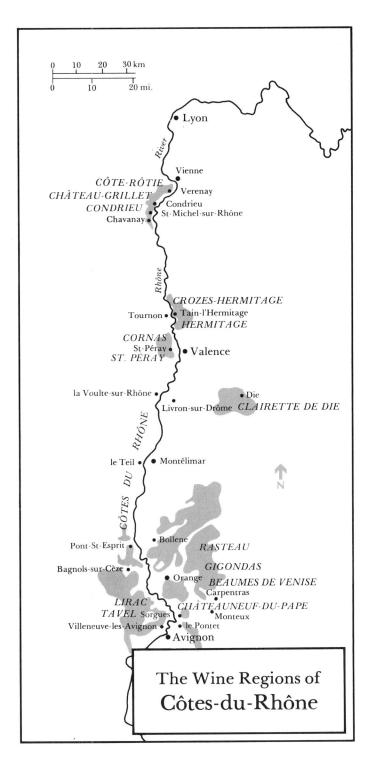

The Wine Regions of
Côtes-du-Rhône

Hermitage stands aloof on its magnificent slope overlooking the Rhône.

Larnage, Gervans, La Roche-de-Glun, Serves-sur-Rhône and Pont-de-l'Isère, makes both red and white wines from the same grape varieties as Hermitage.

Regarded as lesser wines than those of Hermitage, the reds will respond to careful and patient aging, while the whites are best drunk in their early years. Less than Hermitage they may be, but, to my mind, only marginally so.

Saint-Joseph

Directly opposite Hermitage, on the right bank, are the vineyards of Saint-Joseph. This appellation applies to the vineyards on the slopes of the six villages Tournon, Glun, Saint-Jean-de-Muzols, Lemps, Vion and Mauves.

This is a comparatively recent appellation, established by decree on June 15th, 1956. Prior to then they were named the Vin de Mauves because of their purple color.

The red wines are again produced from Syrah grapes, while the Roussanne and Marsanne are used in making white wines.

At their best, the reds of Saint-Joseph are deep-colored, full-bodied, elegant wines similar in style to Crozes-Hermitage. The whites, when young, are attractively light and fresh.

Cornas

Dating back to the Gallo-Roman era, the vineyards of Cornas are planted only with Syrah grapes.

Located on the foothills of the Cévennes, the vineyards of Cornas, which means "scorched ground" in Celtic, are well exposed to the sun.

The wines have a very dark ruby, almost black, color and are not pleasant when young, but they more than reward those with the patience to lay them down and wait for at least three to five years for them to mature.

Saint-Péray

Just to the south of Cornas, and still on the right bank, the vineyards of the appellation of Saint-Péray also trace their origins back to the Gallo-Roman era.

Here, however, only white wines are made from the Roussanne and Marsanne grapes. Because of the narrowness of space between the vines on the steep slopes, much of the ground has to be tilled by hand.

The still, dry white wines of Saint-Péray are somewhat lighter than other whites from the north part of the Côtes du Rhône. Since 1829, a sparkling wine has been made in the same manner as Champagne. Today, sparkling wine accounts for the greater part of the appellation's production.

Rasteau and Beaumes-de-Venise

On the left bank of the Rhône, between the rivers Aygues and Ouvèze, the parish of Rasteau is planted exclusively with Grenache grapes which are allowed to become highly matured before being harvested and fermented into naturally sweet wines. Once the wines reach at least 15 per cent alcoholic content, alcohol is added to control the fermentation so that the wines retain their sweetness.

To the south and east of Rasteau the vineyards of Beaumes-de-Venise are planted with Grenache grapes which yield a light Côte du Rhône wine; but they also grow a Muscat vine which has small berries, and from these is made a naturally sweet wine in the same manner as that of Rasteau.

Gigondas

Located on the left bank of the Rhône, between Rasteau and Beaumes-de-Venise, the vineyards of

Syrah *grapes produce a fragrant wine reminiscent of raspberries or violets.*

The Grenache *grape has attained popularity in the Rhône region where it grows on both sides of the River Rhône.*

Gigondas are composed of layers of sand and pebbles on a series of flowing slopes that reach from the Montmirail towards the Ouvèze valley.

The main grape is the Grenache, but Syrah and Mourvèdre grapes are also grown. It is the blending of these varieties that gives Gigondas wines their distinctive character.

Full-bodied and flavored with an intense bouquet, the wines of Gigondas are capable of long aging. They can take their place not only as some of the great wines of the Rhône, but also of France.

Châteauneuf-du-Pape

No other wine of the Côtes du Rhone is more widely known than Châteauneuf-du-Pape. Located about ten miles north of Avignon on the left bank of the Rhône, the vineyards flow over a group of hills dominated by the ruins of the old summer palace of the Popes.

The vineyards of Châteauneuf-du-Pape have been strictly regulated since 1923, and it was the success achieved through that regulation which gave birth in 1936 to the national appellation controlée system. One of the area's prominent growers at the time, Baron Le Roy, made a proposal, which was adopted, to identify the most suitable growing land, determine the permitted grape varieties, and establish rules for pruning, quality, and strength.

The most striking thing about these vineyards is that there is absolutely no soil visible. Instead the ground is covered with a sea of large pebbles in a variety of colors. The vines grow without the support of either trellises or stakes.

In all, thirteen grape varieties are used to make this wine. The seven principal varieties are: Grenache, Clairette, Mourvèdre, Picpoul, Terret, Syrah and Cinsault, while the six secondary varieties are: Rousanne, Counoise, Muscardin, Vaccarèse, Picardin, and Bourboulenc.

With a higher alcoholic strength, 14.5 per cent, than most French table wines, Châteauneuf-du-Pape is a warm, full-bodied wine, reflecting the warmth of the Provençal sun. It ages well and is

The vines of Châteauneuf-du-Pape seem to spring from the pebbled ground without benefit of support or soil.

worth cellaring for five to ten years. A little white Châteauneuf-du-Pape is made. It has a deep golden color, and, although light on the nose, it is very full-flavored on the palate.

Tavel

Located on the stony soil of the harsh plain of Gard, beyond the Rhône to the southwest of Orange, Tavel produces the most famous dry rosé wine in the world.

Grenache and Clairette are the principal grape varieties, but Cinsault, Picpoul and Bourboulenc are also grown.

Although it has the strength to live for at least three years, it is best drunk while it is still young and fresh.

Lirac

The vineyards of Lirac are planted alongside those of Tavel on the right bank of the Rhône. It overflows into the neighboring villages of Saint-Laurent-des-Arbres, Roquemaure and Saint-Geniès-de-Comolas.

The main grapes grown are Grenache, Cinsault and Clairette along with Mourvèdre, Syrah, Counoise and Maccabeo. Lirac produces red, white and rosé wines. The red is comparatively light and matures while quite young, and the rosé is at its best while fresh and young. Only small quantities of white wines are made, but they are worth seeking out because of their unique character and distinctive perfumed bouquet.

Côtes-du-Rhône Villages

This appellation was introduced in August 1967 and can be applied to the wines of Gard, Drôme and Vaucluse. Strictly controlled, the wines must be made to present the qualities of their districts.

A final appellation of the region is the simple designation of Côtes du Rhône, which can be applied to any wine along the Côtes.

CHAMPAGNE

BEYOND QUESTION, Champagne is the wine of choice for all manner of celebration. It is used to launch ships and marriages, and to mark anniversaries, birthdays and any special occasion.

Champagne is the most northerly of France's wine-producing regions. There are two distinct elements to the Champagne wine trade — the growers and the merchants. There are over 15,000 growers who tend many small parcels of vines. Each year, the grapes are bought by the merchants who make the wine and nurse it through its long period of production until it is ready to be sold.

Only three grape varieties are permitted to be used in the making of Champagne. They are the Pinot Noir and Pinot Meunier, which are black, and the Chardonnay, which is white.

The region is divided into four zones, the Montagne de Reims, Vallée de la Marne, Côte des Blancs and Aube.

The Montagne de Reims runs roughly east to west between Reims in the north and Epernay to the south. The vineyards are planted on both the north and south slopes of the Montagne, and one of the great mysteries of the wine world is that the grapes grown on the north-facing slope attain such a high quality.

The vineyards of the Montagne and those of the Vallée de la Marne, which are to the south of the Montagne, are the primary vineyards of Champagne.

To the south of the Marne is the Côte des Blancs, which runs north to south, and south of that again are the vineyards of Bar-sur Aube and Bar-sur Seine.

The soil of Champagne is a vital element in the success of the vines. Below a thin layer of soil lies a chalky subsoil that ensures perfect drainage but also serves to absorb heat, which it then reflects evenly back to the vines to bring the grapes to full ripeness.

The harvest in Champagne is merely the beginning of a long process that will take at least two years, and usually longer, before the wine is ready to be sold.

Firstly, the black grapes must be crushed with

great care so that only their white juice, and none of the color from their skins, is collected for the primary fermentation. This usually stops during the cold winter months before starting again with the coming of spring.

At this point, the wines have reached a critical stage in their development. The majority of Champagne is non-vintage, and the merchants each sell their wines under brand names whose continuity they wish to ensure from year to year.

To accomplish this, a cuvée, or blend, is made, often incorporating wines from earlier vintages, as well as those of the current crop. Once a satisfactory blend is achieved, the wines selected are thoroughly mixed together, and a liqueur of pure cane sugar dissolved in wine is added. The blend is then bottled to go through a second fermentation.

It is during this second fermentation that the sparkle is created as the bubbles of gas resulting from the enclosed fermentation in the bottle are trapped in the wine.

During the second fermentation, the bottles are carefully stacked in the cellars to lie quietly until the fermentation is completed. At this point, the bottles are placed in *pupitres*, double-sided boards that have holes to accommodate their necks.

This stage in the production of Champagne is the *remuage*, and the purpose of it is to collect the sediment formed during the second fermentation in the necks of the bottles. This is accomplished by giving the bottles an eighth of a turn and gradually moving them from the horizontal to the vertical, neck down. Once it is completed, the sediment is collected against the cork. The men who carry out this operation are highly skilled, and the best of them can turn as many as 30,000 bottles each day.

The wines of Champagne owe much to its chalky soil, which retains heat and helps the grapes to ripen.

Overleaf: *The gentle slopes of Champagne roll into peaceful valleys.*

Left, above: Dégorgeur freezes the neck of a Champagne bottle.

Left, below: The grapes must be crushed with care to avoid coloration by the skins.

Right: Remueur turns Champagne bottles to collect sediment. The best remueurs can turn up to 30,000 bottles each day.

The next stage in the wine's life is *dégorgement*. This process is carried out by a team: the *dégorgeur*, the *doseur*, the *boucheur* and the *ficeleur*.

When the bottle reaches the dégorgeur, he freezes its neck so that when the cork is removed, the pellet of sediment is ejected with little loss of wine.

The bottle is then passed to the doseur, who adds the *liqueur d'expédition*, a mixture of sugar, still Champagne and brandy. The wine melts the sugar, which is used to sweeten the wine; the brandy is added to stop the sugar from starting fermentation. The composition of the liqueur d'expedition is determined by the degree of sweetness that is wanted in the finished wine. For a Brut Champagne it can be as little as 0.5%. In the case of Extra Sec it is about 1%, 3% for Sec and 5% for Demi-Sec.

From the doseur, the bottle passes to the boucheur who drives in the cork which has to be squeezed to half its natural size to fit. It then passes to the ficeleur who squashes the part of the cork above the neck. He then attaches a wire muzzle over the cork and secures it to the ring around the neck of the bottle.

The bottles are then returned to the cellars where they lie until needed. The last task is carried out only when the wine is ready to be shipped.

The bottles are sent to the *cellier* where they are washed and dressed in the traditional foil capsule, which covers the cork and neck of the bottle, the neck label and main label. It is then packed in cartons and shipped.

The high cost of the grapes, amongst the priciest in the world, and the long, complex process involved in the making of Champagne, are the main reasons that the wine is always expensive.

Sparkling wines are made in every part of the world. While it would be wrong to say that all Champagne is of exceptional quality, it is, at its best, the world's finest sparkling wine. Particularly in the New World, many wines are called Champagne, but they rarely measure up to the quality of genuine Champagne.

THE LOIRE

ONE OF THE OLDEST wine-producing regions of France, the Loire is peculiar in that of the important wine regions, it is the only one to run east to west.

It is also one of the most picturesque parts of France and, although it has no great wines, it produces many wines of sound quality.

No one can say when the vine was first grown in the Loire, but it was already there when the Romans arrived in 22 A.D. It is hardly likely that the vines were growing in neatly cultivated vineyards at that time, but they were most certainly growing wild.

The Loire is blessed with a comparatively reliable climate and vintages are, consequently, of less importance than in other parts of France. The vignerons, however, have done a great deal of work over the centuries to upgrade the quality of their vines.

This has been done through clonal selection, the development of new varieties, and the importation of vines.

A classic example is the development of a wild Lambrusco black grape which was first cultivated to produce a red vine which was known as Pineau d'Aunis. It is thought that at some unknown point, through further clonal selection, this vine yielded the white grape variety, Chenin Blanc, or Pineau de la Loire.

The Sauvignon, grown in Pouilly-sur-Loire, Quincy and Reugny, presents a mystery as there are no records to indicate if it was native to the region or if it was imported.

The Muscadet grape, grown in the Nantes area, was almost certainly brought from Burgundy where it was known as Melon. It appears to have been widely planted after 1709 when the winter was so bad that many of the established vines were frozen.

Burgundy was almost certainly the source of several other varieties including the Pinot Noir, Pinot Beurot and Meunier.

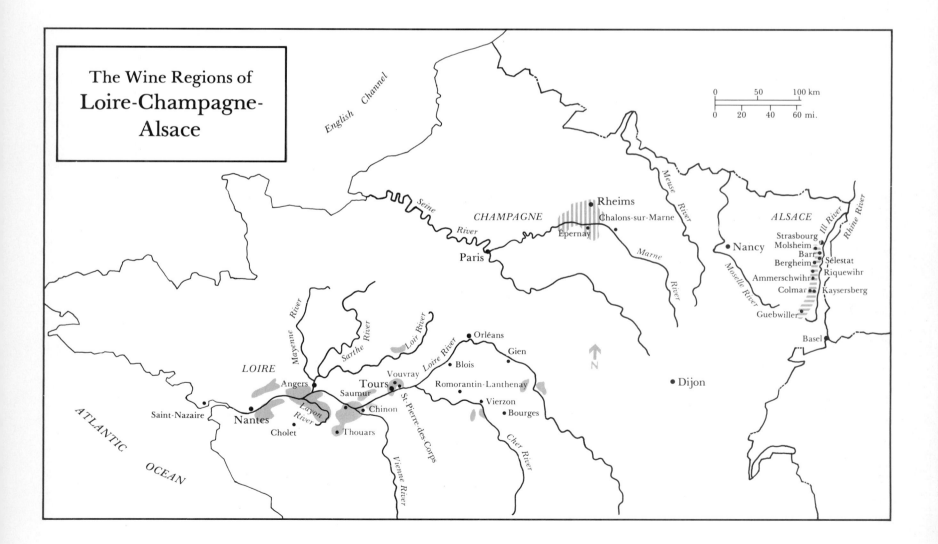

The Wine Regions of
Loire-Champagne-Alsace

The countryside of Nantes is largely planted with Muscadet grapes, originally brought from Burgundy.

Cultivation in Sancerre is mainly of the Sauvignon and Pinot Noir grapes. Its white wines have a distinctive gun-metal character.

Overleaf: *The best red wines of Chinon, mainly from the Cabernet Franc grape, are mellow and warm, with a hint of sweetness.*

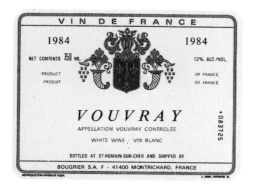

Likewise, the Cabernet Franc and Côt, the local name for Malbec, originated in Bordeaux.

Another import is the Gros Plant which was brought from Charentes. Initially, its wine was distilled, but today it is used to produce an attractive dry white wine.

The Groslot de Cinq-Mars, or Grolleau, on the other hand was developed locally about 200 years ago through cross-breeding of Chenin Blanc vines.

The Loire is the longest river in France, and the wine-growing region of the same name stretches along its banks for 600 miles from Central France all the way to the Atlantic Ocean. Along the way there is a great diversity of soils, micro-climates and grape varieties, which diversity in turn yields a corresponding range of wines.

The Loire comprises four major regions: The Centre (around Orléans and Nevers), Touraine, Anjou-Saumur and Muscadet (around Nantes).

The Upper Loire

On the Upper Loire, just to the north of Nevers, the wines of Pouilly and Sancerre are grown on chalky hills which gives them both a distinctive gun-metal character.

Wines of Pouilly made with only Sauvignon grapes are called Pouilly-Fumé, while wines made with Chasselas grapes, whether or not they are blended with Sauvignon wines, are sold as Pouilly-sur-Loire.

To the west of these areas are Reuilly and Quincy which lie on the Loire tributary, the Cher River, at the point where it is joined by the Arnon River. Quincy, on the right bank of the Cher, is planted primarily with Sauvignon vines which yield a crisp, dry white wine. Reuilly, on the right bank of the Arnon, also produces a pleasant white wine, either dry or semi-dry, from Sauvignon grapes on a mere 62 acres of vineyards. Most of this wine is consumed locally.

Menetou-Salon, to the north of Bourges, was granted appellation controlée status only in 1959. The vineyards also yield a white wine from Sauvignon grapes, but it does not have the fineness of the wines of Pouilly or Sancerre. Red and rosé wines, however, made from the Pinot Noir grape are very pleasant and attractive drinking.

Touraine

The vineyards surrounding Tours produce the wines of Vouvray, Montlouis, Côteaux de Touraine, Chinon, Bourgueil and Saint-Nicholas-de-Bourgueil.

The primary white grape of Touraine is Chenin Blanc, although Sauvignon grapes are also grown.

The wines of Vouvray are the best known of Touraine's wines. The Chenin Blanc, grown in chalky soil, yields a delicate, light still wine which is surprisingly long-lived. Vouvray also produces sparkling wines made by the Champagne method. The quality of these wines is very high, and they are amongst the top rank of the world's sparkling wines.

Montlouis makes wines that are similar in style to Vouvray, but they are inclined to be slightly softer in nature.

The Côteaux de Touraine is a large area that sweeps in a curve from the north bank of the Loire to the south bank of the Cher. Most of the wines are white, and again the Chenin Blanc is the principal vine. The wines are full-bodied and similar in style to Vouvray.

The vineyards of Chinon, Bourgueil and Saint-Nicholas-de-Bourgueil are mostly planted with the Bordeaux grape, Cabernet Franc, which produces both red and rosé wines. The lower vineyards are gravelly, while the higher vineyards grow in a yellow chalk soil known as Touraine Tufa. The reds from the lower vineyards have the freshness and fruit of a quality Beaujolais, while those from the higher slopes, especially in Bourgueil, develop a style similar to that of a light Médoc. The rosé wines also have a pleasant character.

Anjou and Saumur

These two appellations are very closely linked, and Saumur is decreed as part of Anjou. In fact, the wines of Saumur can be sold under the Anjou appellation; however, the reverse is not the case. There are also four sub-regional appellations:

Vineyard in Anjou. Where harvesting has been mechanized, rows of vines are widely spaced to allow the passage of machines.

Côteaux du Loir, Côteaux de la Loire, Côteaux du Layon and Côteaux de l'Aubance.

The white wines of Anjou are made with the Chenin Blanc. They range from dry to very sweet, luscious dessert wines, which are the best white wines of the area.

In the vineyards on the banks of the parallel rivers Layon and Aubance, the Chenin Blanc also yields sweet wines of high quality. These two areas also grow the Cabernet from which they produce a light red wine and the fine Rosé de Cabernet d'Anjou, which is an elegant, delicate wine.

The Chenin Blanc again dominates the vineyards of the Côteaux de la Loire, but in this location, it is the dry wines that are the finest.

Pays Nantais: Muscadet

Muscadet is not a region; it is the grape grown in the vineyards around Nantes from which the name is derived.

The wine tends to be acid, but, rather than being a flaw, that is what gives it its lively character.

The other grape grown to any extent is the Gros Plant, which also yields an acidic wine, but again the acidity provides balance.

Around the town of Ancenis, the Gamay grape is grown and a pleasant, light red wine is produced.

ALSACE

THE VOSGES MOUNTAINS effectively isolate Alsace from the rest of France, to the point where it seems more naturally to be part of Germany. In fact, it has been under German occupation on several occasions, most recently from 1870 to 1918.

During that period, the wines of Alsace were deliberately downgraded by the German authorities, who were intent on eliminating Alsace from competing with their own wines.

Alsatian wines are, in many ways, German wines made in the French style. The Alsatian vintners seek strength in their wines, whereas the Germans look for more lightness and sweetness. The wines of Alsace have the expected flowery bouquet associated with the grape varieties they grow, which leaves the palate completely unprepared for the dry, almost austere, character of the wines.

The vineyards are planted on the east-facing slopes of the Vosges overlooking the river Ill from which the region's name is derived. To the Romans, the river was the Elsus and to the Germans, the Elsass. The vines are grown from Mulhouse in the south to Strasbourg in the north.

The vineyards run for a total of 70 miles, but it is the small portion between Guebwiller in the south and Ribeauvillé in the north that yields the best wines. The principal city of this area, and the wine-trading capital, is Colmar.

The vines are planted at altitudes ranging from 600 to 1,200 feet and run like a ribbon, rarely more than a mile wide, along the slopes of the Vosges. These protect the vineyards from the rainfall coming from the west, just as the altitude keeps the vines above the fogs that are prevalent on the valley floor.

The permitted grapes in Alsace are the Riesling, which is responsible for their finest wines; Sylvaner; Muscat; Pinot Gris, known as Tokay d'Alsace or Rutlander; Pinot Blanc, known also as Weissklevener or Burgenberg; Gewürztraminer; and the lesser varieties of Chasselas and Knipperle.

Vosges Mountains overlook harvest time in Alsace.

The Riesling grape is medium-small, round and greenish-yellow, with russet dots. It rivals Chardonnay in terms of the quality white wines it yields.

PRODUCT OF FRANCE
PRODUIT DE FRANCE
VIN D'ALSACE
APPELLATION
ALSACE
CONTRÔLÉE
WINE OF ALSACE
1982
Pichet d'Alsace
LAUGEL
MIS EN BOUTEILLE PAR
MICHEL LAUGEL
A E 67 520 MARLENHEIM FRANCE
e 750 ml - 10 % alc./vol.

ALSACE
APPELLATION ALSACE CONTRÔLÉE
LÉON
BEYER
Léon Beyer
MARQUE DÉPOSÉE
Vin d'Alsace
RIESLING
1982
750ml   PRODUCE OF FRANCE
Produit de France   12% Alc./vol.
Mis en bouteille par : LÉON BEYER - NÉGOCIANT A EGUISHEIM (HAUT-RHIN) FRANCE
Alsace white wine / Vin blanc d'Alsace

The vineyards of the Alsatian valley are planted with Muscat and Riesling grapes which yield wines that are strong and fresh.

The wines made from the last two grapes are never exported and, in fact, are seldom even bottled. They are used as carafe wines by cafés in the region and for such culinary purposes as pickling red cabbage.

The vast majority of Alsatian wines are named according to the grape variety from which they are made. The exceptions to this are blended wines that carry a brand name.

Sometimes a vineyard name will be used on the label, but the vineyards of Alsace are not classified in the same way as they are, for example, in Burgundy.

All of the wines of Alsace have one common denominator — the Alsatian style of wine-making, which involves the pursuit of naturalness almost to the point of fanaticism. They abhor any process that involves adding anything to their wines. Rather than filtering, they keep the wines undis-turbed in huge wooden vats and rack it as little as possible until it is clear.

The result of their dedication is wines that strike an amazing balance between strength and fresh-ness. In the main, Alsatian wines are dry, but if the vintage warrants it the grapes will be left on the vines to develop high concentrations of sugar for such wines as Auslese or Beerenauslese, which are labelled with German designations, or Ven-dage Tardive, the more appropriate Alsatian designation.

There is only one appellation controlée in Alsace. As in Champagne, there is no complex appellation structure identifying exact vineyards or communes. The wine trade is in the hands of merchants who buy their wines from all along the region to make their blends, which are sold either under the name of the grape variety or under a brand name.

PROVENCE

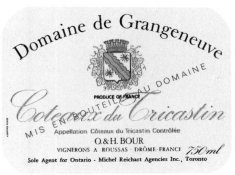

THIS IS A HUGE REGION in southeast France stretching in a wide band from Marseille in the west to Nice in the east. The principal output of the region is a vast quantity of red, white and rosé wines of the Vins Délimités de Qualité Supérieure (VDQS) caliber. There are a few small areas that have earned full appellation controlée status.

A considerable assortment of grapes are grown in the region. Red wines are made with Cinsault, Carignan, Mourvèdre and Tibouren grapes, while Bourboulenc, Ugni Blanc and Clairette are used for the whites.

Among the better known VDQS wines are the Côtes du Lubéron, Côteaux de Pierrevert and Côteaux du Tricastin.

The small fishing village of Cassis, to the east of Marseille, is entitled to an appellation for its white wine, while, further along the coast towards Toulon, Bandol produces red wines with appellation status. Palette, to the north of Marseille, carries an appellation for its red, white and rosé wines, as does Bellet near Nice.

Languedoc and Roussillon

The majority of wines produced in this vast region, which stretches from the estuary of the Rhône in the east, through a wide sweeping curve, to Cerbère to the southwest, is the most prolific wine producing region in France, but the majority of these wines are of such low quality that they are blended with stronger imported wines and sold as vin ordinaire, a term that might have been specifically created for them.

Dotted about amongst this sea of mediocrity, however, are a few pockets of more distinguished wines.

In Languedoc, the areas entitled to VDQS status are: Corbières, Corbières Supérieures, Minervois, Picpoul-de-Pinet and Côteaux-du-Languedoc. The latter appellation covers the extensive areas of Hérault and Aude and the sub-appellations of Cabrières, Côteaux-de-Vérargues, Faugères, Côteaux-de-la-Méjanelle, Montpeyroux, Pic-Saint-Loup, Saint-Chinian, Saint-Christol, Saint-Drézéry, Saint-Georges-d'Orques, Saint-Saturnin, la Clape and Quatourze.

In Roussillon the principal VDQS areas are Corbières du Roussillon and Roussillon-des-Aspres.

Languedoc also boasts some full appellation controlée wines which include those from Fitou, Clairette du Languedoc; the white wines of Blanquette de Limoux, which are usually sparkling wines; and the Muscat wines of Frontignan, Lunel, Mireval and Saint-Jean-de-Minervois.

In Roussillon, the only appellations controlées are applied to the naturally sweet wines of Banyuls, Rivesaltes, Muscat de Rivesaltes, Côtes-d'Agly, Maury, Côtes-du-Haut-Roussillon and Grand Roussillon. To call them naturally sweet wines is something of a misnomer, as alcohol is added to stop the fermentation to retain the high residual sugar.

JURA

THIS SMALL VITICULTURAL AREA lies at the foot of the Jura Mountains about eighty miles east of Burgundy. It was on the wines of Jura that Louis Pasteur carried out the experiments that finally explained the process of fermentation.

The area produces mostly white wines, but also makes reds and rosés from a group of grapes, many of which are peculiar to the area. Red and rosé wines are made with the Poulsard, Trousseau and Pinot Noir grapes, while whites are made from the Chardonnay and Savagnin. Some sparkling wine is also made by the Champagne method.

There are, however, two unique wines made in Jura, *vins jaunes*, yellow wines, and *vins de paille*, straw wines. Vins jaunes are made only from the Savagnin grape, the Gewurztraminer of Alsace, and are vinified in the same way as sherry.

Following a slow fermentation lasting several weeks, the wine is placed in small casks in cool cellars where it remains undisturbed and untreated for six years. During that time, the quantity of wine reduces through evaporation, and a film, known in Spain as *flor*, develops on the surface of the wine.

The growth of the flor, or the veil as it is sometimes called in Jura, is often elusive and there are many unsuccessful casks at the end of the six-year wait, which contributes to the very expensive price of vins jaunes.

Vins de paille are made from the black Poulsard and Trousseau grapes, which are laid out on straw mats to dry for several weeks prior to being pressed.

As the grapes are gathered late, they already have a high sugar content, which is concentrated during the drying process. Usually, the grapes are pressed in January or February and the wine then goes through a slow fermentation. The wines must reach 15 per cent alcohol, and because of the low temperatures at which the wine is kept, this level of alcohol causes the fermentation to stop. The result is a light dessert wine of exceptional quality.

The best vin jaune carries the appellation Château-Chalon which is not a single estate, but a group of designated vineyards.

The appellation L'Etoile is applied to certain vins jaunes and vins de paille.

The area's other two appellations, Côtes-de-Jura and Arbois apply to all types of wines.

SAVOIE

SET IN THE FOOTHILLS of the Alps, hard by the Swiss border, from whence the River Rhône enters to make its east-to-west journey to Lyon, this little-known area produces several very pleasant wines.

There are only two appellations controlées wines in Savoie, Crépy and Seyssel. Several of its other wines have VDQS status, and these are entitled to carry one of the following designations: Vin de Savoie, Roussette-de-Savoie, Vin de Savoie Roussette, Vin de Savoie Mousseux or Mousseux de Savoie.

The designation Roussette de Savoie can be applied only to wines made from the Altesse, Petite-Sainte-Marie, Mondeuse Blanche and Marsanne grapes.

Red wines are made from the Mondeuse and Gamay grapes, but it is the white wines of the region that are its best. In Seyssel, a considerable proportion of the wines are made into sparkling wines.

AUVERGNE

IN THE CENTER of France, between the rivers Loire and Cher, this tiny area produces good fruity red and rosé wines from the Gamay grape.

There are three main production areas, Clermont-Ferrand, Issoire and Riom.

HAUT POITOU

LOCATED ON A 3,000 acre plateau to the south of the Loire, Haut Poitou traces the origins of its vineyards back to 276 A.D. and its most famous vineyard owner was, undoubtedly,

Opposite: *The Jura is best known for its unique* vins jaunes *and* vins de paille.

*Corbières, principal VDQS area of Languedoc. Most
Corbières wines are red.*

In the west of the Provence region are the vineyards of the Côteaux d'Aix-en-Provence and the Baux-de-Provence. These two districts are known particularly for their red wines.

Eleanor of Aquitaine who, two years after her marriage at Poitiers in 1152 to Henry Plantagenet, became Queen of England.

The area's wines were well accepted until the early part of the seventeenth century, after which it seems to have slipped, inexplicably, into obscurity.

The present revival began in 1948, when Jean Raffarin persuaded his neighbors to establish the Cave Cooperative du Haut Poitou in Neuville-de-Poitou, which is at the region's centre. Initially, only Sauvignon Blanc vines were planted, but now Chardonnay, Gamay and Cabernet Sauvignon have been introduced. In the early 1960s, the cooperative wines were granted VDQS status.

The still white wines made with the Sauvignon Blanc and Chardonnay are of very good quality, as is the sparkling wine, Diane de Poitiers Dame aux Serfs, which is made by the Champagne method using only Chardonnay grapes.

Of the red wines the Gamay, which achieves a deep red color, is the best, while the Cabernet Sauvignon is more like a rosé, as the grapes will not produce the depth of color they do in more southerly Bordeaux.

DURAS, MARMANDAIS AND BUZET

THESE ARE three small areas that lie along the southern fringes of Bordeaux.

Duras is the most northerly, being tucked in a little wedge between Bergerac and Entre-Deux-Mers. Its white wines are its best and they are made with Sémillon, Sauvignon, Muscadelle, Mauzac and Ugni Blanc. Although they are made with the classic Bordeaux grapes, Cabernet Sauvignon, Merlot and Malbec, the red wines are rather plain.

Marmandais is something of a neighbor to both Entre-Deux-Mers and Sauternes, but is individual in that it grows a wide variety of grapes to produce both red and white wines of VDQS status. Despite this recognition, they are still rarely seen beyond the region itself.

Buzet is also a VDQS region whose wines are made by a cooperative. Its red grapes are Cabernet Sauvignon, Cabernet Franc, Merlot and Malbec, while white wines are made with the Sémillon, Sauvignon and Muscadelle. The wines tend to be light, but they are of good quality.

CAHORS

TO THE SOUTHEAST of Bergerac is the region of Cahors which produces a red VDQS wine in forty communes mostly located on both banks of the river Lot which forms a great loop around the town.

Made mainly with Malbec grapes, the wine may have a little Merlot and other varieties added. Deep red, almost black, the wine is usually matured for three to five years before being bottled, after which it will continue to develop and reach its peak five to ten years after that, by which time it will be a well-balanced, full-bodied wine with an intense bouquet and excellent flavor.

Minervois produces some of Languedoc-Roussillon's best wines.

A vineyard in Cahors, where forty communes are clustered on the banks of the Lot River.

The most important of Corsica's vine-yards are planted on slopes overlooking the Mediterranean Sea.

GAILLAC

To THE SOUTH OF Cahors, almost halfway to Roussillon, is the region of Gaillac which is best known for its sparkling, *perlant* (lightly sparkling) and dry white wines.

The dominant grape is the Mauzac and the oddly named l'En de l'El, as well as such better-known varieties as Sémillon and Sauvignon.

Sparkling wines are made by a rural method that produces a sparkle without the addition of sugar. Fermentation is gradually stopped through filtration and the wine is then left for two or three years to mature.

Perlant wines are made by fermenting the wine in the same manner as a dry white wine, then allowing it to stay undisturbed for several months until a second fermentation begins, and at that point it is bottled.

The dry still white wines are nicely balanced and make pleasant light drinking.

Red grapes are also grown, but the resulting wines are quite undistinguished.

FRONTON

THIS SMALL AREA to the north of Toulouse produces a deeply-colored red VDQS wine from the Négrette grape blended with Gamay, Malbec, Cabernet, Fer and Syrah. Some white wine is also made using Mauza, Sémillon and Chalosse grapes.

JURANÇON AND ENVIRONS

THE FIVE SMALL REGIONS of Jurançon, Tursan, Madiran, Bearne and Irouleguy are clustered in the southwest corner of France close to the Spanish border.

Jurançon is the most significant appellation controlée in the southwest. The vines are grown on the foothills of the Pyrenees and the grape varieties are peculiar to the region. They are the Petit-Manseng, Gros-Manseng and Courbu which are harvested very late to yield a golden-colored white wine with a strong, sweet aroma and a slight spiciness in its flavor. A little red wine is also made, but it is drunk locally.

Tursan produces mostly white VDQS wines in a cooperative at Geaune. A local grape, Baroque, is the principal variety used to make a very dry, crisp wine. A small quantity of red and rosé wines are made using Tannat grapes blended with Cabernet Franc and Fer, which yields a dark red, full-bodied wine that is high in tannin.

Madiran produces a strong red wine using the Tannat grape, softened out slightly by the addition of Cabernet Franc grapes to the blend. An appellation controlée wine is made by blending the Tannat with Bouchy and Fer.

Béarn is a VDQS region nestled in the Pyrenees. There are red, rosé and white wines which are usually made at a cooperative. The reds and rosés rarely leave the area and are blends on the Tannat with Fer, Bouchy, Manseng and Courbu Rouge grapes added in small quantities. The dry white wines of the area are also blends of Baroque, Sémillon, Courbu Blanc and Claverie grapes.

Irouléguy is a small VDQS area not far from the Spanish border on the Atlantic coast. Again, the Tannat is the dominant grape and Bouchy and Fer are its companions in producing a dry red wine of deep color with a full, fruity flavor.

CORSICA

THE VINEYARDS of this island are planted with several native varieties. The principal of these are the Vermentino, Malvoisie, Nielluccio, Rossola, Bianca, Sciaccarello, Barbarosso and Carcajolo.

During this century other varieties have been introduced from continental France, and these include the Grenache, Cinsault, Carignan, Alicante and Muscat.

The most important vineyards are in the coastal areas. Amongst the most notable wines are those of Patrimonio, which was granted appellation controlée status in 1968, Sartène, Ajaccio, Piana and Bonifacia.

The dry white wines are very fragrant and have a power and smoothness that is very attractive. The reds are powerful, heady wines which again have an intense bouquet, while the rosés are warm and fruity. At Cap Corse, the Muscat and Malvoisie are blended to produce a sweet wine that is delicate and intensely perfumed.

Germany

WINE HAS BEEN MADE in Germany for almost 2,000 years, and many of its ancient vineyards have clung to steep slopes, frequently overlooking rivers, throughout that entire time. Indeed, the Romans built ships to convey the wines of the Mosel back to Rome where they were highly prized. A replica of one of these ships can still be seen at the Landesmuseum in Trier. It was found at Neumagen and had been the tomb of a Roman wine merchant.

Only the United States, Canada and the U.S.S.R. grow wines in the same northerly latitudes as Germany, and in consequence, it is the climate, rather than soil conditions, that is the strongest influence in determining the final quality of the wine possible with each vintage. The different types of soil found throughout, and within, the wine regions do, of course, contribute significantly to the quality and characteristics of the wines, but it is the weather that makes the biggest difference in vintages. Both at the beginning and end of the growing season, frost can have devastating effects on the vines. Late frosts can kill many buds, thus immediately reducing the potential yield, while rains near the end of the growing season can inhibit the development of noble rot, known in Germany as *Edelfäule*, thus making it impossible for the vintage to produce any outstanding wines.

Geographically, the vineyards of Germany are amongst the most picturesque in the world. To sail along the Rhine or Mosel is to see some of the most spectacular and breathtaking scenery anywhere. Indeed, whatever the form of transportation used, magnificent views are to be seen almost everywhere in the wine country, where many ancient castle ruins crown the mountains above the vineyard slopes.

Germany is fortunate in that the rivers bordering many of the vineyards, besides adding to the country's scenic beauty, do double duty as mirrors in reflecting the scant hours of sunshine back into the vines.

The entire German wine industry was revolutionized in 1971 when new wine laws were introduced to control strictly the quality of the wines. Unlike France, where the vineyards are classified at a specific quality level, every vineyard in Germany has the opportunity to produce a first class wine.

The wine law is based on the degree of sugar in the must, unfermented grape juice. The must weight determines the quality of wine that will finally be produced.

There are four main categories of German wine, and, in ascending order, they are: *Tafelwein, Landwein, Qualitätswein* and *Qualitätswein mit Prädikat* (QmP). Tafelwein is ordinary wine that can be made from the grapes of any region. Landwein was introduced in 1978 to indicate a wine of superior quality to Tafelwein, but not of a high enough quality to attain Qualitätswein status.

Qualitätswein is where strict controls come into play in the German wine laws. A specific must weight has to be met, and the wines must come from a specific region and be made from certain grape varieties. The finished wine must also be submitted for government controlled inspection, and, if it passes, the wine will be issued an *Amtliche Prüfungsnummer*, usually known as an A.P. number.

The category Qualitätswein mit Prädikat indicates a wine of special distinction that has been made without the addition of any sugar, and such wines must also be submitted, tested and issued an A.P. number. These wines must be from a specific region and must be made from an approved grape variety. Within this category, there are several subcategories indicating the degree of sweetness in the finished wine. Those categories, from the driest to the sweetest, are: Kabinett, Spätlese, Auslese, Beerenauslese and Trockenbeerenauslese. In

Opposite: Müller-Thurgau, *the most abundant grape variety grown in the Rheinhessen.*

Many differences in flavor can be traced to the type of soil on which the vine grew. This sparse, slaty soil results in a spritely, delicate wine.

Wine tasting is subjective: how we are feeling, the food we have eaten, how much sleep we have had, all influence how we feel about a wine.

essence, the sweeter a German wine is, the higher is its quality. A Beerenauslese or Trockenbeerenauslese will rival any sweet wine in the world.

To determine which quality of wine the grape juice will produce, it is measured by weight. In real terms this means that the sugar level and the degree of acidity are used to determine the weight of the must. In Germany the must is measured against the Oechsle scale. A legal minimum must weight is set for each category of wine. These weights range from a low of 44 degrees Oechsle for Deutscher Tafelwein to a minimum of 150 degrees Oechsle for Trockenbeerenauslese.

Although the sugar content of the juice also determines the alcoholic strength that the wine can attain, in Germany, unlike many other countries, greater emphasis is placed on the potential alcoholic content. The reason for this different emphasis is that given enough natural sugar, the wine maker can arrest the fermentation to retain the desired level of sweetness. By stopping the fermentation to retain sugar, the wine maker is also producing a wine with a lower level of alcohol than it would develop if allowed to ferment until

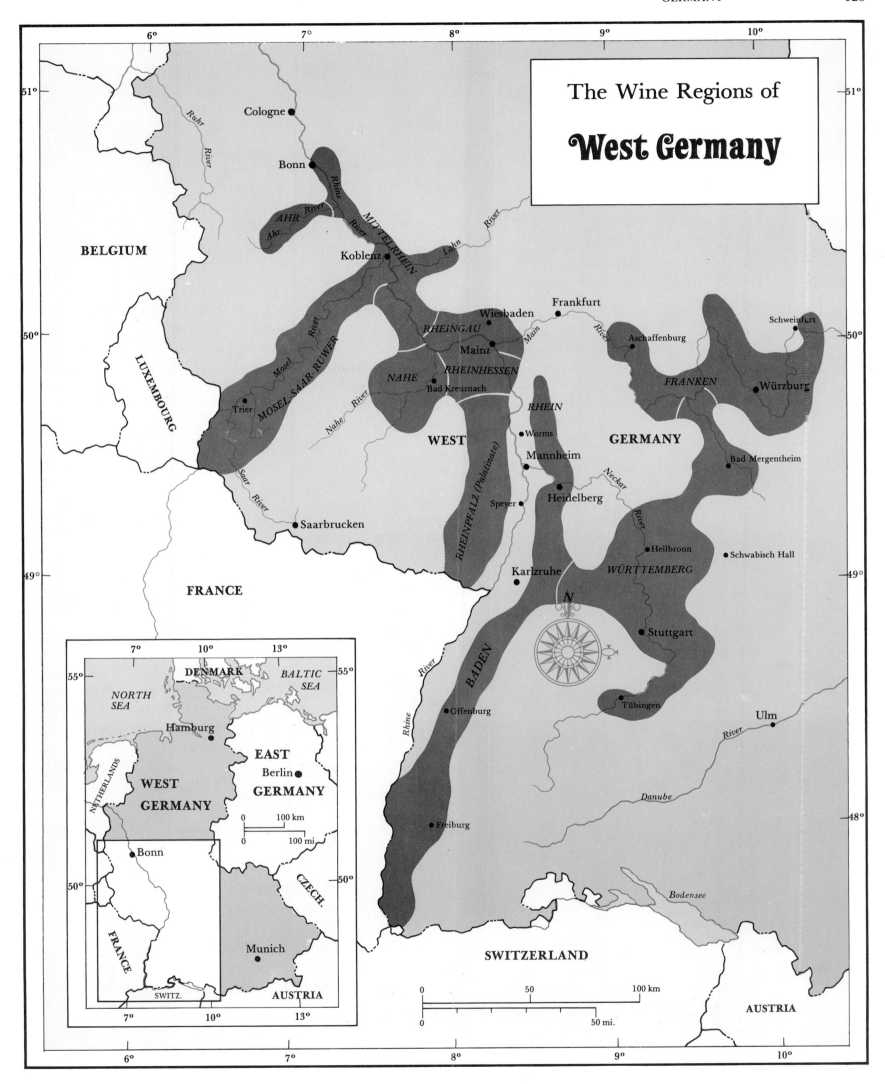

The Wine Regions of

West Germany

The Deinhard Stammhaus (parent company), at Deinhardplatz in Koblenz. Below these buildings are situated three storeys of deep cellars.

One of Germany's jewels, the famous Bernkasteler Doktor vineyard, acquired by Deinhard in 1900 at the price of 100 gold marks per square meter.

all of the sugar was converted into alcohol. It is this technique that yields the flowery, slightly sweet white wines for which Germany is justifiably famous.

In recent years, the German wine producers have shown increased interest in making drier wines. These are designated either as *Trocken* (dry) or *Halbtrocken* (semi-dry) on the label. The word Trocken means dry, but should not be confused with its sense in the name Trockenbeerenauslese, which is a sweet wine. In this case, the Trocken refers to the grapes, which are partially dried on the vines before they are crushed.

Personally, I do not know why the Germans pursue this style of wine, as they do from time to time. They last did so in the 1930s. To my mind, the result is usually a rather flat wine lacking in the liveliness that makes the majority of German wines so attractive.

There are also great quantities of sparkling wines made in several regions of Germany. The German term for sparkling wines is *Sekt*, and that is the word to look for on the label. Sekt labels are worth a close look for another reason — to make sure the wine is in fact German. A great deal of still white wine is imported and made into sparkling wines. A genuine German Sekt, particularly those made with the Riesling grape, is an excellent sparkling wine, and it is worth a bit of searching to find the real thing.

As well as wine, the must is also used to make *Süssreserve*. Süssreserve is unfermented grape juice that is added to the wine prior to bottling to give it the required level of sweetness. This practice is commonly used for wines up to the level of Spätlese. There are several benefits derived from the use of Süssreserve. Its use has simplified bulk storage problems, has allowed a reduction in the levels of sulphur dioxide and has made it possible for producers to increase the supply of the moderately priced wines which are in the greatest demand.

It is for white wines that Germany is most renowned, and the noblest of these are made from the Riesling grape. The two other most widely planted are the Sylvaner and the Müller-Thurgau which is a cross of the other two. Other white varieties include the Scheurebe, Kerner, Weisser Gutedel and Morio-Muskat. The vast majority of German wines are best drunk while young, but

Auslese, and in particular Beerenauslese and Trockenbeerenauslese, will live for many years, and reward when laid down.

A little red wine is also made in Germany and the best of these are made with the Blauer Spätburgunder which is the Pinot Noir responsible for the fine wines of Burgundy. Other red varieties include the Ruländer, Blauer Portugieser and Blauer Trollinger.

The Müller-Thurgau grape is particularly interesting. It was developed at Geisenheim in the Rheingau by Professor Dr. Müller from the Swiss Canton of Thurgau in 1860, about the same year as the automobile was invented. Originally thought to be a cross between Riesling and Sylvaner, it is now generally believed to be a cross between two Riesling clones. This new grape, however, was not as readily accepted as the automobile, and it is only in comparatively recent years that it has been planted extensively. Now one of the major German grape varieties, it does not produce

wines with the distinction of the Riesling, but it does make very sound, pleasant wine much of which forms the basis of many of the inexpensive blends that are so popular around the world.

The wine law of 1971 established eleven wine growing regions (*Anbaugebiete*). They are: Ahr, Mosel-Saar-Ruwer, Mittelrhein, Rheingau, Nahe, Rheinhessen, Rheinpfalz, Hessische Bergstrasse, Franken, Württemberg and Baden.

The law also established 31 districts (*Bereiche*), 130 general sites (*Grosslagen*) and around 2,600 individual sites (*Einzellagen*) to enable consumers to establish a wine's origin.

A Bereich is a grouping of Grosslagen and Einzellagen and is usually the largest sub-district within a region. All of the wines made within its boundaries can use the Bereich name on their labels. Wines bearing only a Bereich name can generally be relied upon to be pleasant everyday drinking, but nothing more.

A Grosslage is a combination of vineyards

Rain and fog, prevalent during the late summer, help to protect the vines from early frost. Mist also provides the right amount of moisture so that noble rot can develop.

centered around one or more villages or towns. Again, all of the wines linked to the Grosslage can incorporate its name on their labels; for example, wines made around the Mosel town of Piesport will carry the word Piesporter on their labels, and possibly the name of an individual vineyard. The Grosslage designation allows the wine merchants to produce large quantities of wine with a similar style and quality under one name. These wines are generally of sound quality, but again are rarely more than slightly superior everyday wines.

An Einzellage is an individual vineyard entitled by the law to sell its wines under its own name. The current 2,600 such vineyards range in size from as little as an acre to over 600 acres. Einzellagen are permitted to produce only Qualitätswein and Qualitätswein mit Prädikat (QmP) wines under their own names. All of Germany's best wines come from Einzellagen, and the best of these come from vineyards with single owners. Where several owners are involved, there is likely to be a variation in quality.

In a very real sense, the label on a bottle of German wine is its birth certificate. The lower qualities such as Tafelwein and Landwein carry less information than QmP wines, which will carry their full pedigree on their labels. The only information that is not required to appear on the main label is the vintage, which may be carried on a neck label instead.

For example, the information typically carried on a QmP wine label would give the name of the region and below that the name of the village and vineyard. Underneath that the vintage will appear. The next line on the label will name the grape variety and the quality distinction, e.g. Kabinett, below which the quality category will appear, followed by the A.P. number. Below this the word Erzeugerabfüllung may appear. It means the wine was estate bottled, and this will be followed by the name of the bottler and his address. The liquid content of the bottle will also be stated, as will be the country of origin.

This may sound complicated, but studying a few German wine labels will reveal the simplicity of the German wine labeling system which is one of the clearest in the world.

As only a few German wines are actually exported, the best way to learn about the full range of German wines is to visit the regions where they are produced.

The scenery alone makes such trips worthwhile and there are *Weinstrassen* (wine roads) marked with road signs usually bearing some wine-related symbol to guide visitors through the most appropriate route in each region.

Unlike France where cellars frequently display welcoming signs with the invitation, "Visitez nos Caves," German wine cellars are not quite so open to visitors. This is not to imply that the Germans

In Ahr, the most northerly German wine region, the vines ripen because gravel and volcanic rock store up warmth and release it at night. This gives the red Spätburgunder its fine, fiery, velvety-soft character.

are inhospitable; on the contrary, they are usually happy to welcome visitors. It is preferable, however, to make prior arrangements either by letter or telephone. Most cellars will arrange for tours and samplings during the normal working day, which is between 9 a.m. and 5 p.m. during the week.

There are also an incredible number of wine festivals held in each region, particularly during the months of August and September. Likewise, there are several wine museums devoted to wine relics and wine history that are of great interest in revealing the origins and development of Germany's wine industry.

AHR

THE MOST NORTHERLY wine region in Europe, Ahr is, strangely enough, Germany's principal producer of red wines. Situated almost midway between Bonn to the north and Koblenz, the tiny River Ahr flows west to east to meet the mighty Rhine.

The Ahr also has the distinction of being the country's second smallest wine region. Only the Hessische Bergstrasse is smaller.

Along about the last fifteen miles of the Ahr's tumultuous course, the vineyards of Ahr are planted on the slaty slopes on both sides of the river. The slate absorbs the heat of the sun during the day, and releases that heat back to the vines during the night, assisting the grapes to ripen in this otherwise unlikely viticultural region.

The main grape is the Blauer Spätburgunder which, in a good year, produces a rich, velvety wine with an attractive individual character. The Blauer Frühburgunder and Blauer Portugieser are also grown for red wine production, while the Riesling and Müller-Thurgau are used for white wines which do not generally measure up to those of the more prominent regions.

For the most part, vine growing is a part-time job in the Ahr valley, and much of the wine is made by cooperatives. The people of the Ahr have no illusions about their wines and do not make any serious attempts to compete with the more illustrious wines of Germany. As a result, little Ahr wine is seen outside of the region itself where most of the wine is consumed.

MITTELRHEIN

STRETCHING ALONG the River Rhine, from Bonn in the north to Bingen, the vineyards of the Mittelrhein extend some 65 miles on both banks, although the total area under vines is only about 2,400 acres.

Most of the vineyards are on steep slopes, but there are frequent breaks where north-facing hillsides are left bare as they are not conducive to viticulture.

Dotted along the high ground of this picturesque region are numerous castles that either peer down upon the vineyards, or seem to spring from their midst.

Although not considered one of the prime German regions, the Mittelrhein has three principal grapes, the Riesling, Sylvaner and Müller-Thurgau. The Sylvaner yields a mild, palatable wine that is hard to fault but is equally unlikely to excite. The Müller-Thurgau wines are distinctly aromatic and, in good years, quite attractive, while the Riesling produces a wine that is often surprisingly flowery, yet has a crisp, clean edge and clean finish.

A great deal of work has been done in recent years in rebuilding the terraced vineyards which now form a series of uninterrupted slopes that are most easily worked.

As in the Ahr, the vast majority of the wine is consumed locally.

MOSEL-SAAR-RUWER

FROM PERL, near the Luxembourg border, the River Mosel meanders northeast to Koblenz where it joins the River Rhine. Along its banks, and those of its tributaries the Rivers Saar and Ruwer, extends an almost unbroken ribbon of

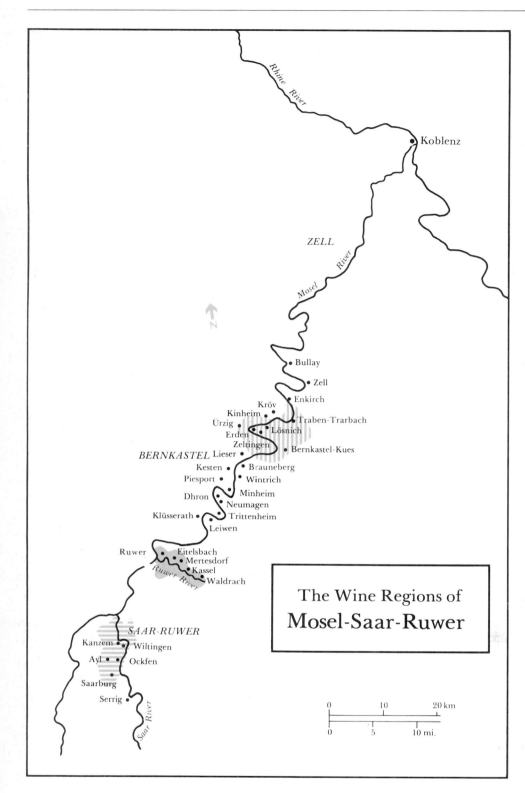

The Wine Regions of
Mosel-Saar-Ruwer

vineyards that produce some of the best-known and finest wines from a northern region. As an added bonus, the scenery revealed at each turn of this serpentine river is amongst the most stunning in Germany.

The main grape is the Riesling, followed by Müller-Thurgau and the ancient Elbling. A few recently developed varieties, Bacchus, Optima, Kerner and Reichsteiner have been planted, especially in some of the valley sites.

A great number of the vineyards are on steep, slaty slopes that are perfect in providing ripening conditions for the vines, but make working the vineyards a costly proposition. In recent years, most of the old walled terraces which accommodated only small numbers of vines have been modernized to improve their economic viability, both in regards to the number of vines that can be planted and in the ease with which the vineyards can be worked.

In the best years, Mosel-Saar-Ruwer wines are racy, elegant wines of great style. An added burden for the wine growers on the Saar, however, is that good years occur only three or four times each decade. In the worst years, the wines are so poor and high in acid that they can only be sold to the Sekt makers to be turned into sparkling wines.

In all, there are over 30,000 acres planted with vines, but the prime vineyards are located on the Middle Mosel where it twists back and forth in a series of loops between Klüsserath and Zell.

Downriver from Klüsserath, the river makes a long but tight loop to form a peninsula near the end of which is the village of Trittenheim. Here, on the steep slopes on both sides of the river, are the vineyards of Altärchen and Apotheke, two Einzellagen, individual sites, as designated by the 1971 wine law. (Prior to that time there had been many individual vineyard names.) In favorable years, these wines have great delicacy and elegance.

The river flows almost due north from Trittenheim before making a long sweeping curve, on which is located the famous village of Piesport. Its wines are most widely known when the village name appears in tandem with Goldtröpfchen, its most famous vineyard or Michelsberg, its Grosslage. The growing conditions at Piesport are perfect. The vines are grown on a two-mile long, 500 foot high slope facing due south. Piesporter

Goldtröpfchen, especially a Spätlese or Auslese, is a smooth, sweet wine with a fragrant nose and an obvious pedigree.

Beyond Piesport, the river forms another short loop before making another long, sweeping curve, along which the only wine of note is Brauneberg in the Grosslage of Kurfürstlay. Then it changes direction to form an elbow at Bernkastel-Kues, where the ground rises suddenly and steeply to a height of 700 feet to the north of Bernkastel. Here the slopes are clothed in a spectacular five-mile curtain of vines.

At the point where the slope rises, there is one portion that faces directly south. This is the location of one of the Mosel's finest, and Germany's most famous vineyards, the Bernkasteler Doktor — so named because its wines are supposed to have cured Bishop Boemund of Trier of a serious illness in the fourth century.

Irrespective of the veracity of this historical anecdote, the Doktor vineyards, largely under the ownership of the important house of Deinhard of Koblenz, produce wines today of incomparable finesse and breeding.

Unfortunately today, wines made in the area stretching all the way from Schweich to Zell are permitted to use the name of Bernkastel. Many are sold under Grosslage names, such as Bernkastler-Kurfürstlay. Wines labeled simply Bereich Bernkastel are usually largely made from Müller-Thurgau grapes, while a wine sold as Bereich Bernkastel Riesling is generally of better quality. It is, nevertheless, this rather loose use of the Bernkastel name that makes it one of the world's best-known wine names.

At Pünderich, the Mosel begins a sweep to form yet another of its frequent loops on which the famous town of Zell an der Mosel is located. The steep slopes around Zell are largely planted with Riesling vines, and their best-known wines are sold under the Grosslage name of Schwarze Katz. The wines are usually elegant and fruity, although they do not generally possess the finesse of the best wines of the Middle Mosel.

The Mosel-Saar-Ruwer is the most northerly of Germany's major wine exporting regions. Its wines are to be found in almost every part of the world and are highly respected generally, with the wines of the Middle Mosel justifiably held in the highest esteem.

Fairy-tale castles and vineyards character-ize the Mittelrhein region of Germany.

The Riesling is the predominant grape in the Mosel region.

NAHE

THE WINE-GROWING region based around the River Nahe stretches from its meeting point with the Rhine as far as Kirn. The best wines come from the area between Bad Kreuznach and Schlossböckelheim, beyond which the area breaks down into sporadic pockets of vines scattered over a wide area.

The Nahe is not only a viticultural region; it is also a farming area, and many of the wine growers are also involved in general farming activities.

The vineyards lie on a mixture of gentle and steep slopes, and the Riesling reigns supreme on all of the best-exposed sites.

Wines from the area around Bad Kreuznach are generally racy Rieslings with a style comparable to that of the Mosel, although wines from some of the individual vineyards can transcend that comparison to achieve a greater depth without sacrificing any of their delicacy.

The two most highly rated vineyards of the region, however, are upstream from Bad Kreuznach, beyond Bad Münster.

The first is Rotenfels which takes its name from the high cliff, the highest in Europe north of the Alps, which forces the Nahe to make an abrupt change of course. Along the foot of the cliff, on a narrow slope of rock fragment, a layer of red earth has been formed through erosion. It is here that this jewel of the region is planted tightly along this strip in a perfect sun-trap. The wines produced here are steely Rieslings to which a unique spiciness has been added, giving the impression of a wine grown in a warmer climate, but one that has also retained an amazing freshness.

Further upstream, between Niederhausen and Schlossböckelheim, lies the vineyard of Kupfergrube. The vineyard site was created in the early part of this century by convict laborers who were set the task of mining the copper that today gives the vineyard its name. Not long after the mine workings were abandoned, the steep slope was planted with Rieslings. The wines of Kupfergrube possess a perfect balance between fruit, acid and sweetness that still is clean-tasting. In exceptionally good years they achieve an astonishing distinction and complexity.

Some people compare Nahe wines with those of the Mosel, while others consider them to bear a greater resemblance to Rheingau wines. The truth, I feel, lies somewhere in between, but there can be no questioning of the fact that the Nahe produces some of Germany's, and the world's, finest white wines.

RHEINGAU

SHORTLY AFTER passing Mainz, the River Rhine makes a sharp turn to run east to west along the foot of the Taunus Mountains. Along the lower slopes of the mountains lie the highly favored vineyards of the Rheingau which benefit from having a southern exposure overlooking the river, and complete protection from the north wind because of the towering Taunus Mountains which reach a maximum height of 2,887 feet.

Few wine regions have been deluged with praise as has the Rheingau. Napoleon and Queen Victoria were loud in their praise of Rheingau wines, as were the composer Robert Schumann and the poet Goethe.

According to legend, it is also the region where

the potential of making sweet wines in Germany was accidentally discovered.

Permission to begin the harvest had to be received from the sovereign prince. In 1775, the courier who was dispatched from Fulda to inform the Benedictine monks at Johannisberg that they could commence the harvest fell prey to robbers, who held him prisoner for several days. When he finally arrived in Johannisberg, the grapes had already begun to rot on the vines, but the monks went ahead with the harvest anyway. It is contended that these grapes yielded the first Spätlese and Auslese wines.

Whether or not true, it certainly is a pretty story to weave around some of the world's finest sweet white wines, and an excellent illustration of the inadvisability of shooting the messenger! The monks too should be praised for passing on their discovery to other wine regions in the country.

The entire area runs from Hochheim in the east to Lorchhausen in the west, a distance of little more than twenty-five miles, fifteen of which face south across the Rhine.

The principal grape is the Riesling. The Müller-Thurgau and Sylvaner are also grown in small quantities. Surprisingly, about 120 acres of Spätburgunder vines are grown near the western extremity of the region at Assmannshausen which produces Germany's most respected red wine.

It is, however, the white wines produced from Riesling vines that have earned the Rheingau its exalted reputation.

Just to the east, the first of the great white wine vineyards rises on a steep, slaty, terraced slope facing the estuary of the Nahe. This is the Berg Schlossberg at Rüdesheim, whose vineyards sweep around the Rüdesheimer Berg and beyond the town to gain, finally, a southerly exposure. At their best the wines of the Berg display an excellent depth of fruit and a subtle strength. In hot, dry years, these vineyards suffer as their drainage is too efficient. In those years the vineyards above the town produce the best wines.

Continuing upstream, the town of Geisenheim is more famous for its 100-year-old wine institute than for its wines. The most highly regarded of Geisenheim's vineyards is Rothenberg, which was expanded and modernized following the 1971 wine laws. Its wines are big and balanced and have an attractive hint of earthiness in their taste.

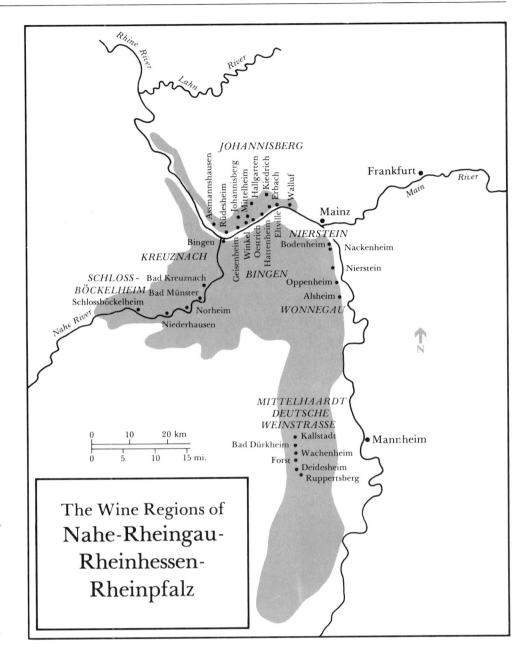

The Wine Regions of
Nahe-Rheingau-Rheinhessen-Rheinpfalz

The Nahe region is known as the "tasting room" of Germany. Different types of soil, many grape varieties and the proximity of both the Rhine and the Mosel lend complexity to Nahe wines.

To the northeast of Geisenheim, is the village of Johannisberg and its other vineyards are completely overshadowed by Schloss Johannisberg. This large estate occupies 86 acres entirely devoted to Riesling vines and according to records was the first estate to take this step in 1716. Most of the buildings were seriously damaged during the Second World War, but have now been restored to their seventeenth-century grandeur. One contributing factor to the quality of this estate's wines is its cool cellars, where the wine is kept in wood to mature. The dedication to quality is clearly evident in the wines which are fine and weighty and truly elegant. Spätlese wines are made only in the best years, and Auslese wines are rare.

The neighboring town of Winkel is likewise dominated by Schloss Vollrads and its 116 acres of vines. The vineyards of the Schloss are slightly further up the slope than most Rheingau vineyards and are protected by the even higher forest.

The wines of Schloss Vollrads possess a distinct acidity allied to fine fruit and a subtle sweetness. The present owner, Erwein Graf Matuschka-Greiffenclau, will not bottle any wines that do not meet his standards; such wines are sold to the wine trade in bulk, but can never carry the name of Vollrads.

One other Winkel vineyard, Hasensprung, does produce one of the best wines of the Rheingau. Covering 247 acres, its Riesling wines are the epitome of perfection and possess all the depth and subtlety that earns the Rheingau its reputation.

Mittelheim, which is linked to Winkel, has no particularly notable wines, but the next village, Oestrich, has two vineyards, Lenchen and Doosberg, that make fine, firm Riesling wines that attain considerable stature during very good years.

The vineyards of Hallgarten are the highest in the Rheingau at 1,000 feet above sea level. The vineyards of Würzgarten and Schönhell, in partic-

ular, are responsible for full-bodied wines with an intense bouquet that are capable of a remarkable amount of aging.

Hattenheim stands on the Rhine, but its vineyards stretch back into the hills. Every other vineyard becomes secondary to Kloster Eberbach. A twelfth century walled Cistercian vineyard, it is the spiritual embodiment of wine growing in the region. Open to the public and very active in promoting wine activities, it also serves as a base for the German Wine Academy.

The neighboring village of Erbach and Hattenheim share parts of one of the Rheingau's best-known vineyards, Marcobrunn, which produces rich, full-bodied wines with a hint of spiciness that show at their best if they are given time to develop in the bottle.

Up the hill from Erbach is the tiny village of Kiedrich. Its most highly regarded vineyard, Gräfenberg, produces yet another elegant, spicy

wine, as does the neighboring vineyard of Sandgrube.

Down by the river, Eltville is an important wine town and headquarters to the Hessen State Wine Cellars. Its vineyards produce good quality wines that command prices similar to those of other leading Rheingau wines.

Behind Eltville, the tiny village of Rauenthal holds a special place for its wines, in a region where there are more special wines than in most places. Typically, a Rauenthaler combines strength with softness and, given bottle age, displays a flowery scent and spiciness that, even in an Auslese, is held in balance with excellent acidity.

The twin towns of Ober-Walluf and Nieder-Walluf and Martinsthal produce wines of excellent quality, but tend to be less well known because of having to live in the shadow of Rauenthal.

At the extreme eastern end of the Rheingau lies the town of Hochheim, from whose name the word

The Rheinhessen has a variety of soils that produce mild, harmonious table wines as well as top-quality vintages.

Hock was derived. Located on the River Main, Hochheim is one of the region's largest wine-growing towns. At their best, the Rieslings of Hochheim's vineyards are of equal quality to the better wines of Rheingau.

RHEINPFALZ

STRETCHING SOME 50 miles from the French border north of Alsace, to the Rheinhessen, this region, which is also known as the Palatinate, has about 55,000 acres under vines.

The region is divided in two with the Mittelhaardt/Deutsche Weinstrasse in the north and the Südliche Weinstrasse in the south.

In the south the grapes are mostly Muscat, Gewürztraminer, Sylvaner and Tokay, and the wines are mostly undistinguished, although they can be pleasant drinking. Much of the production is not even bottled, but is used locally as carafe wine.

The Mittelhaardt is a different story. To begin with, the Riesling becomes the principal grape, and in the area between Ruppertsberg and Kallstadt, the best wines of the region are to be found.

The wines of Ruppertsberg, Deidesheim, Forst and Wachenheim are considered to be the best, but are almost matched by those of Bad Dürkheim, Kallstadt, Leistadt and Königsbach.

Ruppertsberg wines are generally short on depth compared to Forst and Deidesheim. However, the commune is noted for producing a very stylish Scheurebe, as well as good Rieslings and Sylvaners. Its two most highly rated vineyards are Hoheburg and Gaisböhl.

Deidesheim, one of the prettiest towns in the region, is generally acknowledged as the source of many of the best wines, and those made from the Riesling have earned it its reputation. There are several notable vineyards in Deidesheim, including Langenmorgen, Grainhübel, Kielesberg, Herrgottsacker, Leinhöhle and Hohenmorgen, which is probably the best.

Forst is a small, but important wine town which sits in the center of a ring of vineyards where the Riesling grows to produce wines of great depth and infinite charm. The famous Jesuitengarten and Ungeheuer are its most highly rated vineyards.

Wachenheim produces rich, full-bodied wines with great finesse from a cluster of vineyards, mainly to the east of the village. Of these, Böhlig, Rechbächel, Goldbächel and Gerümpel are its most famous vineyards.

Although Bad Dürkheim, Kallstadt, Leistadt and Königsbach produce wines of only slightly lesser stature than the best of the Mittelhaardt, there are no individual vineyards of particular nobility.

Three firms in Rheinpfalz, Dr. Bürklin-Wolf, von Buhl and Bassermann-Jordan, own several estates, or parts of estates, throughout the region, including some of the best, and any wine bearing a label with any of their names reflects the diligence and dedication they bring to wine making.

In general the wines from the Mittelhaardt are of the very highest quality and can take their place amongst the best Germany has to offer. The wines from the south Rheinpfalz, the Bereich Südliche Weinstrasse, are not of the same standard, but they are usually regarded as being of excellent value for their price wherever they are sold around the world.

RHEINHESSEN

THE LARGEST of Germany's wine-growing regions with almost 61,000 acres, the Rheinhessen also produces some of the country's least distinguished wines.

Partly, this lack is due to the fact that the principal grape variety is the Sylvaner. In any case, the plain dullness of the landscape seems also to be reflected in the neutrality of most of the wines.

Much of the wine of Rheinhessen finds its way to market under the name of Liebfraumilch, and every bit as much more is sold, in bulk, to the wine trade to emerge as part of a brand of still or sparkling wine. This region is also the headquarters of the Sichel firm, which exports its famous brand Blue Nun Liebfraumilch to 81 countries.

There are, however, pockets of vineyards that are the region's redeeming features. Mainly, these

The Sylvaner *is the second most abundant grape variety in the Rheinhessen region.*

are the vineyards that are draped like a necklace along the western bank of the Rhine where the vines are either Riesling or Müller-Thurgau.

The best known of these better areas is Nierstein which produces some very pleasant wine of good quality. Sadly, its name has been ruthlessly "borrowed" by the unscrupulous who are content to masquerade in others' plumes.

On either side of Nierstein, the towns of Oppenheim and Nackenheim produce wines from the Riesling grape that can, at their best, rival the fragrance and character of a Rheingau. Nierstein is home to the famous house of Guntrum, which carries on an extensive export business based largely on non-estate-bottled wines.

To the south of Oppenheim, the villages of Guntersblum and Alsheim can be relied upon for good quality wines, while Bodenheim, down river from Nackenheim, also has earned a good reputation.

Around the bend in the river, at the estuary of the Nahe and facing Rheingau, the vineyards outside the town of Bingen produce some wines that are comparable in style to those of the lower Nahe. Its best-known vineyard is Scharlachberg, which yields very fine wines.

*The gracious château and Riesling vineyards of Schloss
Johannisberg in Rheingau. Most of the estate's buildings
were seriously damaged in the Second World War but
they have all been restored to their seventeenth-century
magnificence.*

*The ideal time to visit the Hessische Bergstrasse is in the
spring, when a sea of almond and cherry blossoms give
the area its deserved name of "Germany's spring garden."*

As the largest of the country's wine-producing districts, it is hardly surprising that the Rheinhessen is also amongst the biggest exporters of wines. The wines from the Rheinfront near Nierstein and around Bingen are deservedly the most highly regarded. Away from the river, the best wines make very pleasant drinking, with a few being outstanding. The region does, however, also produce some very plain and very ordinary wines, most of which is sold in bulk to the wine trade for blending and bottling under some brand name.

HESSISCHE BERGSTRASSE

THE SMALLEST of Germany's wine regions, the vineyards of Hessische Bergstrasse cover less than 1,000 acres, about half of which are planted with Rieslings with the remainder being mainly Müller-Thurgau and Sylvaner.

Franken wines derive their powerful, robust character from the chalk, keuper, sandstone and old alluvial soils of the region.

Located inland to the east of the Rhine opposite Rheinhessen, its vineyards produce wines that are similar in character and quality to those of Rheingau.

Many of the smallest vineyards are tended only on weekends, and most of the wine is made at cooperatives. These wines are rarely seen outside of the region itself.

Despite its smallness and the combination of part-time viticulture and cooperative wine making, the wines of Hessische Bergstrasse are generally of such excellent quality that they compare favorably with the wines of the Rheingau, which may explain why they are so rarely found beyond their home region!

FRANKEN

STRADDLING the River Main around the city of Würzburg, the Franken vineyards extend to almost 10,000 acres, about half of which have been modernized since 1954.

The most widely planted vine is the Müller-Thurgau, closely followed by Sylvaner, while plantings of a new crossing, Bacchus, is gaining favor.

The Franconian approach to wine making is different from that of other German regions. It is also the only region which produces a great wine from the Sylvaner grape.

Although sweet wines are made, it is the dry wines made from the Sylvaner that are the region's most noteworthy. Quite unlike any other traditional German wines, they can most readily be compared to white Burgundies in style.

Quality wines from Franken are also peculiar in that they are not sold in the ubiquitous tapered bottle, but are presented in a flagon-shaped bottle called a Bocksbeutel.

One hazard faced by the Franconian vine growers is extremely cold winter temperatures which, in very bad years, can reduce the subsequent vintage by as much as 80 per cent.

Despite such upsets, the Franconian wine makers continue to produce their unique wines which, no matter the grape variety, exhibit a slightly earthy element in their flavor.

WÜRTTEM-BERG

SPRAWLING ALONG the gentle slopes of the River Neckar and its tributaries, Württemberg's almost 23,000 acres of vineyards are planted in almost equal proportions of red and white grape varieties. Almost 70 per cent of the wines, however, are white.

The Riesling, Müller-Thurgau and Kerner are the main white grapes, while the Trollinger, Müller-Rebe, Portugieser, Spätburgunder and Limberger are the red varieties. The Limberger is peculiar to Württemberg.

The red wines are usually light in color and are made in varying degrees of sweetness. The whites are generally rather undistinguished, but are rather pleasant, uncomplicated drinking.

It is hardly surprising that the wines of Württemberg are little known outside the region, as local consumption is three times greater than the total production.

One touching tale, dating from 1140, concerns the town of Weinsberg, which was under siege by Hohenstaufen emperor Konrad III. He guaranteed the women safe passage from the town and permitted them to carry away their dearest possession. When they emerged through the town gate, the women were carrying their husbands on their backs.

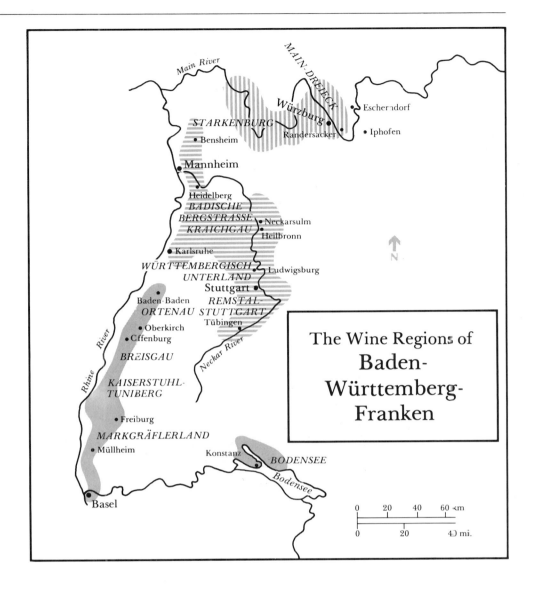

The Wine Regions of
Baden-Württemberg-Franken

BADEN

THE MOST SOUTHERLY of Germany's wine-producing regions, Baden stretches over 180 miles from the Swiss border to the Tauber river in the north.

This vast area, which yields about 15 per cent of Germany's total wine production, is actually composed of seven separate districts which accounts for the wide variation to be found in Baden wines.

Most of the vineyards are planted on flat or

The most southerly German wine-growing region, Baden is the home of fiery, full-bodied wines.

Vines grow on the southern slopes of the Black Forest and on the volcanic soils of the Kaiserstuhl. This region produces nearly a dozen different types of wine, owing to the many types of countryside and of grape varieties.

gently sloping ground, and the Müller-Thurgau is the most widely grown vine. The Ruländer and Gutedel, known elsewhere as the Chasselas, are the other main varieties, while small amounts of Riesling, Sylvaner and other varieties are also grown.

The wines of Baden cover the whole gamut from a light, crisp style to weightier, full-flavored wines. Mainly, the wines of the region, which are mostly produced by cooperatives, are uncomplicated, pleasant drinking.

Part of the reason for the region being capable of such a variety of styles is that the climate is warmer in Baden than in most other parts of Germany. In the European Economic Community wine-making categories, Baden is classed as Zone B, along with some French regions such as Alsace and part of the Loire, while the remainder of Germany's vineyards are classed as Zone A, in common with Luxembourg and Britain.

Among the better wines are those of Kaiserstuhl, a rocky outcropping of volcanic composition which makes a distinctive wine from Ruländer grapes

and a pleasant, light red from the Spätburgunder.

Ortenau, at the foot of the Black Forest below Baden-Baden, makes wines of very sound quality. The best is produced from the Riesling, which is known locally as the Klingelberger.

To the south of Freiburg lies the Markgräferland, which has been noted for its wines for centuries. Its most highly regarded wine today is the light and lively white made from the Gutedel grape.

A final pocket of Baden wines worth noting are those of Bodensee, also referred to as Lake Constance. The vineyards are located on high, steep slopes and benefit from the added warmth and light reflected from the lake. Several varieties of grapes are grown, with the main ones being Müller-Thurgau and Spätburgunder.

The best of Baden's wines are of very good quality, but in common with most regions of the world that produce wines in such quantity, the majority of its wines are rather plain, although they are perfectly enjoyable and agreeable to drink.

Italy

ITALY IS A SMALL COUNTRY that produces more wine than any other in the world — approximately one-fifth of the world's supply.

Until comparatively recent years it was one of the most difficult wine-producing countries to investigate. Just as the Italians themselves are very nonchalant about wine, so their wines have poured through the centuries in an unclassified clutter.

Some wines were named for the grape variety; some bore regional names; others carried the name of a town, while others were simply named out of whimsy. The result of this non-system was that all but a few truly outstanding, or aggressively promoted, Italian wines remained virtually unknown.

Eventually, however, it was recognized that while this situation was all well and good at home where everyone simply drank the local wine, it was not in the least helpful when it came to securing export orders.

Consequently, in 1963 the Italian government stepped in with a wine law bearing a strong resemblance to the French appellation contrôlée system.

This new law set three categories. The lowest designation was *Denominazione Semplice* which was to be applied to ordinary table wines. However, before it could be used, it was rejected by the European Economic Community. The next level of wines was *Denominazione d'Origine Controllata* (DOC), and the highest classification was *Denominazione Controllata e Garantita* (DOCG).

It took several years to introduce this new system and, from a practical point of view, it has been the DOC designation which has proved most significant to date.

To obtain DOC status, a group of wine growers must apply to a committee in Rome for recognition. When applying, they must also suggest a defined area and proposed standards of quality. If a wine is granted DOC status, it must then carry a DOC label, as well as its own, on the bottle.

The first DOC wines were accepted in 1966, and today there are over 200 wines that have been recognized. There are several wines of quality that have not received DOC status. Part of the reason for this is that, rather than apply for recognition, some growers have preferred to remain outside the system.

The DOCG designation is only now, 23 years after the formulation of the law, becoming a reality. Barolo and Barbaresco in Piemonte, along with Vino Nobile di Montepulciano and Brunello di Montalcino in Tuscany, were the first wines to receive that distinction. Chianti in Tuscany has now been accepted for this elevated status, and several other wines are being given consideration.

Wines in the DOCG category are not only authenticated as to place of origin and production methods; they are also guaranteed for quality.

In most parts of Italy, there is enough sunshine and warmth each year to ensure the ripening of the grapes and the development of enough natural sugar. The wine laws forbid chaptalisation, the addition of sugar, but as one candid wine producer, whose wines have to attain a particularly high alcohol level, put it, "In years where the natural sugar is too low, we can always rely on the fairies to steal into the winery at night to add sugar to the wine."

In general, however, the benign climate that prevails in most of Italy's regions ensures that the quality of the wines from vintage to vintage does not vary much. It is also true that, every now and again, there is a remarkable year in which wines of truly superior caliber are produced.

One such year was 1975, when the Chianti of Tuscany was quite remarkable. A British wine writer observed that those who were unwise enough

Opposite: *Tirol Castle, whose vineyards are situated in the steep Alpine valley of the River Adige.*

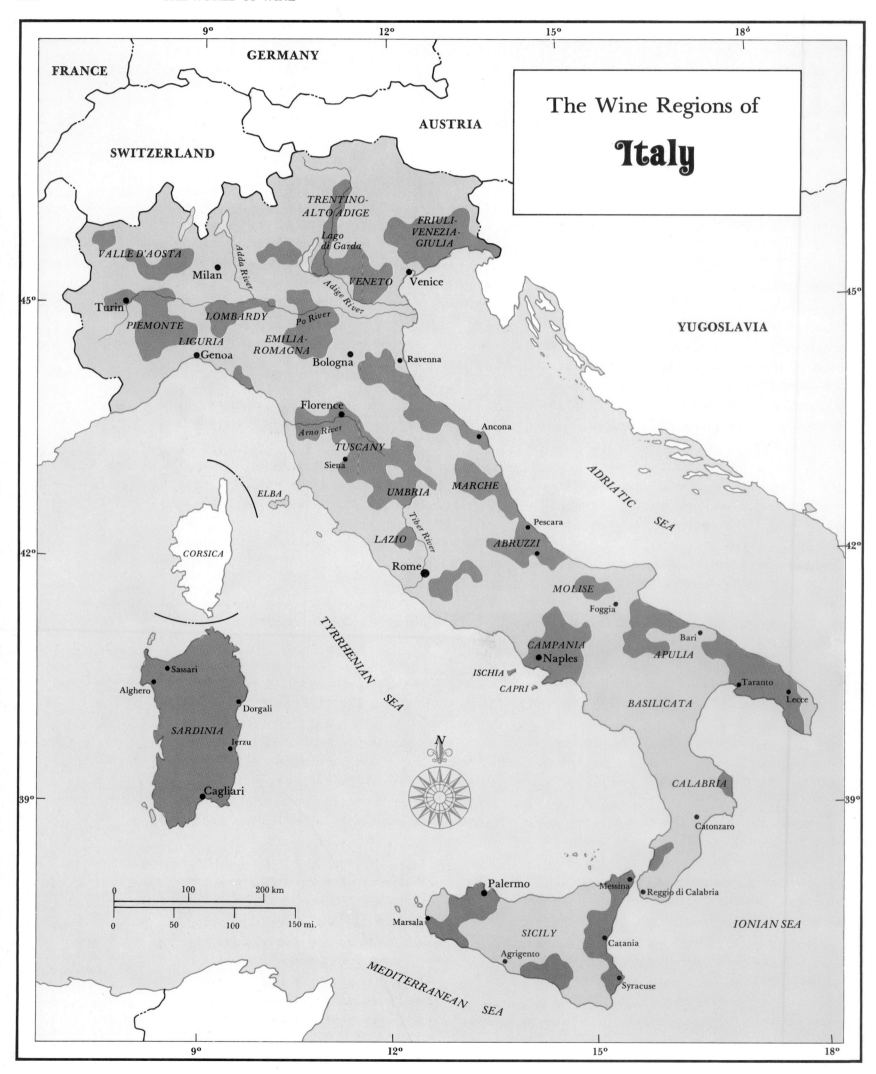

FRANCE

GERMANY

SWITZERLAND

AUSTRIA

The Wine Regions of
Italy

9°   12°   15°   18°

TRENTINO-
ALTO ADIGE

VALLE D'AOSTA

*Lago
di Garda*

FRIULI-
VENEZIA-
GIULIA

Adda River

Milan

VENETO

Venice

Adige River

45°   45°

Turin

PIEMONTE

LOMBARDY

Po River

YUGOSLAVIA

LIGURIA

EMILIA-
ROMAGNA

Genoa

Bologna

Ravenna

Florence

Arno River

Ancona

TUSCANY

Siena

ADRIATIC

ELBA

MARCHE

SEA

UMBRIA

CORSICA

LAZIO

Tiber River

Pescara

42°   42°

ABRUZZI

Rome

MOLISE

TYRRHENIAN

Foggia

CAMPANIA

Bari

Sassari

ISCHIA

Naples

APULIA

Alghero

CAPRI

SEA

BASILICATA

Taranto

Dorgali

Lecce

SARDINIA

Ierzu

N

CALABRIA

Cagliari

39°   39°

Catonzaro

| 0 | 100 | 200 km |

Palermo

Messina

Reggio di Calabria

| 0 | 50 | 100 | 150 mi. |

Marsala

IONIAN SEA

SICILY

Catania

Agrigento

Syracuse

MEDITERRANEAN   SEA

9°   12°   15°   18°

not to lay down suitable quantities of this vintage of Chianti had best have a good explanation ready for their distraught grandchildren!

Although the new wine law has clarified much of the confusion that existed, it is still possible to find the same wine bearing a number of different names. This is usually the result of local tradition rather than any attempt to deceive.

It is hardly surprising that traditions die hard in Italy, where wine has been made since before the days of the Roman Empire, which is generally dated from 753 B.C. There is no certainty as to when and where wine making began, but it is known that the Etruscans were making wine by the ninth and tenth centuries B.C. in what we know today as Tuscany and Lazio.

A great deal is known about the wines of Roman times. They bore no resemblance to the wines of Italy today, any more than do the wines that were being shipped to England by the fourteenth century.

Even as late as the eighteenth century, wines from Florence were apparently still being shipped to England in uncorked casks sealed with oil.

For various reasons — Austrian military tyranny, Church despotism, and trade barriers between principalities — the development of the Italian wine industry was very slow and lagged significantly behind that of the French. Because of the political climate in the very fractured country that is now Italy, there was no incentive for the wine makers to improve upon the wines, as they had no opportunity to gain any profit from such efforts.

For a great many centuries it was common to have a communal wine press set up in the central square, and everyone in the village or town would crush his or her grapes there each year. The importance of these presses may be judged from the fact that when raiders from another community would attack a village, one of their objectives would be to capture the press, which threat, of course, brought out the stoutest defense by the locals.

Gradually, the wine industry moved away from the town squares, and serious wine making began to develop. Many regions, particularly in Northern Italy, began to produce identifiable and individual wines of sound quality.

A giant step forward for the country, and subsequently for the wine industry, was the unification of Italy under King Victor Emmanuel II after March 17, 1861, when the Italian government declared him king of Italy.

This, however, did not result in a magical overnight transformation. Many people, after centuries of cultural isolation and uneasy relationships with their neighbors, had difficulty accepting the idea of being Italian when they had always thought of themselves as Tuscans, Venetians or Calabrians. Indeed, this attitude persists today.

The wine industry, however, continued to develop and began to prosper. New methods were introduced to improve the vines and the winemaking techniques. It was like the awakening of a sleeping giant: exports had been minimal, grew slowly as the wines improved, and then began to soar after 1963 as the results of the DOC laws came into effect, stripping away a great deal of the confusion that had existed, especially in foreign markets.

The success of the DOC laws and the advancement of the wine industry can best be judged by the fact that exports of wine from Italy now exceed six million hectolitres each year, while her wine imports are a mere two hundred thousand hectolitres.

Wine is produced in every region of Italy from an enormous variety of grapes on an equally wide variety of soils. For the most part, the red wines tend to be superior to the whites.

There has been a trend over the past few years to plant vineyards on flat ground where mechanical harvesting is practical. This elicited the observation that, from a financial point of view, only a fool or a hero would continue to grow vines on the hills. Happily for the wine lover there are many people who persist in what may be folly, but they should be more honorably regarded as heroes.

PIEMONTE

LOCATED AMONGST the Monferrato Hills, in northwestern Italy, Piemonte is one of the country's most important wine-producing regions. It is also one of the most productive regions and yields a vast array of wines, the best of which, with few exceptions, are red.

The finest Piemonte wine, and arguably Italy's finest, is Barolo which takes its name from the town of the same name. Made from the Nebbiolo grape, Barolo must be aged for three years, two of those in chestnut or oak barrels, before it is bottled. If it is aged for four years prior to bottling, it is entitled to be sold as a *Riserva*, and after five years of aging in barrels it can be called a *Riserva Speciale*.

A powerful, deep-colored wine, it has a marvellously complex aroma and depth of flavor. It is also dry, full-bodied, and velvety smooth, with all its elements in perfect harmony. It is also capable of maturing in bottle for as long as twenty years.

One of the finest and most important estates in Barolo is Fontanafredda which also has several other points of interest. The vineyards were planted in 1878 by Count Emmanuele Guerrieri, the son of Victor Emmanuele II, King of Italy, and Countess Rosa di Mirafiori, e di Fontanafredda. Originally named Mirafiori Vini Italiani, it is now known as Tenimenti di Barolo e Fontanafredda. The firm quickly earned a reputation for producing fine wines, but its financial fortunes were not as sound, and in 1931 the business was sold to the Monte dei Paschi di Siena Bank. The new owners began renovating the winery and the vast vineyards over a period of ten years, at the end of which time they were not only producing Barolo, but had added Barbaresco, Dolcetto d'Alba, Barbera d'Alba, Moscato and Pinot Bianco.

The buildings on the estate are in reality a small town lying below a ridge of Nebbiolo vineyards. The vineyard and winery workers live in the houses on the estate, and there is also a school and a chapel. Although the firm is justly proud of its century-old cellar and the huge Slavonian oak casks used for aging some of their wines, the winery is a fully equipped, high-tech operation. The tasting room attached to the winery is one of the finest tasting facilities to be found anywhere.

One small mystery surrounds the peacocks that roam freely around the grounds. They have been there for so long that no one knows who brought the birds to the estate.

If there is a wine of the same caliber as Barolo, it is Gattinara, which is named for the main town of the Vercelli province. Made with the Nebbiolo grape and aged for four years before being bottled, it is slightly lighter in color than Barolo, but it has greater subtlety and fragrance.

Barbaresco, also made with the Nebbiolo grape and named for its village, is similar in many ways to Barolo except that it has a lighter and slightly softer style. Its aging requirements are, sensibly, one year less than those of Barolo.

Other wines of note that are primarily made with the Nebbiolo are those of Alba, Boca, Bramaterra, Carema, Fara, Ghemme, Lessona and Sizzano.

The most prolifically grown vine in Piemonte is Barbera, which also gives its name to the wine that accounts for almost half of the entire production of Piemonte. In this vast quantity of wine there are four that carry DOC status: Barbera d'Alba, Barbera d'Asti, Barbera dei Colli Tortonesi and Barbera del Monferrato. Yet these account for only a very small proportion of Barbera wines. There are non-DOC wines sold as Barbera del Piemonte; many of these bear more specific geographical designations.

There is also a Barbera Rosata and a Barbera Bianca which, although it is not common, is made either by vinifying the grape juice off the skins or is made with the Barbera Bianca grapes which are still grown in the Asti, Alessandria and Cuneo areas.

The generous Barbera has created problems because of the huge quantity of grapes that are produced annually. This led the region and the producers, beginning in 1979, to pursue a program of experimentation to devise ways of using the Barbera grape to produce something different from the existing Barbera wines.

The result of these experiments has seen the introduction of a Chiaretto del Piemonte, a natural Chiaretto del Piemonte Frizzante and a Chiaretto Brut Spumante, all of which are vinified partly off the skins. The program has also caused the emergence of a Chiaretto di Moncalvo, a natural Chiaretto di Moncalvo Frizzante and a Moncalvo Chiaretto Brut Spumante. A Barbera Spumante Rosato has also been created as has a nouveau, Barbera Novello di Piemonte. Finally, there is a Barbera in Bianco and Passum which is a dry, red raisin wine.

The traditional Barbera d'Asti and Barbera d'Alba are both made entirely from Barbera grapes. Ruby red when young, they become garnet with age. The wine has a delicate bouquet and is dry and full-bodied, with a good balance between fruit, acid and tannin. Barbera dei Colli Tortonesi can have up to 15 per cent of Freisa and Bonarda Piemontese grapes used in the blend, while Barbera del Monferrato can have between 10 and 15 per cent of Freisa and/or Grignolino and/or Dolcetto in its blend. The Colli Tortonesi is a lively, robust wine that becomes full and round with age. The Monferrato is a lighter, medium-bodied wine that can be quite fizzy on occasion. All four of the DOC Barberas are generally at their best when they are between four and six years old.

Another important grape is the Dolcetto, which is somewhat misleadingly named. Literally translated as "little sweet," the wines are, however, completely dry. Easy-drinking, pleasant wines, they could be likened to Beaujolais in style, although the Dolcetto imparts a completely different flavor than does the Gamay. Several villages produce Dolcetto, and their names can be linked with it on the label. There are seven Dolcetto DOC wines: Acqui, Alba, Asti, Diano d'Alba, Dogliani, Langhe Monregalesi and Ovada.

One red wine which seems out of step with other Piemonte wines is Grignolino, which is light, dry, freshly scented and a refreshingly satisfying wine when drunk young and slightly chilled. The wine has two DOC examples, Grignolino d'Asti and Grignolino del Monferrato Casalese. A considerable amount of wine is sold simply as Grignolino del Piemonte, while others carry more specific geographical designations including Castellinaldo, Cioccaro, Migliandolo and Vezza d'Alba.

The Malvasia grape is widely grown throughout Italy, and in Piemonte two sub-varieties, Casorzo and Schierano, are used. The first is responsible for the DOC wine Malvasia di Casorzo d'Asti, while the second is used for the DOC wine Malvasia di Castelnuovo don Bosco. About 80 per cent of the grapes are sold under the non-DOC designation of Malvasia del Piemonte, and there are some liqueur wines made from the Malvasia as well. Ranging in color from ruby red to cherry, the wines are fragrant, sweet and slightly aromatic.

Another sweet red wine from the region, Brachetto d'Acqui, is made from the Brachetto grape and is the only DOC wine that can have up to 10 per cent of Aleatico and/or Moscato Nero in its

Capo di Ponte Monastero.

blend. A ruby-red, fizzy wine, it has a musky odor and a soft, delicate flavor.

The Erbaluce is used to produce two DOC white wines, Erbaluce di Caluso and Caluso Passito. The Erbaluce di Caluso is a dry wine with a delicate aroma and a fresh, crisp flavor, while the Caluso Passito is a golden-colored wine with a light bouquet and a full, sweet and velvety character.

The most important white grape in Piemonte is the Cortese which is thought to be native to the province of Alessandria. There are three DOC wines made from this grape, Cortese dell'Alto Monferrato, Cortese dei Colli Tortonesi and Cortese di Gavi. It is a clean, crisp dry wine that is both refreshing and elegant. The best known of these wines is the Cortese di Gavi, which is well worth seeking out.

One of Piemonte's most famous wines is the sparkling wine, Asti Spumante, which is made from the luscious Moscato grape. Because of the intensity of natural sugar in the grape, Asti Spumante has always been a sweet wine, but in recent years, there has been a trend towards making a less sweet wine. Unlike Champagne, where it is necessary to add sugar to promote fermentation and a liqueur to add a degree of sweetness, Asti Spumante is an entirely natural sweet wine. There is a little wine made by the Champagne method, but mostly it is made by the Charmat method. Here, the second fermentation takes place in closed tanks, rather than in bottles, and the wine is bottled under pressure when it is ready. One of the advantages of this method is that it takes less time, with the result that the wine is less expensive. The Moscato grape gives the wine a distinctive and intense fruity bouquet that carries through in the flavor; however, although the wines are sweet, they are not cloying. The traditional sweet wines are best either with desserts or on their own, while the newer, slightly dryer style gives the wines a greater versatility.

VALLE D'AOSTA

TUCKED INTO the northwest corner of Italy and Piemonte, the Valle d'Aosta has the distinction of having the highest vineyards in Europe. Some of them are as much as 3,500 feet above sea level below the snow-capped peaks of the Alps. The wine growers here must work hard to gather a decent crop from their reluctant vines.

Oddly enough, the primary language of this region is French.

The region boasts only two DOC wines, Donnaz and Enfer d'Arvier. Donnaz is made with the

Nebbiolo in a blend that can contain 15 per cent of other varieties. A brilliant red in color, it has a light, attractive bouquet and is soft and quite light-bodied. The Enfer d'Arvier is made with the Petit Rouge which can also be blended to a maximum of 15 per cent with other varieties. The result is a cherry-red wine with a light bouquet, light body and pleasantly bitterish taste.

The remaining small amount of both red and white wines produced are charming in their own way, but none of them is of outstanding character.

LIGURIA

To the south of Piemonte, this region stretches along the coastal strip of the Italian Riviera all the way from Imperia to La Spezia.

Around La Spezia, in the area known as Cinque Terre, the steep, laboriously terraced vineyards sweep down to the sea and the harvest must be transported by boat.

The region has a total of only three DOC wines: Cinque Terre, Cinque Terre Sciacchetra and Rossese di Dolceacqua. The two Cinque Terre wines are white and are made with the Bosco grape which must make up 60 per cent of the blend. This is then completed with Albarolo and Vermentino grapes.

Cinque Terre is a pale yellow, dry wine with a light nose and pleasant flavor. Cinque Terre Sciacchetra is a golden-colored wine with a more pronounced bouquet. Typically it is sweet and of pleasant character, although there are some dry versions made also.

From the opposite end of the region behind San Remo, the Rossese di Dolceacqua is made with the Rossese grape which can have 5 per cent of other red grape varieties added to it. The wine is ruby red with an intense, yet delicate bouquet and a soft, aromatic flavor.

Liguria produces other red and white wines of sound, if not remarkable, quality which are mainly consumed by the flood of tourists that annually swells the population of the coast.

LOMBARDY

Although it is about the same size as Piemonte, Lombardy produces a small amount of wine by comparison. Much of its wine is consumed locally, and much is never even bottled as it is bought by the region's restaurants and hotels as house wines. There is also a brisk trade with city dwellers, especially from Milan, who buy their wine by the demijohn for home consumption.

The upshot of this situation is that the wines of Lombardy are little known outside of the region and neighboring Switzerland.

Bordered to the north by the Alps, and the land just beyond the River Po to the south, the majority of the region's wines are red, although some good white wines are also made.

One part of the region that produces notable wines from the Nebbiolo grape is the Valtellina, which is in the Alpine area to the north of Lake Como. The vineyards are as much as 2,500 feet above sea level and, in some parts, the vines are grown in narrow strips amongst rocky crags in soil that has been carried from below by hand, or more accurately, by back.

The result is red wines that are rather harsh when young, but acquire a great delicacy on maturing. According to the location in which they are produced, Valtellina wines are known as either Sassella, Grumello, Inferno or Valgella.

At the opposite end of the region to the south of the River Po, the Oltrepò Pavese district produces some of Lombardy's best wines.

The denominazione actually covers nine wines, six red and four white, all conjoined with the name Oltrepò Pavese. They are: Barbacarlo, Barbera, Bonarda, Buttafuoco, Cortese, Sangue di Giuda, Moscato, Pinot, and Riesling.

The Barbacarlo, which is a blend of Barbera and Croatina grapes, and the Bonarda, made from the grape of the same name, are slightly sweet red wines, while the Sangue de Giuda is a decidedly sweet red. The Barbera, which is the most widely produced wine, is a dry wine that is slightly lighter in body than the wine made from the same grape in Piemonte. Buttafuoco is made mostly from

Barbera and Croatina grapes and is also a dry wine.

The Moscato is a sweet wine with an intense bouquet. It is made both as a still wine and as a delightful Spumante. The Cortese is a crisp, dry wine of modest character. The Pinot can be either red, white or rosé; the white is made with the Pinot Grigio and the red and rosé from the Pinot Nero. All three are pleasant, easy-drinking wines. The Riesling is a blend of Renano and Italico Rieslings. This is a fragrant wine that is also made as a Spumante.

The quality of Oltrepò Pavese wines is generally high. This is partly because a great portion of the wine is made by modern, well-equipped cooperatives that strive very hard to maintain a high standard. This is emulated by the area's small growers.

EMILIA-ROMAGNA

A VAST REGION, Emilia-Romagna is one of Italy's largest wine-producing areas. There are over seventy-two grape varieties grown that yield an incredible range of wines. Yet the region is renowned more for its food than its wine.

The region is divided into eight provinces: Ravenna, Forli, Bologna, Modena, Reggio nell'Emilia, Piacenza, Ferrara and Parma.

The most highly regarded of its wines is Albana di Romagna. A white wine made with the Albana grape, it can be either dry or sweet, still or sparkling. The dry is not bone dry, nor is the sweet version richly sweet. At best, however, they can be regarded as good quality wines of a fairly neutral character. These wines are produced in Ravenna, Forli and Bologna.

The most widely planted grape in Ravenna is the Trebbiano, which yields a pale yellow, dry wine that has a light bouquet and a nicely balanced flavor. Another important Ravenna grape is the Uva d'Oro which, despite its name, is a black grape. It is planted in the Comacchio area, where

it is used to produce a deep red, dry wine with a powerful, grapy bouquet and a good flavor that shows a good balance between fruit and acid.

The Sangiovese is Ravenna's other important red grape. It produces a ruby-red, dry wine with a delicate bouquet, fruity flavor and a slightly bitter aftertaste. These wines can also be a bit high in tannin.

Forli's main red grape variety is the Sangiovese. As in Ravenna, the Trebbiano is widely planted for white wines, as is the Albana. The quality and characteristics of Forli's wines are almost identical to those made with the same grapes in Ravenna.

Bologna also relies heavily on the Trebbiano and Albano for its white wines, while the Sangiovese is again the major red grape. It is for its Colli wines, however, that the district is probably best known. There are actually six DOC designations for these wines, with two being red and four white.

Colli Bolognesi Barbera is a blend of 85 per cent Barbera and 15 per cent Sangiovese. A dry, dark ruby wine, it has a grapy bouquet. The taste shows a nice balance between fruit, acid and tannin.

Colli Bolognesi Merlot has 85 per cent of that grape, while the balance is made up of other non-aromatic red grape varieties. A ruby-red wine, it can be either dry or slightly sweet. In either case, the wine is fruity on the nose and soft and balanced in the flavor.

Colli Bolognesi Bianco is a white wine made with between 60 and 80 per cent Albana grapes with the balance being Trebbiano. Again, it can be dry or

The vineyards of northern Italy yield nearly half the country's total output of wine.

slightly sweet. The Albana grape dominates on the bouquet. The flavor is quite attractive, and there is a hint of tannin.

Colli Bolognesi Riesling Italico is composed of 85 per cent of that grape, with the remainder being Trebbiano. A pale yellow wine, it can be either dry or slightly sweet. It has a delicate, flowery bouquet and is harmonious on the palate.

Colli Bolognesi Pinot Bianco uses that grape and 15 per cent of Trebbiano in its blend to produce a pale white wine with an elusive bouquet and a comparatively neutral flavor in both its dry and moderately sweet versions.

The final wine in this group is Colli Bolognesi Sauvignon, in which the named grape is again augmented by 15 per cent of the ubiquitous Trebbiano. A pale yellow wine, it has a light, delicately aromatic bouquet, good body and a fresh, balanced flavor in both the dry and slightly sweet styles.

The region's most controversial wine is probably Lambrusco, which is produced in the provinces of Modena, Reggio nell'Emilia, Piacenza, Ferrara and Parma. Made from the Lambrusco grape, of which there are several sub-varieties, sometimes blended together and sometimes blended with still others, Lambrusco is a rosé-to-red wine that is either dry or sweet and always fizzy. Years ago it was a dry wine, but the sweeter style was developed to conquer the vast United States market, which it did overwhelmingly well. There are those who consider it the most horrid of wines, while others find it perfectly delicious. In truth, as with all other wines, it is a matter of personal taste. The people of Bologna hold the view that Lambrusco is a special regional wine, the thinness of which is ideal with their traditional, heavy pork dishes.

These three provinces also make a wide range of other wines, with the Barbera being used for many reds and in Piacenza. The Malvasia is widely grown to produce a very pleasant range of dry white wines.

Ferrara, in common with the other Lambrusco-producing areas, also has a number of good wines of which its Trebbiano is a particularly pleasant dry white wine.

Although Ferrara's name has long been associated with cheese and ham, it also exerts a strong influence on the wine scene. Apart from its Lambruscos, it has always enjoyed a sound reputation for its Malvasia wines in particular, although many other grape varieties are grown.

The commune of Merano, in the Trentino-Alto Adige district of northern Italy, produces a wide range of red and white wines.

TRENTINO-ALTO ADIGE

THESE TWO REGIONS were linked together for purely political reasons. Trentino, to the south, is Italian, while Alto Adige, or South Tyrol, is German-speaking. This is hardly surprising, as it was under Austrian rule until 1919.

Set in the narrow, steep-sided Alpine valley of the River Adige, the vineyards are planted everywhere from the valley floor to the snowline.

A wide range of both red and white grapes are grown, and they yield an equally extensive array of quality wines.

For once, the DOC regulations tend to cause more confusion than clarification. The DOC Alto Adige applies to sixteen different varietal wines, while ten varietal wines are entitled to the Trentino DOC. In the case of Alto Adige the confusion applies to all of their wines, as each has its Italian and its German name, either of which can appear on the label.

In Alto Adige, the wines made with Cabernet Sauvignon, Cabernet Franc or a blend of both are generally regarded as being the best of the reds. At their best, they have strong varietal character and can develop a Claret-like style.

Not surprisingly, vines that do well in northern climes give the best white wines in Alto Adige: Riesling Italico, Riesling Renano, Riesling Sylvaner, and Traminer Aromatico. This last is thought to have originated near the village of Tramin (Tremeno in Italian) before making its way to Alsace, Germany and several other countries, where it is usually called Gewürztraminer.

With the exception of the Sylvaner, which is a rather flat and unexciting wine, the white wines from Alto Adige are well worth seeking out.

In Trentino, the red wines covered by the DOC are: Cabernet, Lagrein, Marzemino, Merlot and Pinot Nero, while the whites are: Riesling, Moscato, Pinot and Vin Santo. The Riesling DOC applies to Renano, Italico and Riesling-Sylvaner, while the Pinot covers both Bianco and Grigio. Vin Santo, made from the region's white grapes, is a luscious, sweet dessert wine that is made from grapes that are partially dried out before being pressed, often not until the Easter following the vintage.

In Trentino-Alto Adige, the most widely grown grape is the Schiava and its sub-varieties, which yield red wines of varying degrees of lightness. These are usually of a refreshing nature and pleasant disposition.

All in all, and personal preferences aside, the region of Trentino-Alto Adige wines are of sound to excellent quality.

VENETO

STRETCHING ALL THE WAY from Lake Garda in the west to the gulf of Venice in the east, the Veneto region's very fertile soil supports a sea of vines and other crops which grow in lush profusion whether on mountain, hill or plain.

The region's two most famous red wines are Bardolino and Valpolicella. Both wines are made with a blend of the same grape varieties, with the principal grapes being Corvina Veronese and Rondinella.

Bardolino is produced in the area on the western shore of Lake Garda. A light-bodied, fruity wine, it has a fresh, soft flavor. Wine produced in the original heart of the area can use the term *Classico* on its label.

Further east across the River Adige, Valpolicella is produced from vines grown in the heavy clay soil of the hills just outside of Verona. A fuller-bodied and flavored wine than Bardolino, it is harmonious and velvety on the palate. Again, wines made in the district's heart can use the term Classico. Likewise, wines that are aged for a year and achieve at least 12 per cent alcohol can adopt the designation *Superiore*.

Another kind of Valpolicella is made only with grapes from the ears, or top outside, of the bunch. Recioto della Valpolicella is made in two styles. A sweet wine is made after the grapes have been partly dried out prior to pressing. The fermentation is arrested to retain a high level of sweetness. Complete fermentation, however, results in the dry version, which is best known as Amarone. This is a sturdy, full-bodied, strongly flavored wine that will take considerable aging in bottle.

Vineyards cover the volcanic hills near Padua in the Veneto district.

Cellarmasters in Veneto sample a glass of Amarone, a dry, full-bodied red made only with grapes from the "ears" of the bunch.

Opposite: House and vineyards dominate a hill in Torreglia, near Padua.

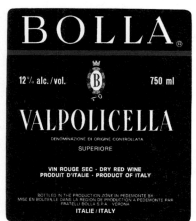

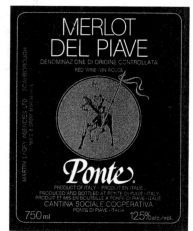

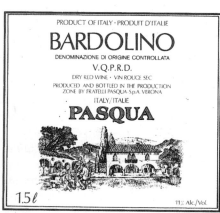

The sub-district of Valpantena, adjacent to the Classico area, produces wine that can also achieve Classico status under the Valpolicella DOC.

The region's best-known white wine is Soave, which is made from Garganega grapes blended with no more than 30 per cent of Trebbiano Toscana and Trebbiano di Soave. The result is a pale, dry white wine with a flowery bouquet and a firm flavor. It is not a remarkable wine, but it has an undetectable subtle character that makes it appealing.

Another white wine worthy of mention is Tocai di Lison, which is made from Friuli Tocai grapes grown on the plain in the Pramaggiore district of the Province of Venice. A dry wine, it has an attractive, lightly perfumed nose and a crisp, clean flavor.

Apart from these four deservedly better-known wines, Veneto produces an enormous number of good wines from a veritable catalogue of grape varieties. The region's name on a label usually indicates a worthwhile exploration into the world of wines.

FRIULI-VENEZIA-GIULIA

THIS REGION hard by the Yugoslavian border was the center of a dispute between the two countries, who did not reach agreement on territorial boundaries until 1963. Then it finally became possible for the Italians to form the region by linking the part of Venezia-Giulia they retained with Friuli.

The turbulent dispute did, however, give the region an advantage: its DOC regulations are the simplest and clearest in the country. There are six zones and sixteen grape varieties, some of which are used in more than one and even all six zones. The zones are: Aquileia, Collio Goriziano, Colli Orientali del Friuli, Grave del Friuli, Isonzo and Latisana. Of the grape varieties, Cabernet Sauvignon, Cabernet Franc, Merlot, Pinot Bianco,

Pinot Grigio, Tocai and Verduzzo are grown in all six zones.

Malvasia is DOC in Collio Goriziano and Isonzo; Picolit is only in Colli Orientali; Pinot Nero, only in Collio Goriziano and Colli Orientali; Riesling Italico and Ribolla only in Colli Orientali; Riesling Renano in Colli Orientali, Isonzo and Aquileia; Sauvignon in Colli Orientali, Collio Goriziano and Isonzo; Traminer in Collio Goriziano and Isonzo. The remaining grape, Refosco has three varieties; Reforsco del Peduncolo Rosso and Refosco Friuliano, sometimes referred to as Refosco Nostrano, are entitled to the DOC, while Refosco Terrano is not. The two authorized grapes are used in Colli Orientali, Grave, Aquileia and Latisana.

Notable among the region's wines is Picolit, a sweet-to-lusciously-sweet wine. It is made in such small quantities that it has become a rarity.

Most of the region's wines are of sound quality, with Cabernet, Merlot and Refosco being the best of the reds, while Tocai, Pinot Grigio, Sauvignon and Verduzzo are the best of the whites. One DOC wine that does not measure up to the region's general standards is the Collio Goriziano Bianco which is a rather insipid, dumb wine.

TUSCANY

MENTION TUSCANY in regard to wine, and most people will immediately think of Chianti. This is hardly surprising, as Chianti is not only the country's largest DOC area, with close to a million acres of vineyards. It is also produced in great quantities and has made its way to every corner of the globe.

The heart of the Chianti area is more or less contained within the triangle formed by Florence, Siena and Arezzo. This is where wines of the Chianti Classico classification are produced.

Surrounding this area there are six districts that also have a Chianti DOC. They are: Montalbano, Rufina, Colli Fiorentini, Colli Senesi, Colli Aretini and Colline Pisane.

A blend of four grapes has laid the foundation of Chianti as we know it today. The formula was developed by Bettino, Baron Ricasoli, and contains 50 to 80 per cent Sangiovese, 10 to 30 per cent Canaiolo Nero, and 10 to 30 per cent Trebbiano Bianco and Malvasia Bianco. In recent years, however, some producers have removed the Trebbiano and Malvasia grapes from their blends, as they questioned the presence of white grapes in a red wine.

At its best, Chianti is a great wine capable of long aging. At is worst, it is a thin, miserable, biting wine. In the middle ground, happily, there is a huge quantity of very sound wine that can grace any table with pride.

Despite its quality and popularity, Chianti is far from being Tuscany's finest red wine. That distinction unquestionably goes to Brunello di Montalcino, which many people regard as Italy's finest red. Made with the Brunello grape, which is related to the Sangiovese, it is a powerful, dark red wine that must be aged in wood for four years before being bottled. If its time in wood is

Vineyards surround a farmhouse in the Chianti region of Tuscany.

Overleaf: Arezzo, in the southeast corner of the Chianti region, where wines of the Chianti Classico denomination are produced.

Above: *Chianti Classico ages in wood at the Fattorie Nipozzano, Frescobaldi Estates.*
Below: *Chianti Classico Riserva, given proper cellaring, ages and improves in the bottle.*

extended to five years, it may be called a Riserva. It is also said to be the longest-lived table wine; some have claimed that it will live for fifty years in bottle. Whether or not that is true, I do know that even after ten years it is still very tannic although the fruit is showing, all indications that it had lots of life left in it.

Another Tuscan red of great quality is Vino Nobile di Montepulciano, which is made from a blend of grapes similar to that of Chianti. A fine, smooth wine, it responds well to aging in bottle.

The region's most famous white wine is Vernaccia di San Gimignano, a delightful dry wine with great depth of flavor and the capacity to take more age than most white wines. It is made from the Vernaccia grape, which is grown around the picturesque town of San Gimignano, also famous for its thirteen remaining medieval defense towers.

There are two noteworthy red wines that cannot be awarded DOC status because they contain Cabernet grapes, which are not approved in Tuscany. Nevertheless, Sassicaia, made almost entirely of Cabernet Sauvignon with a little Cabernet Franc added, is reminiscent of the best California Cabernets, which are also 100 per cent Cabernet. The other is Tignanello, in which the dominant grape is Sangiovese, blended with Cabernet Sauvignon. A hard wine when young, it ages well. Developed by the Florentine house of Antinori, it is made only in years when the grapes are considered to be good enough.

Another style of wine that is produced in several parts of Tuscany is Vin Santo. Made with white grapes, usually either Trebbiano or Malvasia, that have been allowed to dry in the sun or indoors on racks or rafters within the winery, Vin Santo is a rich, sweet dessert wine. Generally, it is made in small quantities, but it is well worth seeking out. A Tuscan Vin Santo can rival the finest sweet white wines in the world, including Sauternes.

The Tuscan countryside might have been made specifically for viticulture, as about 92 per cent of the land is in the form of hills and mountains. The land is unsuitable for other forms of agriculture, and so the vine reigns supreme. Apart from her better-known wines, such as Chianti, Tuscany literally produces hundreds of different wines, most of which are rarely seen beyond the boundaries of the region.

Vineyards near Siena are planted with Sangiovese, Canaiolo Nero, Trebbiano and Malvasia grapes. These and other, complementary varieties are blended to produce Chianti.

Vino Nobile di Montepulciano

DENOMINAZIONE DI ORIGINE CONTROLLATA E GARANTITA

Riserva 1980

Red Wine–Vin Rouge

Produced in the original wine and bottled by
Produit dans la vino d'origine et mis en bouteille par

BIGI S.p.A.
LAZIBE

IN THEIR OWN CELLARS OF ORVIETO
DANS LEUR ÉTABLISSEMENT À ORVIETO
PRODUCT OF ITALY · PRODUIT D'ITALIE

750 ml.   12,5% alc./vol.

LUNGAROTTI

TORRE DI GIANO®

VIN BLANC SEC   **1983**   DRY WHITE WINE

IMBOTTIGLIATO ALL'ORIGINE DAL VITICOLTORE
CANTINE LUNGAROTTI S.p.A.   TORGIANO - ITALIA

TORGIANO
DENOMINAZIONE D'ORIGINE CONTROLLATA

750 ml.   PRODUIT D'ITALIE   PRODUCT OF ITALY   11.5% alc./vol.

TIGNANELLO

1977

VIN ROUGE   RED WINE

Vino di collina Tosca-
na prodotto con uve
sangiovese e cannaiolo
una ad una, conservato in pic-
coli barili di rovere presso il pro-
duttore, imbottigliato il 12 aprile
1979 a San Casciano

750 ml ℮
12,5% vol.

Val di Pesa da
Marchesi Lodovico e
Piero Antinori di Firenze (R.I. 382/
FI) e successivamente adagiato in
fresche cantine sotterranee per un
ulteriore riposo in bottiglia prima
della spedizione.

Vin mis en bouteille en Italie par   Wine bottled in Italy by

VINO DA TAVOLA DELLA VAL DI PESA

PRODUIT D'ITALIE   MARCHESI L. E P. ANTINORI · FIRENZE   PRODUCT OF ITALY
ITALIA

MARINO

DENOMINAZIONE DI ORIGINE CONTROLLATA

PRODUCT OF ITALY   PRODUIT D'ITALIE

WHITE WINE *Gotto d'oro*® VIN BLANC
DRY - SEC

1ℓ   11.5% alcohol.

PRODUCED AND BOTTLED IN ITALY BY
CANTINA SOCIALE COOPERATIVA DI MARINO
NELLE PROPRIE CANTINE DI FRATTOCCHIE DI MARINO (ROMA)
ITALIA
Sole Agents
J. CIPELLI WINES & SPIRITS INC. TORONTO, CANADA

cod. emb.1217/Roma

FRESCOBALDI®

Viticulteur depuis 1300   Vinegrowers since 1300

Wine **Chianti** *Vin*

DENOMINAZIONE DI ORIGINE CONTROLLATA

Vino di collina prodotto nelle no-
stre Fattorie e imbottigliato nella
zona di produzione. Si consiglia
di accompagnarlo a primi piat-
ti e carni varie dal gusto

delicato e di servirlo alla tempera-
tura di 17/18 gradi. Conservare
la bottiglia coricata in ambiente
fresco, al riparo dalla luce.
Reg. Imb.1726 FI.11.5% vol.

PRODUIT D'ITALIE   PRODUCT OF ITALY

1.5 L   11.5% alc/vol.

Mise en bouteille par - Bottled by Marchesi dé Frescobaldi - Sieci - **Italy**

RACCOLTE * MARCHESI

SASSICAIA

VIN ROUGE   **1980**   RED WINE

VINO DA TAVOLA

TENUTA SAN GUIDO

BOLGHERI

Vin mis en bouteille en Italie par - Wine bottled in Italy by
Marchesi L. e P. Antinori S.p.A. - Firenze et S. Casciano V.P. (382 FI)
ITALIA

750 ml   PRODUCT OF ITALY   12% alc./vol.
PRODUIT D'ITALIE

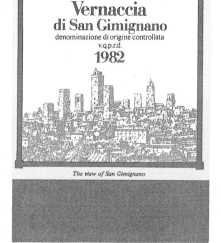

PRODUCT OF ITALY

Vernaccia di San Gimignano

denominazione di origine controllata
v.q.p.r.d.

1982

The view of San Gimignano

Castello della Sala

ORVIETO CLASSICO
DENOMINAZIONE DI ORIGINE CONTROLLATA

VIN BLANC SEC
DRY WHITE WINE

Marchesi L. e P. Antinori
Firenze

VIN MIS EN BOUTEILLE EN ITALIE PAR   WINE BOTTLED IN ITALY BY
MARCHESI L. e P. ANTINORI S.p.A. - FIRENZE et S. CASCIANO V.P. (382 FI) ITALIA
PRODUCT OF ITALY
750 ml   PRODUIT D'ITALIE   11,50% alc./vol.

M.si L. e P. Antinori   Firenze - Italia
Riserva
1975

VILLA ANTINORI®

Chianti Classico

VIN ROUGE   DENOMINAZIONE DI ORIGINE CONTROLLATA   RED WINE

VIN MIS EN BOUTEILLE EN ITALIE DANS LES CANTINE ANTINORI - S.CASCIANO VP (382 FI) - WINE BOTTLED IN ITALY BY CANTINE ANTINORI - S.CASCIANO VP (382 FI)
PRODUIT D'ITALIE
750 ml ℮   PRODUCE OF ITALY   12,5% alc./ml

LUNGAROTTI

SAN GIORGIO

1979

VINO da TAVOLA ROSSO dell'Umbria

Red Wine Bottled By Cantine Lungarotti S.p.A., Torgiano

750 ML.   PRODUCT OF ITALY   ALC. 12% BY VOL.

UMBRIA

ONE OF ITALY'S smallest regions, Umbria lies to the south of Tuscany. Its most famous native is undoubtedly Saint Francis of Assisi.

Umbria's best-known wine is Orvieto, much of which is actually made by the big Chianti houses of Tuscany. Grown around the volcanic outcropping on which the city of Orvieto perches, this white wine was originally sweet, although only really slightly so. In recent times, however, a dry version has been produced. Whether dry or sweet, the principal grape for this wine is the Trebbiano. The dry wine is crisp, clean and refreshing. It is easily one of Italy's best white wines.

Part of the reason that Orvieto develops its special characteristics has to do with the places where it is made. The cellars are often in caves carved into the tufo stone, and the conditions in these cellars ensures the growth of the *muffa nobile, Penicillium glaucum,* a mold that forms on the barrels to give Orvieto its distinctive bouquet.

Although not nearly as well known as its white wine, there is actually an Orvieto Rosso, in which the principal grape is the Sangiovese, which is a ruby-red, dry wine with a pleasant, fruity bouquet and good flavor and balance.

The first Umbrian wines to gain DOC acceptance after Orvieto were Torgiano Bianco and Rosso. The red is made with the same grapes as Chianti, while the white is based on the Trebbiano as is Orvieto, but the other grapes used in the blend yield a softer, fruitier wine. The majority of these wines are made by the Lungarotti family, which sells the white as Torre di Giano and the red as Rubesco.

The hill town of Montefalco has two red DOC wines, Montefalco Rosso and Montefalco Sagrantino. The Rosso is made with between 65 and 75 per cent Sangiovese, to which between 15 and 20 per cent of Trebbiano and 5 to 10 per cent of Sagrantino have been added. The wine is ruby red, dry with a fruity aroma, good flavor and balance.

The Sagrantino is made in two styles, a dry or slightly sweet *passito* made with semi-dried grapes. The dry version is a deep ruby color, has a light bouquet, but a full body and flavor. The lightly sweet version is a robust wine with 14 per cent alcohol. It is pleasant all on its own.

There used to be a maze of names in Umbria's Upper Tiber Valley, but the DOC has simplified

Early spring in an Umbrian vineyard. The shrine in the foreground was built by the Lungarotti family.

matters there by granting the status *Colli Alto-tiberini*. A red and rosé are made with Sangiovese blended with Merlot, Trebbiano and Malvasia grapes. The red is ruby colored, with a grapy bouquet and a dry, round, full and balanced flavor. The rosé is light pink, fruity, fresh and lively. A white wine is made from Trebbiano, Malvasia and other local grape varieties. A straw-colored wine, it has a lightly perfumed bouquet, is dry and has a pleasing flavor and good balance.

The hillside vineyards around Lake Trasimeno produce red and white wines under the DOC designation Colli del Trasimeno. The white is mainly grapes. A clear white, dry wine, it has a light aroma and a pleasant, clean flavor. The Sangiovese is the principal grape for the red, which is again light in aroma, but has good flavor and balance.

LAZIO

WITH ROME at its center, this region lies to the south of Umbria, and all of its better wines are white.

The best known, mainly because of its legend, is Est! Est! Est!!! which is largely made from the Trebbiano.

Briefly, the legend concerns Bishop Johann Fugger, who was travelling from Germany to Rome for the coronation of Emperor Henry V in the year 1110. The bishop sent his major domo, Martin, ahead of the retinue to locate inns with good wine and to chalk the word Est on the door of such inns. On reaching the town of Montefiascone, Martin was so impressed with the wine he wrote Est! Est! Est!!! on the door.

The bishop never travelled the last sixty miles to Rome, but instead remained in Montefiascone, where he eventually died. He is buried in a grave marked by Martin's epitaph which translates as, "On account of too much Est Est Est my master Johann Fugger died here."

In his will, the bishop named the town as his heir, with the condition that a barrel of wine be poured on his grave at the anniversary of his death each year. This tradition was followed until a

cardinal decided to stop such waste and ordered that in future the cask of wine be delivered to the local seminary.

While the bishop's devotion was extreme, it is in fact a very pleasant, easy-drinking wine.

Frascati, to the south of Rome, is the region's other notable white wine. Made mainly with Malvasia Bianca, Malvasia del Lazio and Greco grapes, it is a soft, velvety, dry wine. A sweet version is also made.

In neighboring Marino, a white wine similar to Frascati is made, but it tends to be of a fuller flavor.

Lazio produces many red and white wines of decent and acceptable quality, which come into their own on such occasions as a picnic.

MARCHES, ABRUZZO, MOLISE

ON THE EAST COAST stretching south from Emilia-Romagna, these three regions make a lot of wine that tends to decline in quality on the way south, to the point where Molise does not as yet have any wines of DOC status.

The Marches has undergone a considerable transformation in the past ten to fifteen years. Prior to this change, the vineyards were worked by sharecropping families who used the grapes to produce their own "house wines."

Greater thought has now been put into determining the best grape varieties, and wine making practices have been modernized. White wines are made from a large number of grapes, but the most important are: Verdicchio, Trebbiano, Bianchello, Maceratino, Malvasia, Passerina and Pinot Bianco. There are also some red varieties, with the principal ones being Montepulciano, Sangiovese, Ciliegiolo and Vernaccia di Serrapetrona.

The best-known wine of the Marches, and deservedly so, is Verdicchio. This is also the name of its principal grape, which must be 80 per cent of the blend, although it can be completed with Malvasia and Trebbiano grapes. A dry wine, it is quite full-flavored, refreshing and has a crisp finish. It is also best when drunk young.

In fact, it was the success of Verdicchio in export markets that largely provided the impetus for the region's wine producers to upgrade all of their wines.

Abruzzo too has revised its agricultural outlook, and this is reflected in the vineyards of this mountainous region. The number of grape varieties being used was reduced dramatically. The two principal grapes now are Montepulciano for reds and Trebbiano for whites.

Viticultural techniques were also revised, and the cultivation of low vines was discontinued in favor of trellising. The vineyards were also thinned, and realistic yield quotas were set in an effort to improve the quality of the wines.

In Abruzzo, Montepulciano d'Abruzzo is a powerful red wine made with the Montepulciano grape which is peculiar to the region. The wines are required, under DOC rules, to be at least 12 per cent alcohol, but it is common for them to attain 14 per cent, in which case they are no longer merely pleasantly powerful, but turn into heavyweight contenders.

A white version, Trebbiano d'Abruzzo, is also made. It can also be overly assertive, as it frequently attains alcoholic levels of 12.5 per cent.

Both wines are well made, but caution is advised in making their acquaintance.

Molise has a long wine-making tradition, but historical events have tended to keep it in isolation, a situation that is reflected in the relative obscurity in which the region's wines find themselves.

In a way it is a pity because, for example, the white wines made with the Trebbiano compare favorably with wines made with the same grape in other regions. There is a pleasant, medium-bodied red wine, Aglianico, and a full-bodied, robust red made with the Montepulciano grape.

All of these Molise wines are well made and give a clear statement that it is unwise to fall into the trap of dismissing them lightly. But perhaps it is the Molisani themselves who are responsible for this common attitude — after all, they have been rather reticent about making their wines better known.

CAMPANIA, BASILICATA, CALABRIA

THERE ARE NO TRULY distinguished wines made in these regions, but there is a great deal of perfectly pleasant wine produced, particularly whites. In general, the power of the reds makes them rather overwhelming.

The best-known of Campania's wines is definitely Lacryma Christi, which is made with Fiano and Greco grapes, both as a still white and as a sparkling wine. The quality is consistently good, though not outstanding.

Similar wines are made on the islands of Capri and Ischia. A little red Lacryma Christi and Capri wines are made from the Piedirosso grape, which yields a surprisingly pleasant red wine compared to the southern norm.

Taurasi, made principally with the Aglianico grape which is grown in volcanic soil, is another surprisingly good red that is full-bodied and flavored and will take a fair bit of aging in bottle.

The white wine of Solopaca which relies on the more classic grapes, Trebbiano Toscano and Malvasia di Candia, are quite flowery and of sound quality. Likewise the red and rosé made with a good portion of Sangiovese grapes are pleasant drinking.

The only wine of note in Basilicata is the Aglianico del Vulture. The first part of its name is derived from the grape, while the second part refers to the extinct volcano on which the vines are grown. The wine is light compared to others from nearby, and it has an attractive bouquet and full flavor.

Calabria does not make any wines of note, although some of the whites are quite enjoyable.

View from the Villa d'Este.

APULIA

THIS HIGH-PRODUCTION region, which forms the heel of the Italian boot, stands in some ways as a warning to those who would rush into applying for DOC status.

The wines of Apulia were always very strong, and previously they were shipped in large quantities to strengthen the weaker northern wines.

Beginning in 1968, more Apulian wines have been elevated to DOC status than in all the other southern regions combined.

Whether the region's producers thought of the DOC as a magic wand of acceptance is a matter for conjecture. Today, they can have no such illusions. The strong, fiery reds and powerful whites they have always produced remain unattractive to most outsiders. The Apulians have learned that few people are charmed by their wines, but if they now alter the style or methods laid down in their DOC regulations, they would most likely be downgraded.

The one notable exception in the region is the Castel del Monte rosé. Made primarily from the

Bombino Nero with a little Nero di Troia, the wine is of good quality and is lighter than most of the region's wines. The same DOC regulations apply to a red and white, but they are not up to the style of the rosé.

SICILY

UNLIKE THE APULIANS, the Sicilians did change the nature and style of their wines before submitting them for DOC acceptance.

Not so many years ago, Sicily's table wine trade consisted mainly of supplying northern Italian, French and German producers with strong wines for blending with or stretching their wines. The other major use of their grapes was in the production of the island's famous fortified wine, Marsala.

The Marsala trade was actually begun by two Englishmen from Liverpool, John and William Woodhouse, in 1773 in the western area of the island, where it is still produced today. Made with Catarratto, Grillo and Inzolia grapes, the resulting dry wine is made into Marsala by the addition of wine concentrates. The amount added determines whether the finished wine will be dry, semi-dry, sweet or very sweet. There are different aging requirements for the various grades of the wine. Marsala Fine must remain in oak casks for four months, Marsala Superiore for two years, and Marsala Vergine for at least five years.

It was Admiral Horatio Nelson who brought Marsala to prominence. During his Mediterranean campaigns, Nelson anchored at Marsala, the name of which is derived from the Arabic, *mars-Allah*, meaning Harbor of God. Nelson was so impressed with the wine that he ordered the Woodhouses to supply the entire fleet with Marsala.

It is, however, in table wines that Sicily's producers have brought about a major change.

Their best-known wine is not a DOC, although Corvo, whether red or white, is well up to such standards. A second, lighter white wine, Corvo Columba Platino, is also made as is a sparkling wine Corvo Ala. They also make a sherry-style wine, Stravecchio.

Of the DOC wines, the red, white and rosé of Etna are amongst the best. The red and rosé are both made with the Nerello Mascalese and Nerello Mantellato. The red, although light-bodied, is fairly strong and ages well, while the rosé is a pleasant, refreshing wine when young. The white made from the Carricante and Catarratto is a dry, pale, well-balanced wine, while the superiore version made at Milo is a dark yellow, with a more intense bouquet and depth of flavor.

The red wine of Faro, made with the same grapes as the Etna, is similar in style, but a shade lighter.

All in all, the wines of Sicily are now much more approachable than they were years ago, and are definitely worth trying.

SARDINIA

LIKE SICILY, the wine producers of Sardinia have worked diligently at improving and refining their wines.

The vine grows virtually everywhere on Sardinia. Whether it is beside brushland or upland pastures where pigs and sheep roam, there are innumerable vineyards neatly laid out in apparent contradiction of their surroundings.

Pruning techniques have been improved in recent years to give the vines the maximum benefit from the sun and to limit cropping to yield better wines.

Most of the wine is now made by cooperatives, and there are about forty of them scattered around the island. These cooperatives make more than half of all the wine of Sardinia.

Cannonau di Sardegna, made with the Cannonau grape which is grown only on the island, is a robust wine of pleasant character. After three or more years in cask it becomes a Riserva. There are sweet and fortified versions made, but they are not so appealing.

Another DOC wine of attractive style is the Carignano del Sulcis, made with the grape from which it derives the first part of its name. The red version has a ruby color, vinous bouquet, full flavor and velvety texture. The rosé version is best while still young.

Spain

S PAIN HAS A GREATER acreage of vineyards than any other European country, but their production is far lower than that of either France or Italy. The huge vineyard area was one factor that delayed Spain's entry into the EEC which wanted about half of the country's vines torn up.

The first Spanish wine laws were adopted in 1932. Today, the production of wines in Spain is controlled by the Instituto Nacional de Denominaciones de Origen (INDO), established in 1970, which in turn is responsible to the Ministry of Agriculture. Over and above this, each region has its own regulatory council which is accountable to the national institute.

The Denominacion de Origen (D.O.) laws determine which grape varieties are permitted in each region, and how they will be cultivated, and what the yield will be. Once the grapes are harvested, the laws set alcohol levels and, where appropriate, the length of time a wine must remain in cask before being bottled. The "D.O." is usually written in small letters, or it may be replaced by a seal approved by the regulatory council.

The most important of the D.O. regions include Rioja, Navarra, Penedès, Montilla and the sherry-producing region of Jerez-Xérès-Sherry.

SHERRY

The most famous wine of Spain is Sherry. Grown on a mainly chalky soil in the southwest of the country, the principal grape is the Palomino. Other grape varieties, such as Pedro Ximénez and Moscatel, are grown for use in sweet wines.

Above: *Osborne's sherry cellar, where various awards are displayed.*

Below: *Separating young Sherry from the live yeast, or flor, requires deft handling and a special ladle called a venencia.*

Opposite: *Although few white grapes are regularly used in Rioja wines, Malvasia, Viura, and Garnacho Blanco are sometimes included in blends.*

The grapes ripen well in the region centered around the town of Jerez de la Frontera, from which the wine's name is derived. After harvesting, the grapes are laid out on straw mats in the sun to concentrate the natural sugars before light pressing and fermentation.

In December and January, the wines are critically tasted, and the future style of Sherry that they will become is determined. The driest style of Sherry is Fino; the others, in increasing order of sweetness, are Amontillado, Oloroso and Cream. A separate style of Fino called Manzanilla is produced in the coastal town of Sanlúcar de Barrameda, where the salt air of the Atlantic penetrates the wine during its long aging to give it a distinctive taste. Wines that are rejected go to make brandy, some of which will later be used to fortify other wines to bring them up to the required alcohol level for their style.

It is, however, the unique aging method that chiefly contributes to the character and consistent quality of Sherry from year to year.

The wines are aged in 600-liter oak casks in what is known as a *solera*. This is a system in which the wines of each style are laid out in rows, with each row representing a vintage, the oldest being nearest the floor. Each year, a maximum of 20 per cent of the oldest wine is drawn off for bottling, and the casks are then topped up with the next oldest wine, a sequence that is repeated throughout the system.

A unique, high-quality wine, Sherry is one of that select group of wines that is enjoyed in practically every country in the world.

RIOJA

RIOJA IS BY FAR and away the best-known table wine producing region of Spain. Located in the shadow of the Sierra de Cantabria to its north, the region is divided into three sub-regions. To the west is the Rioja Alta on the highest ground; in the east is the Rioja Baja on the lowest ground, while the central area is Rioja Alavesa.

It is the Rioja Alta and Rioja Alavesa that produce the finest wines. The best of the vineyards

The Wine Regions of
Spain & Portugal

FRANCE

SPAIN

PORTUGAL

RIBEIRO

VELDEORRAS

VALLE DE MONTERRAY

LÉON

NAVARRA

RIOJA

SOMONTANO

AMPURDAN-COSTA BRAVA

Bilbao

Viana do Castelo

Braga

Bragança

VINHO VERDE (MINHO)

Vila Real

Porto

DOURO

Pinhel

ROA Y PENAFIEL

Zaragoza (Saragossa)

CARINENA

CONCA DE BARBERA

Villafranca del Panadés

ALELLA

Barcelona

PRIORATO

PENEDES

Tarragonna

TERRA ALTA

TARRAGONNA

LA NAVA-TORO

Aveiro

Viseu

DAO

BAIRRADA

Coimbra

Madrid

Toledo

Castelobranco

Alcobaça

MENTRIDA

LA MANCHA

MANCHUELA

UTIEL-REQUENA

Valencia

Torres Vedras

Cartaxo

BUCELAS

Lisbon

SETÚBAL

COLARES

CARCAVELOS

Setúbal

Borba

Redondo

Reguengos

Vidigueira

Beja

Ciudad Real

Manzanares

VALDEPANAS

Valdepeñas

ALMANSA

YECLA

JUMILLA

VALENCIA

CHESTE

ALICANTE

CONDADA DE HUELVA

Seville

Huelva

MONTILLA

Montilla

Granada

LAGOA

Tavira

Portimao

Faro

Sanlúcar de Barrameda

MALAGA

Malaga

Jerez de la Frontera

Cadiz

Gibraltar

JEREZ XERES SHERRY MANZANILLA SANLÚCAR DE BARRAMEDA

Douro River

Tagus River

Guadiana River

Guadalquivir River

Ebro River

ATLANTIC OCEAN

MEDITERRANEAN SEA

Strait of Gibraltar

N

0   100   200   300 km

0   100   200 mi.

45°   45°

40°   40°

35°   35°

5°   0°

are 1,500 feet above sea level. The authorized grapes for red wine are the Tempranillo, Garnacho, Graciano and Mazuelo, while the approved white varieties are the Malvasía, Viura and Garnacho Blanco.

The style of Rioja wines was greatly influenced by a number of Bordeaux wine growers who fled south to Rioja when the phylloxera devastated their vineyards in the 1870s. Consequently, some wines of Rioja today may still resemble the style of a Bordeaux of 100 years ago.

The red wines are the region's best and, apart from careful blending, their character is formed by the length of time they spend in casks. After two or three years in wood, the ordinary wines are

bottled, but *reservas* can be kept in cask for up to ten years before being bottled.

There are, essentially, two types of Rioja. Lighter dry wines of great complexity, depth of flavor and slight acidity are referred to as *claretes* and are sold in Bordeaux-style bottles. Deeper-colored dry wines with a fuller, softer flavor and a hint of acidity are called *tintos* and are put in Burgundy-style bottles. Both types of wine will take considerable age in bottle.

Many white Riojas also spend a long time in wood and as a result are deep golden in color, though dull and flat in taste. Younger ones, however, are straw-colored, dry, with a fine balance between wood and fruit.

OTHER SPANISH WINES

T HERE ARE HUNDREDS of different wines made in several regions throughout Spain, a few of which are of particular note.

Navarra

Located to the northeast of Rioja, the red wines of Navarra, which are frequently made with the same grapes, at their best bear a strong resemblance to those of its neighboring region. The region produces some very good rosé wines, which are now beginning to be exported in greater quantity.

Penedès

Enjoying a very favorable location just to the south of Barcelona, the Penedès is one of Spain's oldest wine regions. It is divided into three sub-regions: the Bajo Penedès, Medio Penedès and Alto Penedès.

The Baja has the hottest climate of the sub-regions and produces excellent red wines from the Cariñena, Garnacha, Ojo de Liebre and Samso grapes.

The Medio has the largest production of wine in the region and accounts for about 60 per cent of all Penedès' wines. Most of its wines are white and are made with the Xarel-lo and Macabeo grapes. The bulk is used to make sparkling wines which are quite attractive.

The Alto has a more humid and cooler climate than the rest of the region and is planted almost exclusively with the Parellada grapes which yield some of the finest white wines of Spain.

One Penedès firm whose wines have received considerable acclaim around the world is Torres.

Above: *Rioja wines, first aged in 225 liter oak bordelesas, continue their aging in bottles.*

Below: *New casks that have been used to ferment Sherry must are later sold to whiskey distillers who prize them highly for maturing whiskey.*

Vineyard in Jerez de la Frontera, where the Palomino is the classic Sherry vine.

Limestone soils and a temperate climate help the Penedès region to produce the widest range of wines in Spain.

Not only does the present wine maker, Miguel Torres, work diligently to maintain the high standards set by his forebears, but he is boldly experimenting with such classic grape varieties as Cabernet Sauvignon, Pinot Noir, Riesling and Gewürztraminer.

An important segment of the Penedès production is sparkling wines. Centered on the town of San Sadurni de Noya, many of the wines are made by the same method as Champagne. The main grapes used are the Macabeo, Xarel-lo and Parellada.

The sparkling wines are now called *Cava* (cellars) because they are made and aged in bottles and kept in cellars. As in Champagne, one of the main factors in determining how the finished wine tastes is the blend. Each firm has its own particular formula which it guards jealously.

Sparkling wines made by the closed-tank method for secondary fermentation are not permitted to use the word Cava on their labels.

The high quality of Spanish sparkling wines, and particularly those of Penedès, may be judged from the fact that they are the top-selling sparkling wines in North America, a position they have held since 1982.

Montilla-Moriles

This region lies just to the north of Jerez and is mostly planted with the Pedro Ximénez grape. Unlike the sweet wines made with the same grape in Jerez, the wines of this region are allowed to ferment completely, and the result is a dry fino that does not require fortification as it is naturally high in alcohol.

Rueda

Vega Sicilia is the most noteworthy wine of this region, and it is of such extraordinary character that it deserves special mention. Made on a small estate on the River Duero, it is composed of such grapes as the red Garnacho, white Albillo and Bordeaux grapes which were planted during the phylloxera epidemic in the last quarter of the nineteenth century. None of the wine is sold before it is ten years old, and it has extreme depth in all of its elements — color, aroma and flavor. It is made in small quantities and is expensive, if you can find it.

Portugal

THE MAIN EXPORTS of Portugal are cork and wine, so it is vital to the Portuguese that their wines are viewed favorably in foreign markets.

Their most famous wine, Port, has been strictly controlled for years, and the quality of its various grades has been long established.

In the regions of Vinho Verde and Dão, which produce most of the wines exported, there are wine laws that define the areas within the regions and control both viticultural and vinification methods. Bucelas, Carcavelos, Colares, Bairrada, Douro, Algarve, Setubal and Madeira are also defined regions.

Other than that, however, although wine laws exist and are applied, it is difficult to define other distinct regions.

The country's best-known table wine, Mateus Rosé, while enjoyed worldwide as an easy-to-drink introductory wine, is more of a tribute to a clever marketing campaign than anything else. It gives scant indication of the excellent light wines the country has to offer.

PORT

THE VINEYARDS of the Upper Douro Valley are among the most spectacular and mind-boggling sights in the world of wine. For a distance of fifty miles, narrow, walled terraces follow the curving valley walls and climb high up the mountainous slopes to form something like a gigantic wall garden. To help retain the scant rainfall, not only did the walls have to be built by hand and the slate hewn or blasted, but the earth had to be carried up the hillsides to form a footing for the vine.

Even today, it is impossible to get either machinery or animals into the vineyards. Consequently, the grapes must be gathered by hand and hauled down the treacherous slopes on the backs of the laborers.

Altogether, there are sixteen red grape varieties and six white varieties of grapes grown. But as much as the grapes, the soil and climate determine the style of the wine, not to mention human skills.

Port as we know it today was developed by English merchants in the early part of the seventeenth century to appeal to English wine tastes. The presence of English merchants in Portugal was due to a trade agreement between the two countries whereby Portugal would accept English woolens, while England would accept Portuguese wines.

It is the method of making Port that gives it its unique character. Formerly, the grapes were trodden by foot to extract the fullest possible color, but today this job is done mechanically, and the wine is fermented. Timing is of the essence at this point, as the fermentation must be arrested so that the wine retains the desired degree of sweetness. This is done by putting the wine in casks that already contain a certain amount of *eau-de-vie* (brandy) made from Douro wines. The distillate causes fermentation to cease, and the wine begins its development in cask.

There are various styles of Port, largely determined by the degree of aging.

Ruby is a wine that has been aged for only a few years, and is the least expensive Port. It also has less character than more highly developed wines.

A cheap Tawny is made by blending Ruby and White Ports to give the illusion of the depth of style and character of an Old Tawny.

White Ports are made either in the same style as red Port with a medium sweetness, or they are fermented dry before fortification. In either case, I consider them to be nothing more than interesting oddities.

Old Tawny is a blend of wines from various vintages that have lived in cask for between ten and forty years. They have an attractive amber color

Opposite: *Harvest time on the steep slopes of the Dão region means hard work by hand — and by back.*

Spiky young vines line the granite hills of the Vinho Verde region.

and a smooth mellowness, which reflects the maturity of the wines in the blend.

Late Bottled Vintage is the designation given to wines from a single vintage aged in wood for four years before bottling that are not eligible to become vintage Port, but have enough character to come a close second. They are wines that have been aged for between four and six years prior to bottling. They are intended to be drunk immediately, which makes them very useful, especially in this era when few have the cellaring capacity for a continuous supply of matured Vintage Port.

Vintage Port has to earn its classification. Each vintage is assessed by the shippers who, about three times every ten years, decide that the wine of a particular year is of especially fine quality. They then "declare" a vintage. Vintage Port does not spend long in cask and is typically bottled after two years. What occurs in the bottle, however, is an amazing transformation. When bottled, Vintage Port is often harsh and tannic, but with time, it becomes a very deep-colored wine with an intense flavor. It is also a wine of incredible longevity. Quite attractive when ten years old, it is excellent after twenty years, but will continue to develop and mature for several more decades.

Although Port is the country's best known and most widely distributed fortified wine, it would be a mistake to overlook the table wines of Portugal, many of which are of very good quality.

VINHO VERDE

DÃO

Red wines of the Dão region are given long aging in wood.

ALTHOUGH MUCH RED WINE is made in the Minho region, which is located in the northwest of the country, it is primarily the white Vinho Verde that is exported.

The principal grape is the Alvarinho. Along with the minor varieties used, it is deliberately picked early. The wine is bottled young, prior to its secondary fermentation. It is thus dry and high in acid, with a slight sparkle, due to trapped carbon dioxide from the fermentation which continues in the bottle.

TO THE SOUTH of Minho, Dão produces some of the country's best wines. As in the Rioja, the reds are given a particularly long time in wood with the result that they tend to be rather hard and tannic when young. However, they develop nicely when given time to mature in bottle.

White wines that are given extended wood aging tend to be rather flat and dull, but those that are bottled younger are nicely balanced and flavored wines that make excellent everyday drinking.

Overleaf: Terraced slopes of the Douro Valley yield grapes for Port wines.

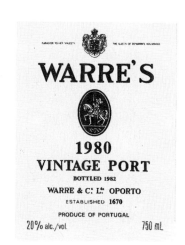

BUCELAS, CARCAVELOS, COLARES, MOSCATEL DE SETUBAL

THE FIRST THREE of these regions are clustered around Lisbon. Carcavelos and Colares are both dwindling regions caught between the expanding capital and the new popular resort towns. Colares is noted for its dark, tannic red wines, while Carcavelos produces a sweet, amber wine.

Bucelas, to the north of the city, is not under the same pressures as the other two regions, and produces a pleasant, dry white wine.

To the south of Lisbon, across the River Tagus, lies Moscatel de Setubal where a sweet, fortified wine of good quality is made from the Moscatel grape.

Few of the wines of these four regions are seen far beyond the Lisbon and Estoril area.

MADEIRA

ALTHOUGH CLOSELY related to Port, Madeira is a unique wine experience, largely owing to the difference in the method by which it is made.

In the early stages of its production, Madeira follows exactly the same process as Port, but once fermentation is arrested by the addition of brandy, the course of a Madeira's life takes a very individual twist.

The casks of wine are placed in *estufas* (ovens), and the temperature is gradually raised to between 33 and 55 degrees Celsius. The wine remains in the estufas for three to six months. If it is to be kept in the estufas for the shorter period the temperature is higher, while a longer stay means a lower temperature.

When it emerges from its ordeal by fire, the wine has acquired the distinctive caramel flavor which is common to all Madeiras.

In fact, Madeira and fire have been associated from the day the island was first settled by the Portuguese around 1420.

When the Portuguese arrived, the island — 500 miles southwest of Portugal in the Atlantic Ocean — was thickly wooded. They apparently did not want to spend the time clearing the land, so they set fire to the woods — a fire that reputedly burned for seven years.

The result was that when the fires finally died out, the potash of the burned forest had been added to the volcanic soil and centuries of leaf mold, creating a very fertile island.

Vines were soon planted and once they reached maturity the first of the island's wines were produced. Unfortunately, the natural table wine of Madeira proved to be rather bitter. With brandy added to stop any further fermentation, Madeira was used as ballast for ships, to be drunk only as a last resort.

It was this practice, however, which led to the discovery of the process by which Madeira is made today. It was found that ships that crossed the equator on their voyages to and from India returned with a wine that, rather than being destroyed by such extensive travel, had been hastened to a desirable maturity. For some years after this happy observation, it became a practice to ship wine aboard India-bound vessels for the purpose of maturing. The wine was bottled after the return voyage and, when sold, it was referred to as East India Madeira.

In time, of course, the Madeira producers developed the estufas technique for maturing their wines, but the voyages of Madeira were not over. It was customary for English ships sailing to the American colonies to interrupt their passage at Madeira where they took on water, provisions and wine.

Wine shippers, even today, can have problems with their wines becoming sick owing to travel. No such plague afflicts Madeira, which is a robust and hearty traveller.

Madeira, probably because of its stability, was considered a fashionable drink in North America until the turn of this century.

A custom that major American shipping families adopted was to sling a cask of Madeira in a rocking cradle in the entrance hall of their offices. It was the duty of everyone passing to push the cradle, and in this way the wine was kept in motion from morning to night, as though it were pitching about in the hold of a ship. The theory behind this practice was that it brought the wine more quickly to maturity.

The principal grape varieties grown on the island are Verdelho, Sercial, Bual and Malvasia. The four major styles of Madeira depend entirely on which grape variety is used.

Malmsey, an English corruption of Malvasia, is the sweetest, richest and, in many opinions, the finest Madeira. It is usually dark brown in color. Production is limited, and finding an Old Malmsey is, in consequence, difficult as well as expensive.

Bual is not as rich a wine as Malmsey. It is a golden brown color, has a fragrant nose and velvety taste.

Verdelho is an even lighter wine with a golden color. It is also less sweet than Bual and tends to impart a silky feeling to the palate. Verdelho is an elegant wine which, it has been suggested, is to Madeira what Amontillado is to Sherry.

Sercial is the driest of all Madeiras. It is produced from grapes grown on higher ground than most other Madeira grapes. Light in color, it is an excellent digestif wine.

One of the most famous brands, Rainwater, is actually a light Verdelho blend. According to some authorities, the name is derived from the fact that the wine is produced from grapes growing on higher slopes, which depend on rainfall for moisture, rather than irrigation systems. Although this sounds like a plausible explanation, the equally plausible and much more romantic suggestion is that the name Rainwater reflects the custom of American shipowners to give a Madeira wine the name of the ship in which it crossed the Atlantic. It is known that one ship engaged in this traffic was the *Rainwater*.

Europe

AUSTRIA

ALTHOUGH AUSTRIA has a wine tradition stretching back for hundreds of years, only in the past fifteen years or so have the country's wine producers begun to realize their potential on the international market.

Up until then, most of their wines were either consumed within the country or exported to Germany, where they have long been appreciated. This is understandable, as many of the grape varieties are the same as those used in Germany. The style of Austrian wines tends to be an attractive combination of the lively, light German style and the more intense style of Hungary.

The growing reputation that Austria had been building for her wines took a severe setback in 1985 when it was found that a small number of growers were falsifying their wines by sweetening them with diethylene glycol, a chemical used in the production of anti-freeze. Perhaps it was inevitable in a country where it is permissible to import wines from other countries and sell them as Austrian wines.

Equally, however, it was unfair to the thousands of honest growers and producers who have devoted themselves to building the reputation of Austrian wines on foreign markets. The Austrian government has acted with commendable speed to introduce new laws that will make such activity very unlikely in the future.

The red wines of Austria are of little consequence, but the white wines are often excellent. All of Austria's wines are grown in the eastern part of the country, and Vienna itself is surrounded by vines. A few vineyards survive even in some of the newer residential districts.

Few of the wines made around Vienna are ever bottled, but of those that are, the best known out-side of Austria come from Gumpoldskirchen, to the south of the city. They are made with Veltliner, Riesling, and Gewürztraminer grapes that are harvested late. These yield delicate wines of varying degrees of sweetness that, however, retain a freshness that makes them very attractive. It should be noted that when an Austrian wine bears only the name Riesling on its label, the grape is the Italian Riesling. When the German Riesling is used the label bears the term Rheinriesling.

To the south of the Vienna region, the wine district of Burgenland, located along the Hungarian border on the shores of the Neusiedlersee, is one of the country's most important. It is particularly famous for its sweet white wines, and of these, the best known come from the wine center of Rust. Ruster wines are reminiscent of Germany's sweet wines, and a Ruster can be in the style of an Auslese or Beerenauslese, or even have the intensity of a Trockenbeerenauslese. Although not as well known, the sweet wines of Apetlon, which faces Rust across the lake, are well worth seeking out.

The other important Austrian wine region is Wachau, which lies to the west of Vienna and is centered around the town of Krems. The vineyards are planted on the steep slopes of the mountains which rise about 1,500 feet above the River Danube. Made from the Sylvaner grape, the region's best-known wines are Schluck and a racier version, Blue Danube. The better wines of the region, however, are made with the native Austrian grape, the Grüner Veltliner, which yields a highly flavored, spicy wine. Not so common, the wines made in Wachau from the Rheinriesling are often nothing short of outstanding.

Austria's best-known wine producer, Lenz-Moser, is located at Röhrendorf in Wachau. One of his greatest contributions was the development of a high-culture system in which the vines are grown on wires at twice the normal height. Moser's system gives higher yields and improved quality.

Opposite: *Grape harvest outside Vienna, Austria.*

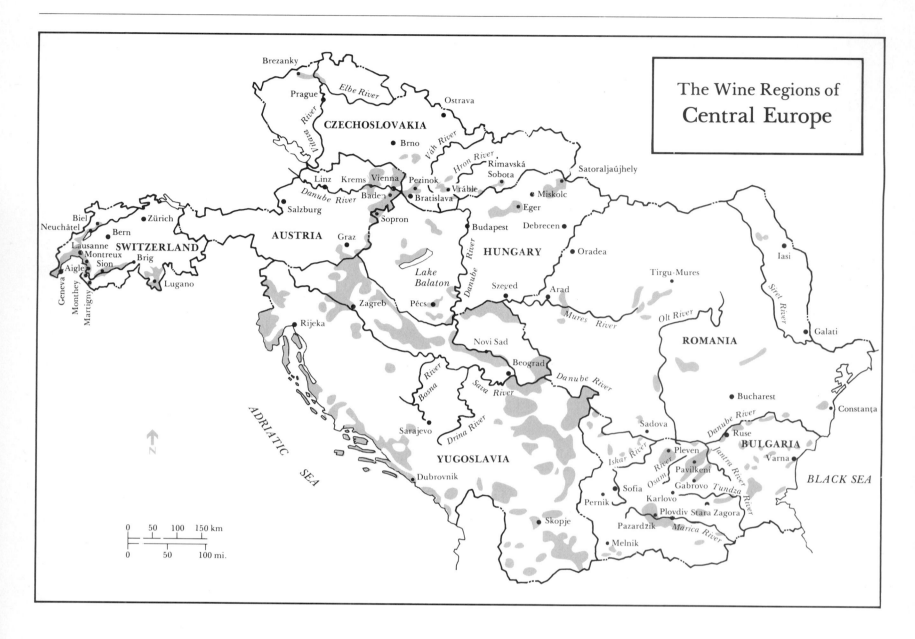

The Wine Regions of
Central Europe

SWITZERLAND

THERE IS ONLY ONE problem about getting to know Swiss wines, and that is that very little of it leaves Switzerland. Except for Germany, few countries import a significant quantity of Swiss wines.

The country's most important regions follow the northern bank of the Rhône valley and sweep along the curving north shore of Lake Geneva all the way to the city itself.

The two most important regions are Vaud and Valais. The principal grape in these chiefly white-wine regions is the Chasselas, which is known in Valais as the Fendant and in Vaud as the Dorin.

Valais is located in the Rhône valley and is

centered around the town of Sion. The area is very dry, and the little rain there is has to be augmented with irrigation. The main climatic problem for the vines are the spring frosts, and if they do no damage, a normal crop is fairly well assured.

One confusing aspect of these two regions is that some otherwise familiar grapes are called by different names. The Sylvaner becomes the Johannisberg, the Marsanne is Hermitage, Pinot Gris is Malvoisie. Along with the indigenous varieties, Petite Arvine, Armigne and Humagne, they are responsible for the white wines of the Vaud and Valois.

The Pinot Noir and Gamay are responsible for the best red wines. In Valais, a superior blend of these two grapes is known as Dôle and in Vaud as Salvagnin. Lesser wines of this type are named Goron.

Vaud is actually divided into three parts. The area to the east of Vaud, between Lausanne and Montreux, is known as Lavaux, and that between Lavaux and Valais is called Chablais.

Another significant Swiss wine region is Neuchâtel, which is located on the northwest shore of the lake of the same name. The region produces both red and white wines. The Pinot Noir is the principal red wine grape and it is used to produce a light wine. White wines are made with the Chasselas; they are vinted to retain a degree of fizziness, and some are produced as full sparkling wines.

Wine is made in almost every part of Switzerland, but the production is so low that the wines are rarely, if ever, seen beyond their own cantons.

HUNGARY

THIS LANDLOCKED NATION produces a wide range of wines and has about 500,000 acres of vineyards, half of which are located to the south of Budapest on the Danube Plains.

Most of the wines made in Hungary are white. They are usually stout, robust wines that are assertive enough to stand up to the spicy cuisine of the land. Their red wines too are mostly sturdy, with a lot of heart. The country's most celebrated wine, however, is definitely the sweet dessert wine, Tokay.

Made in the northeast of the country close to the Russian border, Tokay is produced from grapes, mainly the Furmint, that have been affected by the same noble rot that makes the sweet wines of Sauternes and Germany possible.

There is a technique that gives it its own distinctive style. When the wine is a year old, a quantity of Aszu is added to the 35-gallon barrels. Aszu is a pulp produced from the sweetest grapes which have been kept separately in seven-gallon puttonos. The wines are then graded to degrees of sweetness according to the number of putts that have been added to the casks. A five-puttonos wine is almost entirely Aszu and is as intensely sweet as any wine in the world. If no putts have been added,

the wine is sold as Szamorodni and is dry and rather rough.

Halfway between the Tokay-producing area and Budapest is the town of Eger, where the country's best-known red wine is produced from the Kadarka grape. Egri Bikavér, which translates as Bull's Blood, is a dark, strong, heady wine that has the capacity to develop with age, but most of it is drunk while it is still young.

The vast vineyards of the Danube Plain are mostly planted with the red Kadarka and the white Olaszrizling which is the Italian Riesling. The

Above: *At Hungarovin in Budafok, wines from all districts of Hungary mature in casks in a 16 mile-long cellar system built into the hills.*
Below: *On gentle slopes outside of Budapest, the vine stocks in Etyek Vineyard run in rows farther than the eye can see.*

Above, left and opposite: *Hungary produces stout, robust wines that are well-suited to the country's spicy cuisine. The vineyards of the Danube Plain are planted mostly with the red Kadarka and white Olasrizling grapes. In the northeast near the Russian border, Hungary's most famous wine, Tokay, is produced from the Furmint grape. The other main region lies on the north shore of Lake Balaton and is noted for wine produced from native grape varieties, the Furmint, Kéknyelu and Szürkebarat.*

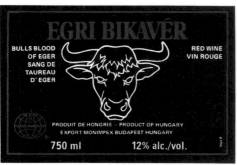

wines produced in this region are not outstanding, but they are the ordinary, everyday wines of the country.

One of Hungary's most interesting regions lies on the north shore of Lake Balaton, Europe's largest lake. A passable white wine is made from the Olaszrizling, but it is the Hungarian white varieties, Furmint, Kéknyelu and Szürkebarát, that yield the region's best wines.

Amazingly sweet-scented, they are robust white wines with a fiery nature. The Kéknyelu is considered to produce the best wines, and the name Badacsonyi on the label indicates a wine of greater sweetness and strength.

There are several other small wine-producing districts in Hungary that make sound, but not remarkable, red and white wines.

Most of Hungary's bottled wines are controlled in state cellars, and the name Monimpex on the label indicates a state wine.

CZECHO-SLOVAKIA

FROM AN INTERNATIONAL point of view the wines of Czechoslovakia are largely unknown. Wines are produced in the provinces of Moravia, Slovakia and Bohemia, but practically all of it is consumed within the country.

By the eighteenth century, Czechoslovakian wines had earned a reputation that put them in the same rank as Hungarian and Italian wines, but after the devastation of the phylloxera disaster, no great effort seems to have been made to restore the vineyards to their former glory.

ROMANIA

BEGINNING IN the mid-1950s, Romania commenced a vineyard expansion program of such dimensions that it could be rivalled only by the commitment of the Russians to the vine. Although Romanian wines do not enjoy extensive world distribution, they have certainly exhibited the potential to produce quality wines.

More than half of the wines produced in Romania are white and the grapes used include Chardonnay, Pinot Gris, Sauvignon, Italian Riesling, Traminer, Furmint, Muscat and an indigenous variety, Feteasca. Red wines are made with Pinot Noir, Cabernet Sauvignon, Merlot and Cadarca.

The Carpathian Mountains run in a southeasterly direction from the center of the country's northern border before sweeping in a curve to the west and running parallel to the River Danube. It is in the eastern foothills of these mountains that Romania's best vineyard regions are located.

The biggest of these regions is Focsani, which is centered around the town of the same name and the towns of Odobeşti and Nicoreşti. Light, dry white wines of good quality are made from the Italian Riesling and Fetească grapes, while some attractive reds are made with Cabernet Sauvignon, Pinot Noir, Merlot and Băbească Neagră grapes.

To the south of Focsani and around the curve of the Carpathians is the region of Dealul Mare, which translates as Great Hill. Again, white wines of sound quality are made from the same grapes as in Focşani and also from Pinot Gris. The reds made with Cabernet Sauvignon, Pinot Noir and Merlot can be good, but sometimes owing to the way they are made, or the high sugar content of the ripe grapes, they can be a little on the sweet side.

Further to the west lie the areas of Piteşti and Drăgăşani, where good quality red and white wines can be found. To the south, the vines of Segarcea grow on the plain near the Danube. As well as red and white wines, this area also produces a rosé which, like so many of the reds, tends to be somewhat sweet.

In the west, along the Hungarian border, the red and white wines of Arad are mostly made from classic grape varieties, while in Banat to the south the principal red grape is the Hungarian Cadarka.

In the northeast of the country is Cotnari, which produces what was once the country's most famous wine, a naturally sweet white dessert wine that is less intense than Tokay.

Near the Black Sea, in the southeast of the country, the region of Murfatlar makes a sweet white wine based on the Muscat grape. It also produces dry table wines with the Chardonnay.

Romania's most famous region, Transylvania, also produces wine. Actually the vineyard region is called Tîrnave, and it is located on the plateau in the center of the country behind the Carpathians. A white wine producing region, one of its more interesting wines is Traminer, made from the grape of the same name.

BULGARIA

THE VINEYARDS of Bulgaria are scattered all over the country and are mostly planted in huge blocks on flat land that allows mechanical harvesting.

While part of Bulgaria is ancient Thrace, where European wine making began, the country has no distinguished wine history, as it was under Muslim rule until just over 100 years ago. In 1949, the Bulgarian government embarked on an expansion and modernization of the country's wine industry. The

result is a state-run grape- and wine-producing organization. On foreign markets, all Bulgarian wines carry the name of the country's wine export organization, Vinimpex.

The country's best white wine is made from the Burgundian grape, Chardonnay. It is a dry wine with lots of flavor and body. The Bulgarians have been equally successful with the Cabernet Sauvignon of Bordeaux from which they produce a dark, full-flavored, balanced wine which is best given a fair time of bottle aging.

Mavrud is a deep red, full-bodied wine that also ages well and is considered to be the country's best. Melnik is an even more powerful version of Mavrud. A lighter and pleasant everyday red wine is Gamza which, if it is not from the same grape as Hungary's Cadarca, tastes like a close relative.

Other than the Chardonnay, some pleasant, but not outstanding, white wines are also made. Hemus is a popular wine made from the Misket grape and ranges from medium to sweet. Other grapes used to produce white wines include the Italian Riesling and Sylvaner, both of which have a pleasant style.

YUGOSLAVIA

THE COUNTRY SHARES borders with several others: Austria and Hungary to the north, Italy, Hungary, Bulgaria and Romania to the west, Greece to the south, and Albania to the southwest.

The country was formed at the end of the First World War through the union of the republics of Serbia, Croatia, Slovenia, Bosnia-Herzegovina, Macedonia, Montenegro, and the two autonomous provinces of Kosovo and Vojvodina. It was not until November 29, 1945 that Yugoslavia was proclaimed a republic; a few months later, on January 31, 1946, it became a federated republic.

To a large extent this turbulent recent history is reflected in Yugoslavia's wines. Each province has its own individual grapes and wine-making style.

The country's best wines come from Slovenia in the north. Those produced in the northeast around Ljutomer on the borders of Austria and Hungary bear a strong resemblance to the wines of these two nations. The Laski Riesling, the local name for the Italian Riesling, is a heady, full-flavored wine which, in good examples, is delightfully rich.

One of the district's best-known wines is sold under the brand name of Tigrovo Mljeko, Tiger's Milk, and is made with the Ranina Radgona grape. A moderately sweet wine, it is very pleasant drinking as an apéritif.

The area around Ljutomer also produces agreeable white wines from Burgundec (Pinot Blanc), and Traminac, although in the case of the last-named grape, better examples are to be found in Vojvodina.

In the western area of Slovenia, the Italian influence is evident, with very decent red wines being made from the Merlot and Cabernet and good, rather heavy whites produced with the Malvasia, Pinot Bijelo and Tokay.

Various vines are planted in the vineyards stretching along the Dalmatian coast between Rijeka in the north and Dubrovnik. The quality is variable; however, rather pleasant red wines are made with the Mali Plavac grape.

In Serbia and Macedonia, the Prokupac grape yields dark red wines that are full-flavored and robust.

Generally speaking, Yugoslavian wines are good value for the money, a fact appreciated by the many Italians near the border who cross over to fill their demijohns with Slovenian and northern Dalmatian wines to serve in their homes.

USSR

I N COMMON WITH many of its other activities, the Russian wine industry remains something of a mystery to much of the West. A very rapid expansion of the vineyards was begun in the 1950s and, as far as can be ascertained, the country is now the world's third largest producer of wines.

The expansion of the vineyards was decreed by the government in an attempt to promote the consumption of wine rather than vodka. How successful this has been within the country, I have no idea; but on my most recent social encounter with Russians, I was disappointed to find that there was no wine, although there was plenty of vodka!

The vineyards, which now cover over 4½ million acres, stretch from Moldavia on the Romanian border in the west through a great, sweeping curve around the shores of the Black Sea to Armenia on the Turkish border.

There are dozens of native varieties of grapes, but a large number of the classic western European vines of France and Germany have also been introduced. Many fortified wines are also made and borrow the names of Sherry, Port and Madeira. There are also considerable quantities of sparkling wines made in the area around Rostov.

The vineyards of the USSR, which stretch from the Romanian border to the Caspian Sea, produce more wine than any other country except Italy and France.

Eastern Mediterranean

GREECE

JUSTIFIABLY REGARDED by many as the mother of the European wine industry, Greece has made no apparent effort to progress or change over the centuries. Her best-known wine, Retsina, although thoroughly enjoyed by the Greeks themselves, is usually viewed as rather horrid by outsiders.

In fact, about half of the wine in Greece is resinated. This treatment is done during fermentation by the addition of pine resin, which imparts a flavor that has been likened to either turpentine or floor polish. Suffice it to say that Retsina has a peculiar taste that appeals to few people outside of Greece.

Other Greek wines are of more general interest. Although there are no truly outstanding wines, there are some that are very palatable. The white wines tend to be fairly neutral and perfectly enjoyable as vins ordinaires. The reds, on the other hand, range from slightly deep-colored rosés to inky black wines that are full-bodied and intense.

Two wines that are worthy of attention are Mavrodaphne and Samos. The first, made from the grape of the same name, is a dark red, sweet dessert wine that is very good, especially when it comes from Patras in the important wine-producing region of Peloponnese. The second is a sweet Muscat made on the island of Samos. At its best, it can take its place proudly amongst the great sweet white wines of the world.

Wines are produced in every part of Greece, including the Ionian islands and Crete and, although they do not enjoy wide international distribution, where they are found they are usually of excellent value for the money.

CYPRUS

IN COMMON WITH Greece, Cyprus has an ancient wine tradition, but unlike Greece it has been very progressive in introducing modern technology. This has caused a tremendous improvement in the quality of its wines.

One part of Cypriot tradition that remains intact is the varieties of grapes that are grown. The land has escaped the ravages of phylloxera, so rather than expose themselves to the unnecessary risk of importing new vines, the growers have stayed with the three varieties that they have always grown: Mavron for reds, Xynisteri for white and Muscat of Alexandria.

In relation to its size, Cyprus has a huge vineyard area extending to over 30,000 acres, mainly to the north and west of Limassol.

The wines often bear such romantic names as Aphrodite, a sweetish white wine, and Othello, a full-bodied red. These are brand names used by the important Limassol firm of Keo.

The island's most outstanding and unique wine is Commandaria, an intense, sweet dessert wine, made predominantly from red grapes, that was first made by the Knights Templar, who established themselves on the island at the end of the twelfth century during the Crusades. In recent years, a moderately aged wine has been marketed, but it does not compare to the traditional long-aged wines which have such a concentration of flavor that drinking them is almost like eating grapes. I recently had the opportunity of tasting a 1947 Commandarie St. John; it was hours before the intense flavor left my mouth.

A great deal of Cyprus wine is shipped in bulk to France and Germany where it is blended into their own wines.

Opposite: The vineyards of modern Greece cover nearly half a million acres, half of which produce wine.

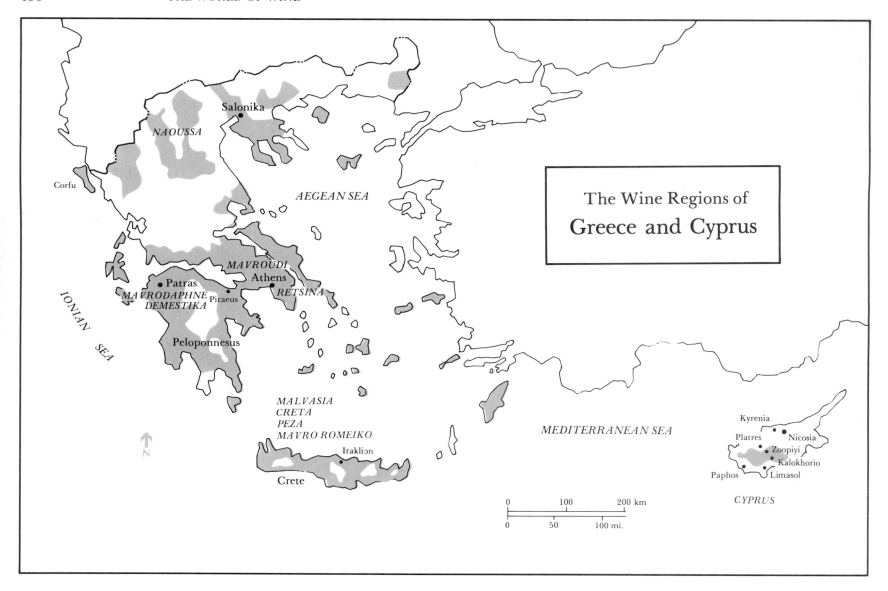

The Wine Regions of
Greece and Cyprus

TURKEY

THE VINEYARDS of Turkey are widely dispersed, but their total gives the country the fifth largest acreage of vines in the world. Only a small percentage of this crop, however, is made into wine. This is a reflection of the fact that the majority of the country's population are Muslims.

As a rule, wineries do not own their own vineyards but buy grapes from farmers. As well as several that are privately owned, there are 17 state-operated wineries.

The quality of the few Turkish wines I have encountered has been very good. I was particularly impressed by a red wine sold under the name of one of the private firms, Doluca. It was quite light, full-flavored and very palatable.

LEBANON

THIS SMALL wine industry, based on Ksara, grows its vines in a cool region some 1,500 feet above sea level. The grape varieties include Cabernet Sauvignon, Cinsault, Carignan and Aramon.

Quality is generally high, and among the most outstanding are the reds of Château Musar. These are largely made with Cabernet Sauvignon and are well-matured in wood. The result is a dark red wine with a huge bouquet and great depth of flavor.

Owing to intermittent conflict with Israel, as well as a civil war now entering its second decade, the growers face additional problems. In 1984, for example, few grapes made it from the vineyards to the wineries, but instead rotted on trucks caught in the conflict.

Filling casks with fortified wine at Carmel Wines. Although Israel produces a wide variety of table and fortified wines, recent trends have emphasized light, dry, European-style table wines.

ISRAEL

BEGUN IN the 1880s by Baron Edmond de Rothschild who sent vine cuttings and a team of experts from Bordeaux, Israel's wine industry is growing rapidly. Rothschild also paid for the building of wineries at Zichrob-Jacob and Richon-le-Zion.

Until fairly recently, the vineyards were planted with such lesser varieties as the Carignan for reds and Sémillon, Clairette and the inevitable Muscat d'Alexandrie for whites. These grapes are used to produce sweet red and white wines, rather un-appealing to many, but which sell well because of local and international demand for kosher wines.

Now such improved varieties as Cabernet Sauvignon and Grenache for reds and Sauvignon Blanc, Chenin Blanc and French Colombard for whites have been introduced. This has resulted in a line of wines of higher quality and wider acceptance.

Mount Carmel is one of the main growing areas, where some of the vineyards are planted as high as 3,000 feet above sea level. Carmel brand wines, a cooperative of more than 800 growers, are Israel's most widely distributed.

Vines are also grown on the Judean Hills, in upper Galilee and along the Mediterranean between Haifa and Natanya.

EGYPT

TWO THOUSAND years ago, Egypt had a healthy wine industry that was highly regarded in the ancient world. However, by the beginning of this century it had diminished to the point of being almost non-existent.

In 1903 an Egyptian, Nestor Gianaclis, began an attempt to re-establish the vineyards on the Nile Delta. It was far from being an overnight success; wine growing never is. But by the early 1930s, fairly respectable wines were again being produced in Egypt.

Production is limited even today, doubtless owing to the prevalence of Islamic values. The wines bear some historic, and romantic, names: Omar Khayyam and Kasr Gianaclis are soft, fairly dry, and have pronounced tannin; Pharaons is somewhat drier, with less flavor. White wines are generally not so good as the reds; these include Nefertiti, Cleopatra, and Gianaclis Villages. There is also a palatable rosé, Rubis d'Egypte.

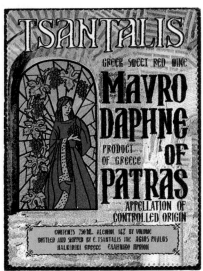

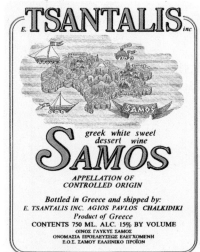

Africa

ALGERIA

THE STORY is told of a cruise ship's captain who asked the wine steward for a taste of the wine he was offering. On tasting it, the captain said, "This is a perfectly fine Algerian wine. Why does it have a Beaujolais label?"

This is a problem that Algeria has always faced because its wine industry, largely built up by the French *colons*, never made a concerted effort to establish its own identity. After the Second World War, Algerian wines were mostly sold to the French for blending, although many were also sold under more illustrious names.

At the time that Algeria became independent in 1962, France, Algeria's main customer, had been working to upgrade the wines of southern France. Between that fact and a few tanker loads of politics, France decided that she would no longer require to buy Algerian wines.

This was a tremendous blow because, in common with other North African wine-producing countries, exports are essential for the industry's survival. Little wine is sold to the local population, which is largely Muslim.

Since then Algeria has put more emphasis on quality, rather than quantity, and more of the vineyards have been established on hilly slopes instead of on the plain as they were previously.

They have also developed new export markets, particularly in Germany and Russia, as well as other African countries.

The red wine grapes are Cabernet Sauvignon, Carignan, Cinsault, Grenache, Pinot Noir, Mourvèdre and Morrastel. Whites are made with Aligoté, Clairette, Faranah and Ugni Blanc.

The reds are, at their best, full-bodied, soft, velvety and extremely good. The country also produces some excellent rosés, but the whites are rather flat and lifeless.

MOROCCO

ALTHOUGH MOROCCO has a long wine history, it was not until after the Second World War that modern vineyards were established.

As in the case of Algeria, the red wines are made with the Cabernet Sauvignon, Cabernet Franc, Alicante, Carignan, Cinsault and Grenache. The quality of Moroccan red wines is outstanding, and they also make some excellent rosés using the Cabernet Franc. A little white wine is made, but it is mostly of poor quality.

Among the better-known labels are Vieux Pape, an intense, full-bodied red; Cabernet (red and rosé), Valpierre (red and white), Oustalet (rosé and white) and Sidi Bughari. Gris de Boulaouane is a specialty wine reportedly distilled from onion skins, but I have not had the opportunity to try it.

Opposite: *Flowers dot the grounds surrounding the Koöperatieve Wijnbouwers Vereniging Headquarters in Paarl, South Africa.*

Below: *Sherry barrels. Nearly half of South Africa's wine goes for distillation.*

Koöperatieve Wijn-bouwers Vereniging at Paddagang, South Africa.

SOUTH AFRICA

THE FIRST VINEYARD was planted in South Africa in 1652 by Jan van Riebeeck, but it was his successor, Simon van der Stel, the commander of the colony, who really established the wine business. It was based on vineyards that he planted to the south of Cape Town in what is now known as Constantia. Stel also gave his name to the town of Stellenbosch, to the east of Cape Town, which is now one of the country's most important wine centers.

The vineyard area stretching northeast from Stellenbosch, through Paarl to Wellington, along with the more southerly district around Franschhoek, constitute South Africa's primary wine-producing districts.

In the eighteenth century, South African wines gained international recognition because of the dessert wine produced at Constantia, which was coveted by the courts of Europe. According to legend, Napoleon asked for a glass of Constantia when lying on his deathbed.

As has been the case in most New World wine industries, South Africa was initially a producer of fortified wines in imitation of Sherry and Port, whose names it blithely borrowed. In truth, however, the South African versions of Sherry are of very high quality and are often difficult to distinguish from the original.

As the industry developed there was a growing effort made to produce good table wines. From the mid-nineteenth to the early twentieth century, the wine growers suffered two major setbacks. The first was the arrival of the destructive phylloxera which was conquered by the introduction of American rootstock. The other was more difficult to battle. The South African government removed tariffs against imports, and the market was flooded with French wines.

The South African wine industry went into a decline that was not turned around until 1924, when the government gave statutory powers to the Koöperatieve Wijnbouwers Vereniging van Zuid-

Although there are no official classifications as there are in France and Germany, the Moroccan government has imposed strict controls, and only sound wines with at least 11 per cent alcohol are allowed to be exported.

TUNISIA

WINE MAKING in Tunisia dates back to the arrival of the Phoenicians over two thousand years ago. After the Punic Wars, the conquering Romans took over the vineyards and wineries; Roman ships left Carthage laden with Tunisian wines, dates, and grains destined for patricians' tables. More recently, the vineyards of Tunisia were largely destroyed by a phylloxera attack, and were never fully replanted after that.

Using much the same grapes, Tunisia produces red wines of about the same calibre as those of Algeria. They also make some palatable rosés. Among the reds, Côteaux de Carthage and Haut Mornag are much enjoyed; Sidi Raïs is perhaps the best-known white.

Tunisia's specialty, however, is Muscat Sec de Kélibia, a "dry-sweet" white wine made with the Muscat of Alexandria. This wine is fragrant, powerful and luscious.

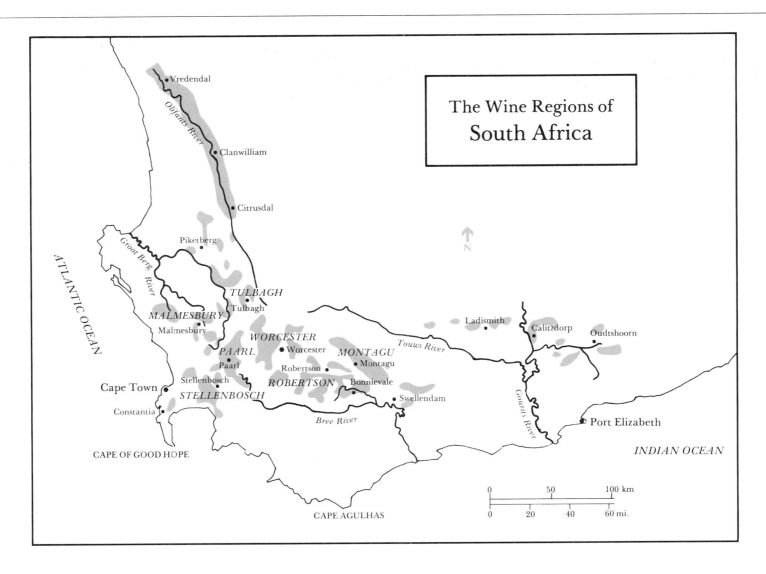

The Wine Regions of
South Africa

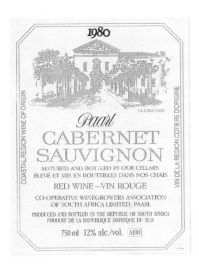

Laboratory at KWV.
Researchers for the
cooperative
developed the
Pinotage vine, a
cross between the
Hermitage and
Pinot, which
combines the best
qualities of both.

Afrika, Beperkt (KWV) which was a cooperative established in 1918. A structure to guarantee minimum prices and set production quotas was introduced, and gradually order emerged from the chaos. The industry began to stabilize.

In September 1973, South Africa adopted wine-of-origin legislation patterned after the French and German systems. Accepted by the EEC, these wine laws are enforced by the Wine and Spirit Board. The laws verify the authenticity of the grapes used in the wines, the vintage declared and either the area of origin or the specific estate where that is applicable. Wines of exceptional quality are permitted to carry the designation Superior on their labels.

The most widely planted red grape is the Pinotage, a cross between Pinot Noir and Hermitage, which is peculiar to South Africa. Pinotage, Her-

mitage and Gamay make soft, round, full-flavored wines. The Cabernet Sauvignon is also grown, but as the wines tend to be hard, it is usually softened through blending. The Syrah of the Rhône yields a spicy red, and there have been experiments with such other varieties as the Californian Zinfandel.

The Steen, a clone of the Chenin Blanc, is the most successful white wine grape and is used either to produce a dry wine or, when late harvested, a sweet wine. The Riesling also makes attractive wines, as does the Clairette Blanche. The French Colombar and Gewürztraminer are also grown, and there are experimental plantings of some of the newly developed German varieties.

The sherry grape, Palomino, is used in the production of sherry wines as well as brandies. In fact, almost half of the wine produced in South Africa goes for distillation.

Lab cellar at KWV.

England

A FEW YEARS AGO any allusion to English wines was likely to be greeted with either disbelief or derision. Neither reaction is justified. There is, in fact, a thriving, and rapidly expanding, wine industry, mainly concentrated in southern England.

This should not be surprising, as there was a very active wine industry in England and Wales until the middle ages, mainly pursued by monasteries. However, the ascension of Henry of Anjou and Eleanor of Aquitaine to the English throne in 1154 made practical the importation of wines from Bordeaux and the Loire. This put the English industry into a decline that ended in its demise.

From then until the 1960s, only odd vines were cultivated, including specimen plants in hot-houses. Amateur wine making survived, but these wines were mostly made from fruits other than the grape, including such unlikely materials as dandelions and nettles. In more recent times, imported grape juice and grape juice concentrate formed the base for commercial and amateur wine makers in Britain. This has given rise to a distinction being made between British wines and English wines, the latter definition being reserved for wines made from grapes grown in English vineyards.

The modern English wine industry was born in 1952 when Major General Sir Guy Salisbury-Jones, having sought advice from the growers in Champagne, planted a chalky slope at Hambledon near Petersfield in Hampshire with Chardonnay, Pinot Noir and Pinot Meunier vines. These now cover a total of 5½ acres.

This solitary pioneer's efforts did not inspire an immediate surge of vineyard planting, but the late 1960s and mid-70s saw a rapid expansion of the acreage under vines.

Today the greatest concentration of vineyards lies in the southern countries, stretching from Cornwall in the west to Kent in the east. To the northeast of London, in Essex, Cambridgeshire and Norfolk, many vineyards have been successfully established. The most northerly vines are found around Leicester in the center of the country, while the Welsh vineyards are found around Pembroke.

Most of the wines produced are white and are of German style. The Müller-Thurgau is one of the most widely planted grape varieties which usually yields a dry, fruity wine. The Sylvaner, Sheurebe and Kerner are also to be found, as are several more recent German hybrids.

Another widely planted white wine variety is the French-American hybrid, Seyve-Villard. There is considerable experimentation going on; one success story is that of Richard Barnes of Biddenden in Kent whose fruity white wine, made with the Ortega grape, has won gold medals two years in a row against other English wines.

Red and rosé wines are made from a variety of grapes including Pinot Noir and Gamay. Experiments are also being undertaken at Pilton Manor in Somerset and Felstar in Essex, to produce sparkling wines made by the méthode champenoise.

Most English vineyards cover fewer than 10 acres, but there are a few that are between 15 and 25 acres.

Most of the grape varieties selected are early ripening. All jokes about the vagaries of the British climate aside, the growing season is very short and, apart from such exceptional years as 1975 and 1976, when heat-wave conditions prevailed, it is difficult to bring grapes to full ripeness every year. Because of this, chaptalisation (the addition of sugar) is a fairly common practice, as it is in Germany and Burgundy.

The English Vineyards Association now has in

Opposite: Wootton Vineyard and winery, Somerset.

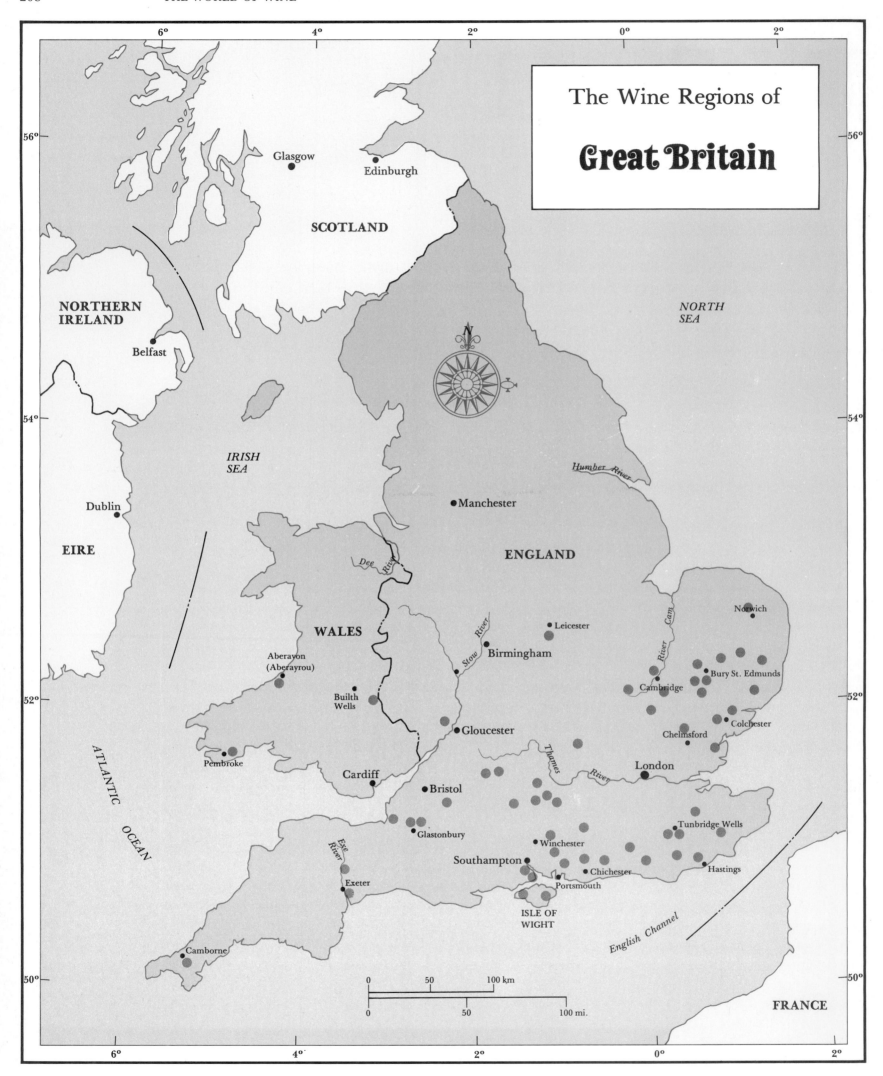

The Wine Regions of

Great Britain

SCOTLAND

NORTHERN
IRELAND

Glasgow

Edinburgh

Belfast

NORTH
SEA

IRISH
SEA

Dublin

EIRE

ENGLAND

Humber River

Manchester

WALES

Dee River

Norwich

Leicester

Stow River

Aberayon
(Aberayrou)

Builth
Wells

Birmingham

Bury St. Edmunds

Cambridge

River Cam

Pembroke

Gloucester

Colchester

Chelmsford

Cardiff

London

Thames River

Bristol

ATLANTIC
OCEAN

Glastonbury

Tunbridge Wells

Exe River

Winchester

Hastings

Southampton

Exeter

Chichester

Portsmouth

ISLE OF
WIGHT

English Channel

Camborne

0   50   100 km

0   50   100 mi.

FRANCE

Gathering the harvest at Waldrons Vineyards in East Sussex, where St. George's English wines are produced.

The five-acre Waldron Vineyards were established in 1979 by Gay Biddlecombe, who manages an all-woman team.

Gathering the grapes at the Merrydown Vineyards in southern England. The Merrydown Vineyards contain vines of the Müller-Thurgau variety. Researchers continually seek vines that are suited to the English soil and climate.

excess of 700 members and, though the industry is still in its infancy, the British wine producers take their business seriously.

One hurdle they face constantly is that the British government imposes the same level of taxation on their wines as it does on imports. In consequence, the wines are necessarily expensive, a fact that has not helped in launching the industry.

The few English wines I have tasted have been very respectable indeed, and their overall quality may be judged from a contest run by *What Wine* magazine, which presented wines from 24 countries in a blind tasting to a panel of its experts. English wines finished first and second.

There is also a healthy competitive atmosphere to the industry, which holds a competition to name the wine of the year. This is awarded the Gore-Brown Trophy.

The European Economic Community ruled in 1980 that in 10 years English wines could be assessed for the establishment of an appellation contrôlée system. In the meantime, all English wines are allowed to be represented only as table wines, irrespective of the level of quality attained.

But quality is the name of the game as far as British wine makers are concerned. They can never obtain high yields and that, along with their unfavorable tax position, has convinced them that if they are to compete with their continental rivals then they must constantly strive for quality.

Although they do take their business seriously, they also have time to indulge the well-developed British sense of humor.

Each year, the vintners organize a lighthearted rally at the English Wine Centre at Alfriston in Sussex. The contestants then set out on a race, and the first to get his or her wine to Paris is declared the winner.

This tongue-in-cheek reversal of the much ballyhooed dash to get the first bottle of Beaujolais Nouveau to London is a clear indication of the confidence that British vintners have in their wines.

At present, the English Vineyards Association enforces its own quality standards, but once an appellation system is established with its implication of guaranteed quality, the British vintners are liable to give many well-established wine producers a serious run for their money.

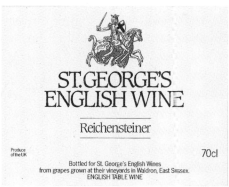

North America

WINEMAKING in North America goes back much further than most people realize. Explorers, missionaries and early immigrants to the eastern United States and eastern Canada found an abundance of wild grapes. These grapes were the native North American species, with *Vitis labrusca, rotundifolia* and *riparia* being the largest groups.

The wines made from these grapes are generally pretty foul, but the probability is that the persistent pioneers didn't have much option if they wanted any wine at all. The first attempts to introduce European vines were made in the eastern United States in the early part of the seventeenth century, and on frequent occasions after that, but these endeavors all failed, as the vines would inexplicably deteriorate and finally die.

Late in the nineteenth century, the reason for the inability of the European vines to survive in the Eastern United States was discovered, but nobody cheered. The discovery was made in botanical gardens in England where native American vines had been planted. The trouble was traced to a species of aphid that lives in the soil of the eastern United States and lives mainly upon the roots of vines.

This tiny creature, Phylloxera vastatrix, was about to change the entire world wine industry. By 1864 it had arrived in France and, in very short order, began a devastation of the vineyards that all but destroyed the French wine industry.

The discovery of phylloxera, and its deadly effect on European vines, also brought out the knowledge that the native American vines had to be immune to attack. It was this observation that finally rescued not only the French wine industry, but the world industry, as it was discovered that European vines grafted to American root stock were then also immune to the predations of phylloxera.

The second great setback for the fledgling U.S. wine industry came in 1919, when Congress voted for Prohibition. This came into effect in 1920, and was not repealed until 1933.

Both in the east and California, the majority of wineries went out of business. Vineyards were plowed under and planted to other crops or table grapes. Those that survived did so by making cooking wines, sacramental wines, tonics, or grape juice concentrates for home wine making.

Repeal did not magically restore the wine industry. In fact, there was no market remaining for table wines. The "dry" generation was more interested in alcoholic content, and the greatest wine demand was for Sherry and Port.

Compounding this adverse situation was the fact that in repealing Prohibition, the federal government left the regulation of the sale and distribution of wines and spirits in the hands of states, counties and municipalities. Some states set up their own stores, which became the only legal outlets for all alcoholic beverages. Even shipping wines made in one state to another state was a complicated matter, requiring importers' licenses and the application of discriminatory taxes by some states to protect their own wine industries.

To overcome the lack of demand, the large wineries embarked on a campaign to demystify wine. Anything that might cause consumer hesitation was eliminated. Vintage dates and varietal designations were dropped in favor of brand names. Corks were often replaced with screw caps, and the gallon jug became the fairly standard package. These wines were, to say the least, not outstanding, but they were consistent and bland. The large California and New York wineries later introduced fizzy, sweet, flavored wines that were supposedly tailored to the taste Americans wanted.

Irrespective of what one might think of these

Opposite: *New York wine aging in redwood tanks.*

wines, they did serve their purpose in introducing millions of Americans to wine, and now that there is enough distance from that era, there can be no question that these wines were successful in bringing about the transition that has made America a healthy wine market.

Behind the scenes of the jug wine era, a lot of work was being done in vineyards, principally in California and the Finger Lakes district of New York State, to grow better grape varieties and produce better wines.

CALIFORNIA

ALTHOUGH WINE was made in California in the early part of the nineteenth century, the industry as it exists today actually dates from the end of Prohibition.

The wine-producing business in California, and indeed throughout North America, is carried out in various ways. Large wineries may or may not grow any of their own grapes; in any case, they also buy grapes from independent growers. Some vineyard owners do not make any wine of their own, but simply grow their grapes to sell to wineries. There are also vineyards where the owners grow their grapes and then make their own wines.

An enormous contribution to the Californian wine industry has been made by the University of California at Davis. Such men as Dr. Maynard A. Amerine and Dr. Albert J. Winkler, along with a host of others, have been very influential in shaping the wine industry into what it is today.

Their work has caused improvements in both the vineyards and the wineries, and they have been a major influence in raising the general quality of Californian wines. Their work has now gained international recognition.

The coastal area to the north of San Francisco is California's best wine-growing district. Within that district, the Napa Valley has earned the reputation of producing the finest wines.

Napa Valley stretches some 25 miles from Napa in the south to Calistoga in the north. It lies between the Howell Mountains to the east and the Mayacamas Mountains on the west. At its widest part, the valley is only five miles across. The southern end of the valley around Napa and Carneros is the coolest area, while the area to the north, around Oakville and Rutherford, is slightly warmer. Continuing north, the climate around Calistoga is warmer still.

A total of 25,000 acres of vines are grown, both on the valley floor and on the mountain slopes. Most of the grape varieties are the familiar *Vitis vinifera* of Europe. Red wines are made from Cabernet Sauvignon, Pinot Noir, Petite Sirah, Gamay, Barbera and Zinfandel, which is something of a mystery grape that is now thought to be related to the Primitivo of Italy. White wines are produced with the Chardonnay, Johannisberg Riesling, Sauvignon Blanc, Chenin Blanc and Gewürztraminer.

In general, Napa's best red is the Cabernet Sauvignon, a big, full-bodied wine of generous dimensions, while the Chardonnay, in more recent years, is yielding its best whites. These are also big, full-bodied, aromatic wines.

There are now over 400 wineries in California, and more than 70 of those are located in the Napa Valley. One aspect of the wine business in Napa, perhaps a reflection of the tone set by the professors at Davis, is the genuine spirit of cooperation that exists between wineries. Advice, information and equipment are willingly shared. They freely trade grapes and batches of wine and will even help each other in wine making.

One of the valley's best-known wine makers, Robert Mondavi, established himself in a new winery at Oakville in 1966 by buying grapes from other growers. He now has about 800 acres of his own vineyards, from which he produces about a dozen vintage-dated varietals each year. His wines are always very good and, on occasion, they are exceptional. Mondavi and Baron Philippe de Rothschild of Bordeaux made a wine together in Mondavi's winery and released it in 1984 under the name Opus I. This California/Bordeaux alliance caused quite a sensation, which can be judged by the fact that people happily paid $50 for a bottle.

The Mondavi family are not newcomers to the valley, having operated the Charles Krug winery near St. Helena since 1943 when it was purchased by Cesare Mondavi, who operated it with his sons Robert and Peter. One of the biggest wineries in the valley, it has over 1,000 acres of vines. The

The Wine Regions of

North America

In springtime tiny green berries that will become the year's grape crop form on vines in California.

The Cabernet Sauvignon grape yields the Napa Valley's best red wines.

Mondavis pioneered the cold fermentation techniques developed by Dr. William V. Cruess of Davis. Today, of course, controlled fermentation techniques are widely accepted and practiced. Cesare Mondavi died in 1959, and after Robert left to open his own winery, management of the Krug operation fell to Peter. About 20 per cent of the wine produced is sold under the Charles Krug label, while the bulk, which is of lesser quality, is branded as C.K. Mondavi.

Sterling Vineyards is a large operation that was established in 1964 when an Englishman, Peter Newton, began buying vineyard land near Calistoga. In 1971, along with partners Michael Stone and Martin Waterfield, he built an impressive winery. The white buildings, complete with bell towers, are located atop a 250 foot hill. Visitors can reach the winery only by riding an aerial tramway.

A winery with very limited production, but extremely high quality, is Stony Hill Vineyards, located about 600 feet above the floor of the valley between Diamond and Spring mountains a little south of Calistoga. The vineyards cover a mere 38 acres and are planted only in white grapes: Chardonnay, Sémillon, Gewürztraminer and

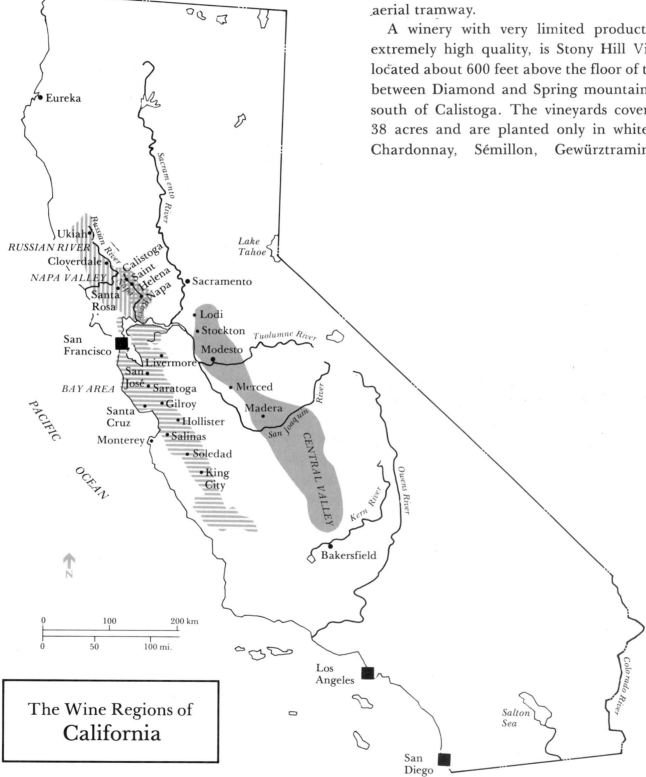

The Wine Regions of
California

White Riesling. The vineyard is really the result of a happy accident. It was purchased in 1943 by Frederick McCrea, a vice-president with the advertising agency McCann-Erickson, who was looking for nothing more than a summer home for his family. They began to experiment with vines, however, and in 1951 the McCreas made their first wines. Production is small and it is absorbed by those people on their mailing list, which includes a few of California's finest restaurants. McCrea died in 1977, but the family continues to run the winery.

Another small operation that enjoys the highest reputation in the valley is Heitz Wine Cellars, just south of St. Helena. Joe Heitz was stationed at Fresno during the Second World War and got a job working in a winery at nights. Bitten by the wine-making bug, he studied oenology at Davis and later taught viticulture and oenology at Fresno. Subsequently, he worked with such huge enterprises as E. & J. Gallo and Italian Swiss Colony. At Beaulieu Vineyards, he worked for seven years as assistant to the legendary wine maker, André Tchelistcheff. Heitz bought his own winery in 1961, but as the only grape planted there was the Grignolino, Heitz began buying grapes from other growers, along with wine for aging and blending. Today, there are many who consider him the best wine maker in the valley, and his Cabernet Sauvignons and Chardonnays are always worth seeking out.

Of the larger Napa Valley wineries, few can compete with the reputation of the Louis M. Martini Winery, located just south of St. Helena. The business was begun in the San Joaquin Valley in 1906 by an Italian immigrant. The present winery was built in 1940 and is now run by the founder's son, Louis P. Martini. The firm owns about 900 acres of prime vineyards in various locations in the Napa and Sonoma valleys. They are particularly noted for their Cabernet Sauvignons, which at their best are superb. I recall a dinner with a Californian friend in 1980; he supplied a 1966 Cabernet Sauvignon Private Reserve from Martini, while I provided a 1966 Château Ducru-Beaucaillou. Both wines were from rather average years, but while the St. Julien had softened and become quite delicate, the Martini wine was still full, fruity, sturdy and frank.

Stag's Leap Wine Cellars is one of a number of small wineries begun in recent years that produce fine wines, but none have sprung to prominence with quite the velocity of this property on the Silverado Trail, established in 1970 by Warren and Barbara Winiarski. Their 1973 Cabernet Sauvignon, released in 1976, took first place ahead of several Bordeaux first growths at a blind tasting held in Paris. That one victory propelled the infant winery to prominence, and it has never looked back.

The largest church-owned wine-making concern in the world is the Christian Brothers, who have three wineries in Napa Valley where they have about 1,500 acres of vines, and two in San Joaquin Valley where they have a further 1,000 acres under vines. They produce about fifty different products each year, although until recently none of it carried a vintage date, and their total production is about 2 million cases annually. Although some of their wines are very good, the vast majority are nothing more than pleasant, uncomplicated drinking.

An interesting innovation to the Napa Valley took place in 1973 when Domaine Chandon was established on about 850 acres near Yountville. A subsidiary of Moët-Hennessey, and the owners of the Champagne house of Moët et Chandon, this new winery has eloquently made the point that it is not necessary to borrow someone else's name to succeed. Marketing their wines simply as Domaine Chandon Sparkling Wine and not as California Champagne, they have already captured top spot for sales of sparkling wine in California.

Of the dozens of other wineries in the Napa Valley, most make wines that are of good quality, while some of their better wines are excellent. Beyond question the finest wines of the Napa Valley can take their place with the best the world has to offer.

On the other side of the Mayacamas Mountains from the Napa Valley is the Sonoma region which has the Pacific Ocean as its western boundary.

This region has had more than its share of ups and downs. By the 1920s, there were about 60,000 acres under vines, but this declined to around 12,000 acres. In the 1970s, there was a renewed interest in planting; there are presently over 20,000 acres again under vines.

There is a considerable variation in soil and climatic conditions throughout Sonoma. In the southern area known as the Valley of the Moon,

Overleaf: Sun-washed field against a backdrop of blue mountains is typical of vineyards in the Napa Valley.

Left: *A lone vine seems to stand silent vigil over sloping acres of choice wine variety grapes in a California vineyard.*

Right: *A grape grower checks ripe grapes for sugar content with a measuring instrument called a refractometer.*

there are the three climatic variations found in the entire length of the Napa Valley, and that variation is again found to the north in the Russian River Valley and the Alexander Valley. This variation in micro-climates is again repeated in lower Mendocino County.

All of the new vineyards are being planted with noble grape varieties, and there is a very definite effort being made to produce much higher-quality wines, mainly vintage-dated varietals, than has been the case in Sonoma in the past.

Two men, living almost a century apart, exerted a tremendous influence on the development of the Sonoma Valley, in particular, and the California wine industry in general.

The first was Count Agoston Haraszthy, a Hungarian with an apparently colorful history that would make a book in itself. He eventually arrived in California in the late 1840s, became San Diego's first sheriff and later was official smelter and refiner of gold for the U.S. mint.

It is, however, for his contribution to the Californian wine industry that he is now remembered. Following several abortive attempts at cultivating vines, he eventually arrived in Sonoma, planted vines and was soon making wine. In 1857 he constructed the Buena Vista winery and began working towards realizing his own prophecy that California could produce as noble a wine as any country on the face of the globe.

In 1861, he was appointed by the governor of California to tour the European wine regions and to report on how their practices could be applied to California. Haraszthy returned with over 100,000 vine cuttings, but the political climate had changed in his absence and he was never paid for the cost of his journey.

Evidently a resilient individual, he simply returned to Buena Vista where he planted some of his European cuttings. He sold the majority of the cuttings to other growers, then gave away those that were left.

Buena Vista became the world's largest vineyard, and Haraszthy opened offices across the United States and in London. He was at the height of his success, but it was not to last. In the mid-1860s, a series of disasters befell him. First phylloxera arrived and began destroying his vines, then stock exchange losses ravaged his capital resources, which were also adversely affected by new taxation. Fire all but destroyed the winery; he then lost his credit.

It is hardly surprising that such a run of bad luck forced Haraszthy to depart California. He went on to Nicaragua, where he won a government contract to distill spirits from sugar.

In July 1869 Haraszthy disappeared completely. What became of him no one really knows, but legend — and he was a man of legends — has it that met his demise when he fell from a tree overhanging an alligator-infested river.

It has become fashionable to downplay Haraszthy's contribution to the Californian wine industry, but had he done nothing more than engender enthusiasm for and confidence in the capability of California to produce fine wines of the highest caliber, he would still have to be regarded as a giant of his era.

The second man to make an indelible mark on the Californian scene by establishing a winery in Sonoma was James K. Zellerbach, Chairman of the Board of the Crown Zellerbach Paper Company and United States Ambassador to Italy.

Zellerbach's favorite wines were Burgundies, particularly Montrachet and Romanée-Conti, and his driving passion was to prove that wines of equal excellence, and not mere copies, could be produced from the Chardonnay and Pinot Noir grapes.

Not short of funds, Zellerbach was able to pursue his ambition in the grand manner. First he called in the experts from the University of California at Davis to identify the most suitable vineyard location for the propagation of Chardonnay and Pinot Noir vines. The site chosen in 1951 was a rocky slope overlooking the Valley of the Moon. Zellerbach named the property Hanzell, a contraction of his wife Hanna's name and his own surname. Coincidentally, it was just a short distance from Haraszthy's Buena Vista winery.

With the site chosen, planting soon began on the terraced slope 700 feet up the mountain. In 1956 a winery was constructed in an architectural style reminiscent of Clos de Vougeot, but the interior was a thoroughly modern and completely equipped wine-making and laboratory facility.

In the vineyards of Hanzell, the vines were severely pruned so that the yield would not exceed 1¼ tons per acre. When it came to the harvest, Zellerbach demanded that only perfectly ripened bunches be picked, and, not content with that, he further insisted that these bunches be inspected to eliminate any unripened berries. Laudable as these standards may be, they are not practical on a large scale.

Cold fermentation was the rule at Hanzell, as was the use of inert gas to reduce the wines' contact with air when they were being transferred, stored and bottled.

Considerable research had been done by the University of California biochemistry graduate, Bradford Webb, hired by Zellerbach to determine the best methods to adopt for the making of Hanzell's wines. The primary motive behind the

Harvest time at a California winery. Picking may be done either mechanically or by hand.

research was to minimize the risk of any unknown factors entering the process and affecting the final quality of the wine.

At Zellerbach's insistence, Burgundy casks made with Limousin oak were imported for use in aging the wines. There were many who were of the opinion that Zellerbach was incurring unnecessary expense for no good reason, and that American oak barrels would have the same effect.

Hanzell's first vintage Chardonnay in 1956 clearly showed that Zellerbach's decision to use Limousin oak was wise indeed, as the wine did taste like a French wine.

Hanzell continued to produce truly great Chardonnays, and it became apparent that Zellerbach's goal of producing great wines in California was a realistic one.

Zellerbach died suddenly just before the 1963 vintage, and the winery was closed until it was sold by the estate in 1965. Although now operating under its third owner, the methods established by Zellerbach remain virtually unchanged.

Haraszthy and Zellerbach built their wineries with the sole ambition of proving that California was capable of producing fine wines. Both of them won their points and have undoubtedly inspired others to equal and improve upon their successes.

In the same vicinity as Buena Vista and Hanzell is one of California's largest family-owned wineries, Sebastiani. Established in 1904 by Samuele Sebastiani, an immigrant from Tuscany, it grew to become one of the largest wineries on the

Italian Swiss Colony, located at Asti on the Russian River, was established in 1881 by Andrea Sbarbaro, a grocer turned banker, whose idea was to assist Italian and Swiss immigrants to America by establishing a colony of vineyard workers at the winery.

He purchased a total of 1,500 acres, but the original scheme proved impractical. He then converted it to straight private enterprise and soon had a successful business.

Today it is part of the Allied Grape Growers, a cooperative of about 1,600 growers. Their marketing arm, United Vintners, is now owned by the giant Heublein Inc. which also owns Beaulieu and Inglenook in the Napa Valley as well as several others.

Sonoma is very much in a state of transition. Such older wineries as Geyser Peak, Souverain, Sonoma Vineyards and Château St. Jean are making rapid progress in entering the vintage-dated varietal wine market, while retaining their jug wine business.

These wineries are now being joined by a rapidly growing number of others. The newcomers are mostly smaller operations, and most of them are aiming at the fine wine market. A money-is-no-object winery in the Zellerbach tradition is Jordan, which is the 270-acre property of oilman Thomas Jordan. He set out to produce only one wine, a fine Cabernet Sauvignon. The first vintage made in 1976 and released in 1980 proved somewhat short, but the wines are now showing improvement. A Chardonnay was added with the 1979 vintage.

The San Joaquin Valley, also known as the Inland or Central Valley, runs north and south for three hundred miles between the Sierra Nevada Mountains and the coastal range from Lodi in the north and Bakersfield in the south.

The climate in the valley is too hot for the production of fine wines. The area is best known for its ordinary table wines, dessert wines and brandies.

The northern area around Lodi incorporates the Sacramento Valley and Sierra foothills which were established vineyard areas prior to Prohibition. They went into a decline, but are again being revived. Likewise, the vineyards of the Shenandoah Valley in Amador County are again attracting considerable attention, particularly for their Zinfandels.

Three times each day, cellar workers at Beaulieu Vineyard in California's Napa Valley break apart and pound down the cluster of grape skins called a "cap," which rises to the top of each tank during fermentation. Greater juice contact with the grape skins gives the wine more intensity and depth of color.

north coast. Sebastiani survived Prohibition by producing sacramental wines and tonics. Unlike Haraszathy and Zellerbach, Sebastiani concentrated on producing large quantities of sound, everyday wines. By the time of his death in 1944, he had succeeded, handing on a substantial business to his son August, who twenty years later began producing varietal wines, including a very reliable Zinfandel and a very good Barbera. He also secured a substantial share of the varietal jug wine market. When he died, the business was handed on to his sons Sam and Don. Although highly successful, the Sebastianis have remained an unpretentious family.

To the south, and strictly speaking beyond the Central Valley, the district of Cucamonga, east of Los Angeles, produces mostly ordinary table wines, but is most noted for its good Zinfandels. Urban sprawl is the biggest threat to this region's future. Greater emphasis is now being placed on the Temecula district in Riverside County near San Diego, where the cooler climate makes it possible to produce some fine wines.

The really massive vineyards of the San Joaquin Valley, however, are those lying between Modesto and Fresno. This area produces two-thirds of all the wine made in California, and most of that is made by the two giant firms of E. & J. Gallo and United Vintners.

The story of Ernest and Julio Gallo is remarkable. With absolutely no wine-making experience,

they rented a warehouse and fermentation tanks in Modesto in 1933. Their only guidance came from a couple of small pamphlets from the local library, but they succeeded in making sound wine. Two years later, they built their own winery on the outskirts of Modesto. The original winery has been expanded to become the world's largest winery complex, and they have also built new wineries at Fresno and Livingston. They have a total capacity of about 250 million gallons of wine, and their Modesto plant includes their own plant for bottle production. Perhaps the most remarkable thing is that in building this empire, Ernest and Julio have retained sole ownership of everything.

Gallo wines are generally good quality, reliable wines at very reasonable prices, and a large part of their success is due to their clever and aggressive

Fermentation tanks at one of California's newer wineries.

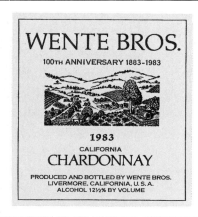

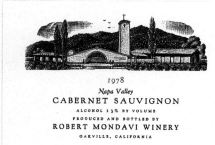

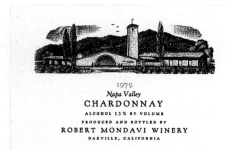

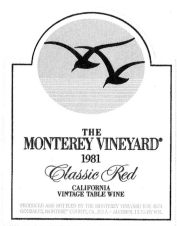

marketing strategies. They are also very forthright about their wines. I recall a few years ago tasting one of their Sauvignon Blancs and remarking that it was unpleasantly high in acid. My observation drew the simple and clear explanation that this was due to the fact that the vines were only three years old, and that the wine would be better in future years as the vines matured.

There are some Gallo wines that are less than ordinary. These are their high-alcohol flavored wines such as Thunderbird and pop wines such as the Boone's Farm line. These wines are usually sold under brand names rather than the Gallo label, but all the labels name Modesto as the place of origin. It is for their sound-quality table wines, however, that the Gallos have earned a deservedly good reputation.

United Vintners is in many ways the complete opposite of the Gallo operation. The second largest wine producer in the United States, United is part of the complex and diversified Heublein conglomerate. United Vintners has eight wineries in California, with the largest being at Madera where, like Gallo, their facilities include their own bottle manufacturing plant.

United Vintners sell their wines under a diversity of labels including Inglenook, Beaulieu, and Italian Swiss Colony for the best of their table wines, which are generally of good, or better, quality. They also put out a line of pop wines under the Annie Green Springs label that are as sickly sweet and fruity as all the other wines in this category produced by themselves and others.

Large winery operations are the norm in the San Joaquin Valley. Although overshadowed by the gigantic Gallo and United Vintners operations, Guild Wineries and Distilleries, California Wine Company, East Side Winery, Franzia Brothers Winery and Bear Mountain Winery, are sizable operations by any standard.

A notable exception is Ficklin Vineyards, which is one of California's smallest and most highly regarded wineries. Established by Walter Ficklin in 1946, the winery has built its reputation on one wine — Port. Using the classic Portuguese varieties, Tinta Madeira, Souzao, and others, they produce a ruby-style Port of extremely high quality. The fifty acres of vineyards also have plantings of two grape varieties developed by Davis for hot climates, the Ruby Cabernet and Emerald

Riesling, both of which have earned Ficklin a high reputation and have shown others that it is possible to produce fine wines even in a hot climate.

South of San Francisco there is a vast vineyard area that begins at Livermore in Almeda County in the north and, heading south, incorporates the Santa Cruz Mountains, the Santa Clara Valley, the Salinas Valley and Monterey.

There is an incredible variation in soils and micro-climates throughout this vast region, which produces an equally astonishing variety of fine wines.

In the Livermore Valley, one of the pioneering wineries, Concannon Vineyard, was established by the Irishman James Concannon in 1883. It was originally solely concerned with the production of sacramental wines, a course that assured the winery's survival during Prohibition. Today, the winery has a solid reputation for its wines, particularly its Sauvignon Blanc. Other whites that are deservedly of high repute are the Johannisberg Riesling and Muscat Blanc. Two of the winery's reds, Petite Sirah, which Concannon pioneered in California, and Cabernet Sauvignon are produced in limited quantities and are much sought after.

In the same year that James Concannon established his winery, Carl Wente, an immigrant from Germany, set up his winery just across the road from Concannon's.

Wente is particularly noted for white wines and did, in fact, obtain cuttings of Sauvignon Blanc and Sémillon from Château d'Yquem. Wente Bros. were the first Californian winery to be acclaimed for their Chardonnay; they are also noted

In this cool aging cellar at a historic California winery, wines slumber for months and years in wooden casks before they are ready for bottling and further aging.

The great variation in soils and micro-climates throughout California produces a wide variety of fine wines.

for their Grey Riesling and Blanc des Blancs, which is a blend of Ugni Blanc and Chenin Blanc. Occasionally they produce a Late Harvest Riesling that can be quite exceptional. Although the winery also makes some red wines, it is on their whites that their reputation has been built.

Wente Bros. have always been reticent about the use of wood, and their attitude was perhaps best summed up by the late Karl Wente, grandson of the founder, who said, "I want to make wines that taste of the grape and not a two-by-four." Indeed, one of the hallmarks of Wente wines is that the emphasis in the flavor is definitely on the fruit.

Paul Masson Vineyards is one of the best known from the area south of the bay, and deservedly so. Because of family involvements, there was a strong link between Paul Masson and Almadén. In 1852, Etienne Thee planted some vineyards that were inherited by his son-in-law Charles LeFranc who, in turn, invited his son-in-law, Paul Masson, into the business. In 1892, Masson bought out LeFranc's share of the firm and established the Paul Masson Champagne Company. Then in 1896 he built his own winery in the Santa Cruz Mountains.

Masson succeeded in surviving Prohibition by

receiving permission to market "medicinal Champagne." Three years after repeal, he sold the winery to Martin Ray. In 1941, a major fire caused Ray to abandon the project and establish his own winery on another mountain site.

In the following year, the Paul Masson winery was acquired by Joseph E. Seagram and Sons, under whose ownership it has grown into one of the largest premium wine companies in California. Masson now has four wineries and six thousand acres of vines.

For the longest time, Paul Masson, which markets some four dozen products, was producing wines that were nothing more than pleasant, but ordinary, table wines of no particular distinction. But since the late 1970s, they have begun to produce an increasing number of vintage-dated varietals aimed at the fine wine market. In this regard, they are relying to a considerable extent on their vineyards in Monterey.

Almadén, initially a relative of Paul Masson and now owned by National Distillers, has continued to expand, with some 7,000 acres of its own vineyards and a further 10,000 acres under long-term contract.

The Almadén line consists of over five dozen wines. The majority are honest, clean wines with no particularly exciting character. But in relatively recent years, they have begun to produce a series of fine vintage-dated varietals under the Charles Le Franc Founder's Wines label.

There are many older and newer wineries in this vast region, making everything from basic everyday wines to fine wines from single-cask bottlings. Notable amongst these are Mirassou Vineyards, Ridge Vineyards, David Bruce, Mount Eden Vineyards, Chalone Vineyard and Monterey Vineyard. Of these, David Bruce is the greatest innovator. His 37 acres of premium vines located at 2,000 feet in the Santa Cruz Mountains yield fine grapes. Bruce, in addition, follows his own personal dictates in wine production. He will not use filters or fining and still offers wine that is the product of only one cask.

Although he is by no means alone, Bruce's individualistic attitude perhaps is as clear an indication as any of the open-minded, adventurous, and still very much pioneering attitude that prevails in the Californian wine industry.

NEW YORK STATE

ALTHOUGH IT IS the second most important wine-producing region in the United States, New York's production is only a fraction of California's. Whereas California has some six hundred thousand acres under vines, New York has a mere forty thousand acres.

The Eastern United States, in common with the Niagara Peninsula in Ontario, Canada, is unique in that it makes wine from three different families of grapes. The most widely planted are the native labruscas, while there are only small plantings of the classic vinifera vines and a growing acreage of hybrids of the other two species.

The most important New York region is the Finger Lakes, followed by the Hudson River Valley. There are also wines grown in the western part of the state around Chatauqua and Niagara near Lake Erie and in the east on Long Island.

The native North American grapes, such as Concord, Catawba, Delaware and Elvira produce wines of a nature that are euphemistically described as "foxy," although some discriminating palates have favored them with less complimentary epithets.

Both in New York and Ontario, the standard way of compensating for a short growing season and the off flavors has been to add sugar to offset the high acid and low sugar content of the grapes, and to add water to dilute the otherwise peculiar taste.

The advent of the hybrid grapes has greatly altered the nature of the wine industry in New York State, as has the limited introduction of vinifera varieties.

In the United States, the first proponent of hybrid varieties was Phil Wagner, an editor with the *Baltimore Sun*. Wagner had been making wine at home with grapes shipped from California during Prohibition, but when repeal was enacted, that source of grapes no longer existed. He then tried making wines with native grapes, but did not like the taste. As a result, having heard about the hybrid vines, he began to experiment and found

Left: *A man with his "thief" tastes the aging wine periodically to determine when it is ready for bottling.*

A flash of early autumn foliage surrounds a New York vineyard.

*Visitors to the Taylor Wine Company, Inc. of New York
enjoy a wine tasting in the Taylor cellars.*

The Taylor Wine Company, Inc. of Hammondsport, New York.

that he could make pleasing wines with these grapes.

In 1945, he and his wife Jocelyn bonded Boordy Vineyard in Riverwood, Maryland. His results were such that his wines soon became favored locally. In fact, his red and rosé were pleasant wines, but his white was little better than the wines made with the native varieties.

Nevertheless, no one can ever detract from the contribution the Wagners made to the development of the wine industry in the Eastern United States. Their pioneering efforts, and Phil Wagner's crusading spirit, spread throughout the eastern states and up into Canada, where similar research programs had been initiated in the mid-1930s.

Adoption of the hybrid vines was, and remains, a very slow process in the United States, but an even greater reluctance can be found in the introduction of Vinifera vines.

Dr. Konstantin Frank, a Russian-born German, who had been exposed to vinifera viticulture in the Ukraine, arrived in the United States in 1951 and was unsuccessful in convincing the experimentation facility at Geneva, New York, that it was possi-

ble to grow these varieties commercially in New York State.

After a frustrating period, Charles Fournier, of Gold Seal Vineyards, finally allocated him vineyard space in 1953 for experimentation with vinifera vines. Frank soon showed that he knew what he was doing. To begin with, he grafted the vinifera vines onto Canadian rootstock, causing the vines to blossom later and the grapes to mature earlier.

Having proven his point, Frank branched out in 1963 and established his own vineyards and winery above Lake Keuka. He very pointedly named his new enterprise Vinifera Wine Cellars.

Despite the contribution of Wagner and Frank, almost 90 per cent of the vines planted in New York State are still native varieties. In consequence, a great proportion of the products sold are apt to be somewhat disappointing.

However, there are some interesting wines and wineries in New York State. The most important wine-growing areas are those along the shores of lakes Keuka, Seneca and Canandaigua. The town that is the main center is the village of Hammondsport, at the southern end of Lake

Century-old wine casks at the Taylor Wine Company.

Keuka. The village is rather rustic and certainly does not, on the surface, give the impression of being an important wine center.

Amongst the most important New York wineries are The Taylor Wine Company, Inc. and Great Western, the latter sometimes referred to as the Pleasant Valley Wine Company. Both wineries were established in the second half of the nineteenth century. In 1977 both wineries became part of the Coca-Cola Company and again changed hands on November 1, 1983 when they were purchased by Seagram.

Taylor, with over thirteen hundred acres of vineyards, buys additional grapes from about 450 other growers to make up the quantity they need to produce the thirty different wines they market. Their wines are made with native grape varieties as well as hybrids.

They make sparkling wines with the native Delaware grape, which has only a slight labrusca flavor and yields pleasant wines. Many of Taylor's wines made with labrusca grapes are very heavily scented and flavored with the typical foxiness that marks wines made with these varieties. Some of

their more pleasant wines are a blend of Californian wine and New York wine. The vast majority of Taylor wines have screw caps rather than corks.

Great Western, like Taylor, produces about 36 different wines from both native and hybrid varieties. Regarded as the premium division of Taylor, their best products are their sparkling wines, which they call Great Western New York State Champagne. Their table wines are of about the same quality as Taylor's, although some of their varietal wines made with hybrids are of good quality.

The Bully Hill Wine Company, located not far from Great Western, was established in 1970 by Walter Taylor, who was ejected from the Taylor Wine Company in the same year because of his loudly proclaimed objections to the use of out-of-state wines for blending.

The Taylor Wine Company won a court decision that prohibited Walter from using the Taylor name on his wine labels. At first Walter simply used a felt-tip pen to scratch out his name, but was eventually compelled to create new labels.

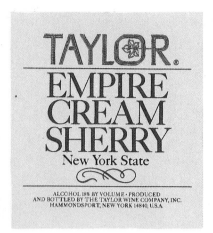

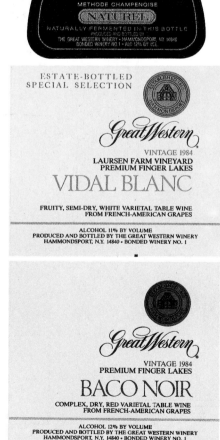

Unbowed, Walter asserted that they might get his name, but they could not get his goat. To emphasize his point he came out with a whimsically labeled wine called Bully Goat. He has since produced a whole line of humorously named wines.

But there is a serious side to Walter Taylor, who is a firm believer in the hybrids that he maintains can produce fine wines. Most of his wines are unblended varietals, but where the wine is blended, the exact ratio of grapes used is shown on the label. Taylor is still firmly opposed to the use of out-of-state wines and to the common practice of adding water to temper the flavor of labrusca wines. He has even gone so far as to coin the motto, "Wine without water" for his winery.

Although Bully Hill wines are all well made and very palatable drinking, Taylor still has a long way to go to prove that the hybrids can produce fine wines in New York State.

Gold Seal Vineyards have the distinction of being the first New York winery to make wines with vinifera grapes. Their Chardonnay and Johannisberg Riesling are their best vintage-dated vinifera wines, but they make them only in favorable years. The winery also has a considerable reputation for its Blanc des Blancs New York State Champagne.

Vinifera Wine Cellars, founded in 1962 by Dr. Konstantin Frank, is a 78 acre estate planted entirely with vinifera grape varieties. Although ten wines are produced, they are all made only in small quantities. One of his more remarkable wines is his Johannisberg Riesling Natur Spätlese. He has also had considerable success with Gewürztraminer and Chardonnay.

There are dozens of other varieties in New York State, but although some pleasant wines are made, most of the State's wines are undistinguished.

OTHER STATES

APART FROM the better known regions of California and New York, wine growing has spread far and wide across the United States. An interesting aspect of this developing situation is that the greatest interest is being shown in the hybrid and vinifera varieties, rather than the native vines.

Beyond question, the most exciting developments in wine production in the United States center in Oregon and Washington. Both states have long grown grapes, but until comparatively recent years, they were perceived as being capable of growing only native North American varieties.

Washington state has a long history of grape growing, although even today a considerable portion of the crop is the native Concord which is used to produce grape juice. That situation is changing, however, as the state has a rapidly expanding wine industry based on both vinifera and hybrid vines and, after California, is now the second largest wine producer in the United States. There are now about sixty wineries, four times more than there were in 1980, and more than ten thousand acres of vinifera vineyards, mainly centered in the Yakima Valley and Columbia River Basin, close to the Oregon border, and east of the Cascade Mountains which are a major influence in determining the quality of wine grapes that can be produced.

To the west of the Cascades, about one hundred inches of rain falls on the coastline each year, while the interior valleys receive about forty inches of rainfall. To the east of the Cascades, however, the climate is much drier with less than ten inches of rain each year being recorded in the Yakima Valley. This arid condition makes irrigation necessary, but that is not a problem as there is a more than adequate supply of water available from the Columbia River.

During the growing season, the vineyards receive as much as seventeen hours of sunlight daily. The temperatures can soar to one hundred degrees Fahrenheit, a factor that would normally eliminate

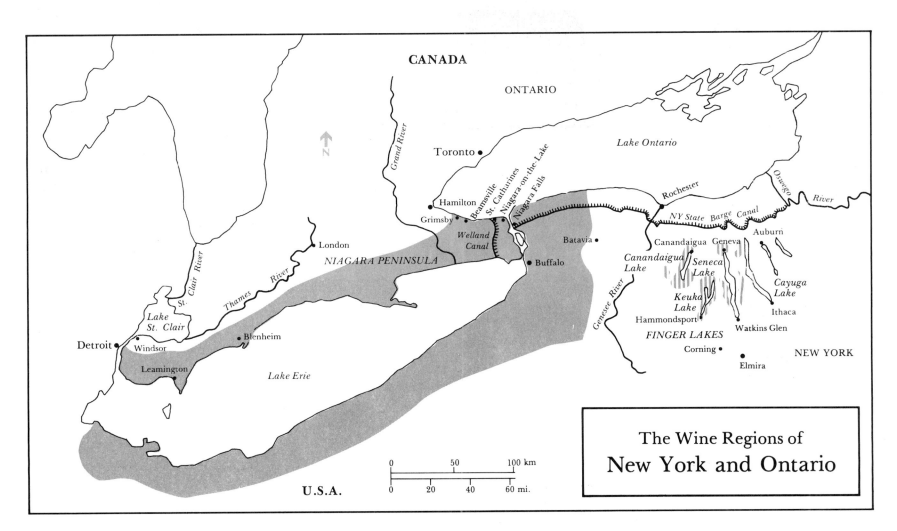

The Wine Regions of
New York and Ontario

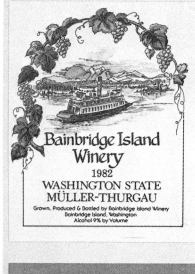

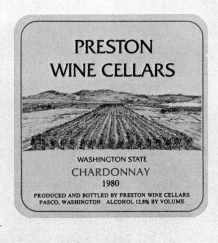

acidity almost completely in the grapes. In Washington, however, these daytime temperatures are moderated by cool nights that preserve a good balance between fruit and acidity in the ripe grapes.

The main climatic concerns for Washington growers are autumn frosts and cold winters. The frost can cause the leaves to fall from the vines, robbing the grapes of carbohydrates and making it impossible for them to ripen further, while the winter can either kill the vines completely or significantly reduce the number of living buds for the next growing season. One interesting aspect of vinifera vine growing in Washington is that, as the state has never been affected by phylloxera the vines are grown on their own roots, making it one of the few places in the world where this can still be accomplished successfully.

The vineyards are located on approximately the same latitude as Burgundy and Bordeaux. Obviously, allowance has to be made for climate and soil differences, but the precise importance of latitude for grape quality has yet to be fully explored. Some indication of the contribution the state's location makes to the wines may be drawn by comparing the style of Washington and California wines made with the Cabernet Sauvignon grape. Cabernet Sauvignon wines from California display a tremendous intensity of fruit and shortness of acidity. Washington Cabernet Sauvignons, while equally intense, show a greater balance between fruit and acid and a style closer to that which is achieved in Bordeaux with the same grape.

The principal white grape varieties grown are the White Riesling, Chardonnay, Chenin Blanc, Sauvignon Blanc and Gewürztraminer, while the main red varieties are Cabernet Sauvignon, Merlot and Grenache. Other varieties which have been successfully introduced include the Pinot Noir, Muscat, Semillon and Müller-Thurgau.

For a considerable number of years the only winery of significant size was Château Ste. Michelle which began planting vinifera and hybrid vines in 1970. Today, the firm has expanded to over five thousand acres of vines and three wineries, making it by far the largest wine operation in the state. In 1984 they produced about one and a half million gallons of wine and, through vineyard expansion, anticipate that within the next year their production will have increased to two and a half million gallons a year.

Vineyard in Washington state. As the state has never been affected by phylloxera, it is one of the few areas of the world where vines are grown on their own roots.

They operate Grandview Winery in the Yakima Valley, River Ridge in the Columbia River Valley and Headquarters Winery in the Seattle region. The firm produces consistently high quality wines and has been particularly successful with Riesling, Sauvignon Blanc and Fumé Blanc white wines, while their Merlot is a highly acclaimed red wine.

Château Ste. Michelle now has many worthy competitors, and vineyards have spread to every part of the state. Apart from the Yakima and Columbia valleys, the vine is now grown in the Walla Walla area in the south, and in the regions of metro Seattle, Spokane, Olympic Peninsula and Puget Sound to the north. While most of the newly emerged wineries are small family operations, one of the longer-established and larger wineries, Associated Vintners in Seattle, has built its reputation on a particularly outstanding dry and spicy Gewürztraminer.

These two major winery operations have received many awards for their wines. Several other Washington state wineries have also won acclaim in both national and international competitions. In the Yakima Valley, Hogue Cellars, Quail Run Vintners, Hinzerling Vineyards and Kiona Vineyards have all won awards for their wines, as has Leonetti Cellar in Walla Walla. In the Columbia Valley Preston Wine Cellars and Champs de Brionne Winery have produced medal-winning wines, as have Worden's Washington Winery, Arbor Crest and Latah Creek Cellars in the Spokane area. Demonstrating the quality that can be achieved in every part of the state, medals have also been awarded to wines from Haviland Vintners from the Seattle area, Neuharth Winery on the Olympic Peninsula and Mount Baker Vineyards and Snoqualmie Falls Winery of Puget Sound.

It is estimated that the total acreage in Washington suitable for grape growing is 150,000 acres. It will be many years, if ever, before that acreage can be put into production, but the rapid growth of the area would indicate that a substantial portion of that acreage will indeed become vineyards.

Washington state is very young in winemaking terms and, despite their successes to date, the winemakers of the area are still very much involved in experimentation. They are still trying to determine which vines perform best in which areas, a process which took centuries in Europe. It will not take the Washington vintners as much time to reach their conclusions because of the modern viticultural knowledge available to them, and their own determination to progress. They have also not yet established a consistent style. To a large extent they still allow the grapes to determine how the wines will turn out. Several winemakers, however, are beginning to juggle what nature gives them in an effort to establish well-defined winemaking guidelines such as those that exist in Europe and California. Where this search will lead remains to be seen, but the successes to date indicate a bright future for Washington state wines.

The rapidity with which progress can be made in Washington is perhaps best illustrated by a 1967 incident. André Tchelistcheff, the octogenarian dean of American winemakers who earned his reputation in California, tasted a Gewürztraminer that had been made in a basement by the late Phil Church, a University of Washington professor. Tchelistcheff pronounced the wine to be the finest Gewürztraminer produced in the United States. That was enough to convince Church and colleagues to begin marketing their wines and they sold their first in 1969 as Associated Vintners. It has since grown to be the fourth largest winery in the state. Associated is noted to this day for its bone dry, spicy Gewürztraminer — the wine which was responsible for the launching of the firm.

Expansion and experimentation, allied to the quality of wines already being produced, assure Washington wines a place on the world's wine map. They will be a force to be reckoned with in the future, even by the prestigious wines of California.

In Oregon the principal variety is Pinot Noir, with Chardonnay and White Riesling being the next most significant varieties. The cooler climate of Oregon has been found to allow winemakers to produce a Pinot Noir that is closer to the European style than is achieved in California, where this Burgundy grape has not been particularly successful.

An important aspect of the Oregon wine industry is that in 1977 it was able to convince the State Liquor Commission to enact wine laws that are much more exacting than the federal laws require. The labeling standards are particularly precise. It is illegal to use any terminology that refers to any geographical location such as Burgundy, Chablis, or Rhine. Likewise, grape varieties named on labels cannot carry any geographic inference. As a result, Gamay Beaujolais is named as Gamay and the term White Riesling is permissible, while Johannisberg Riesling is not.

If a grape is named on a label the wine in the bottle must be at least 90 per cent of the named variety. The exception to this rule is Cabernet Sauvignon where the minimum content is 75 per cent, but the other 25 per cent must be composed of other Bordeaux varieties.

Since 1981, it has also been illegal to raise the sugar level by more than 2 per cent before fermentation. In the best years chaptalization is not needed. The addition of water is completely banned.

The intent of this very rigid legislation is to create a quality image for the wines being produced in Oregon.

The vast majority of the state's wineries are located in the Willamette Valley and around Portland where the climate is cooler than in the other main areas to the south in the Umpqua and Rogue River Valleys.

It was, however, in the Umpqua Valley that the first vinifera vines were planted when Hillcrest Vineyard was established in 1963 by Richard Sommer. Since then, he has had considerable success in particular with White Riesling, Gewürztraminer and Cabernet Sauvignon.

Tualatin Vineyards in the North Willamette Valley is the state's largest producer of vinifera wines. Initially, they made their wines with grapes brought from Washington and Idaho, but now that their own plantings are mature they are growing their own grapes. Two interesting wines from this winery are a delicate Pinot Noir Rosé and a very attractive Muscat.

Although Oregon's wine industry is small, and likely to remain so, the emphasis on quality augurs for a bright future.

On the east coast one of the oldest wineries is Boordy Vineyard at Riverwood, Maryland which was established in the 1940s by Philip and Jocelyn Wagner to pioneer the growth of hybrid vines in the United States.

Since that time, the wine industries of Maryland and Virginia have experienced considerable growth. One of the most significant Maryland operations is Mowbray Wine Cellars to the northwest of Baltimore where the vineyards established by Dr. G. Hamilton Mowbray are planted with both hybrid and vinifera varieties.

Another winery completely committed to vinifera grapes is Byrd Vineyards which are located at the opening of the Catoctin Valley. Begun in 1972 by Bret Byrd, the vineyards and winery occupy about fifty acres. He has had considerable success with his Chardonnay in particular.

There is a healthy wine industry in Virginia where the Italian firm of Zonin purchased about eight hundred acres near Charlottesville in 1976 and began planting vinifera vineyards. Two years later a similar development took place with the arrival of Dr. Gerhard Guth from Hamburg, Germany. On his fifteen hundred acre farm near Culpeper he began planting vinifera, mostly Riesling.

Many Virginia growers have been attracted to the all-vinifera crosses developed in Germany. The German objective in propagating these crosses was to produce a grape strain that would be more dependable and earlier ripening than the Riesling but still produce fine wines. It appears that the Kerner variety has considerable promise and if the Virginia experiments are successful this variety may well be adopted by producers in other eastern states.

In New Hampshire, White Mountain Vineyards is making wines with hybrid grapes, while there are experimental plantings of vinifera in Connecticut. Massachusetts also has a small wine industry; one of its wineries, Chicama Vineyards, which concentrates on vinifera, is located on the island of Martha's Vineyard. Rhode Island also has a developing wine business, and both vinifera and hybrid varieties are being grown.

In Pennsylvania the greatest grape-growing activity was based on the native Concord variety which was used for making juice rather than wine. That picture has changed dramatically, and there are now over two dozen wineries making wines with both hybrid and vinifera grapes.

The first of these wineries was begun in 1963 when Melvin Gordon planted his ten-acre Conestoga Vineyards. In 1978 the wine industry received permission from the state, which controls all wine sales, to sell their own wines. This freedom was all the encouragement several people needed to open wineries and begin a healthy growth of the industry.

There are also a few small wineries near the shore of Lake Erie in Pennsylvania and Ohio. The lake creates a micro-climate that makes the weather milder than is the case further inland.

Wine producing has expanded considerably in the Midwest, and besides Ohio, wines are now made in Michigan, Indiana, Illinois and Missouri. Michigan has long been the largest wine-producing state in the Midwest, with a number of large and small wineries which are mostly located in the southwest area of the state near Lake Michigan. Two of the larger operations are the Bronte Champagne and Wines Co. and Warner Vineyards. Both of these firms have introduced both vinifera and hybrid grapes to their plantings in an effort to improve the quality of their wines. In common with these large producers, many of the small wineries have also concentrated their efforts on vinifera and hybrids.

Western Ohio remains one of the Midwest's largest growers of the native variety Catawba, mainly used in the production of fortified wines in the Sherry style. The growers, however, are beginning to give serious attention to the introduction of improved grape varieties.

The same is true in Illinois, Indiana and Missouri, where wine production has come to depend on finer grapes.

The distinction of being the Midwest's largest winery goes to the Mogen David Wine Corporation of Chicago which is best known for the production of kosher wines made with native labrusca grapes.

In the southern and western states experimental plantings have been made almost everywhere from Florida to New Mexico. The grape has even spread as far afield as Hawaii, where vinifera plantings have been made.

The experimental hybrid and vinifera plantings in Texas and Arkansas are particularly encouraging. The largest winery operation in the Southwest is Wiederkehr Wine Cellars at Altus, Arkansas. Their production is still very limited, but they have had success with several vinifera varieties, particularly White and Johannisberg Riesling.

CANADA

THE FIRST REFERENCE to wine making in Canada occurred in about 1535 when Jesuit missionaries made sacramental wines using the wild native grapes in what is now Quebec. It is generally considered, however, that Johann Schiller, who planted a 20 acre vineyard on his property at Cooksville, Ontario around 1811 was the first commercial wine maker in Canada.

The Ontario wine industry today is centered in two areas. The most important is the Niagara Peninsula, where the vineyards are located in the area just east of Hamilton to Niagara Falls. An escarpment runs the length of the peninsula, and vines are grown both above the escarpment and on its slopes which face Lake Ontario in the north. The second area is close to Lake Erie in Essex and Kent counties, and is centered around the towns of Blenheim and Leamington.

The modern Canadian wine business was born in 1873 when George Barnes opened a winery at St. Catharines with the longish name of The Ontario Grape Growing and Wine Manufacturing Company. Today, the winery, which is the oldest continuously run wine-making business in Canada, is more simply named Barnes Wines.

But Barnes was soon joined by Thomas G. Bright, who opened a winery in Toronto in 1874 named the Niagara Falls Wine Company. Sixteen years later the company did move to the town of Niagara Falls, where they are located to this day.

Wineries began to spring up in the area between Toronto and Niagara Falls, and after a series of mergers and takeovers, the firms of Château-Gai and Jordan emerged.

In September 1916, the Ontario Legislature passed the Ontario Temperance Act, which was similar to the soon-to-follow Prohibition in the United States. But Ontario's vociferous grape growers lobbied the government, with the result that native wines were exempted from the act. Wineries had to obtain permits from the Board of Licence Commissioners who, it seems, were prepared to issue permits to anyone who asked, because by the time the act was rescinded in 1927, there were 57 wine-making operations in existence.

There were some rather bizarre aspects to this situation. It was legal to sell wine only at the wineries themselves, and even then only a minimum of five gallons or two case lots could be sold. So-called wineries sprang up overnight in the oddest and most ill-equipped conditions. Barns, basements and even a former pig pen were all used to house wine-making operations. The vast amounts of wine being made were doctored by the many unscrupulous and unskilled license holders whose only objective was to make a fast dollar in what was a captive market. Their existence began to cause concern. In 1928 the government created the Liquor Control Board of Ontario to set and maintain quality standards and to market wines and spirits. Today, the LCBO controls all wine and spirit sales in the province, except those that are sold through stores owned by the wineries.

Gradually, order emerged from the chaos. Brights and Jordan, in particular, bought up several of the spurious wine licenses, and the number of wineries dropped from 51 to eight. The reduction in numbers, however, did not suddenly result in the remaining wineries producing good-quality wines. In fact, the majority of their wines were high-alcohol, Sherry- or Port-style wines; even their table wines were high in alcohol and not very palatable.

Brights changed hands and came under the ownership of Harry Hatch who brought chemist and wine maker Vicomte Adhemar de Chaunac de Lanzac from the firm's Quebec plant to Niagara Falls. De Chaunac made experimental batches of dry table wines with Catawba and Delaware grapes, and Hatch was so pleased with the results that in the mid-1930s, he gave de Chaunac a budget of $3 million to pursue the propagation of some of the New York and French hybrids in Bright's vineyards. These later came under the direction of George Hostetter. In 1946, the first vinifera plantings were established.

Thousands of vines were planted and, not surprisingly, there were more failures than successes, but a number of vines finally emerged and yielded better wine-making grapes that could survive the severe Canadian winter. Sadly, however, these experiments did not result in a marked improvement in Ontario's wines. Indeed, when Andrés, first established in British Columbia, reopened the Beau Chatel winery at Winona in 1970, they

Opposite: Headquarters of Inniskillin Wines, Niagara-on-the-Lake, Ontario.

Above: *Vineyard of Barnes Wines in St. Catharines, Ontario.*

Below: *Barnes offices, established in 1873.*

caused a remarkable change of course in the Ontario industry.

Light sparkling wines with only seven per cent alcohol had been on the Ontario market for some years, but in 1971 Andrés launched a pink, fizzy wine of this style called Baby Duck. It was so successfully promoted that it earned record sales. It also earned the envy of the other wineries, with the result that the market was soon flooded with this type of wine, to the point where there were almost 80 of them. They all had two things in common. They all bore the name of a bird or an animal and formed what can best be described as a menagerie of wine. They all also tasted very sweet.

But while the large established wineries were battling it out in the pop wine market, other people were formulating completely different plans.

The first to arrive on the scene was Inniskillin Wines at Niagara-on-the-Lake, which was granted a winery license in 1974. It was the first such license issued since 1929, and its owners, Donald Ziraldo

and Karl Kaiser, had a different vision than anyone before them. Their plans were to operate a cottage winery, producing only wines made with hybrid and vinifera grapes. They were also determined to make wines of high quality.

In their first year, they made only three wines. There were 500 bottles each of Maréchal Foch and De Chaunac, and 5,000 bottles of a wine named Vin Nouveau, which was a blend of the other two wines plus some Chelois and Chancellor. They were all red wines because no white grapes had been available. The wines were made by Karl Kaiser in a tin-roofed barn on Ziraldo's farm, which was to be home for the winery until 1978, when they moved to their present facility, a thoroughly modern winery housed in a pretty, Spanish-American style building.

Inniskillin's wines quickly gained a high reputation and wide acceptance by the public. This led to two consequences. Firstly, the large, established wineries suddenly realized they had been left at the post, and they too began serious attempts to produce superior wines. Secondly, several other wineries with the same high ideals as Inniskillin emerged.

The first actually received its license only 24 days after Inniskillin. The Podamer Champagne Company located at Beamsville, and the owner, Karl Podamer, whose family was in the sparkling wine business in Hungary, began producing sparkling wines of a high standard. A separate label, Montravin Cellars, has since been established; it produces still table wines.

Then, in rapid succession, more cottage wineries were established. Charal Winery and Vineyards opened in 1975; Château des Charmes came into existence in 1978 at Niagara-on-the-Lake; Newark, now Hillebrand Estates Wines, also at Niagara-on-the-Lake, was begun in 1979.

The newcomers included Château des Charmes, operated by Paul Bosc, an Algerian who received his formal training at the University of Dijon and

White grapes for wine making have been cultivated successfully in Ontario for over 40 years, but only in recent years have the vine plantings been expanded on a commercial scale.

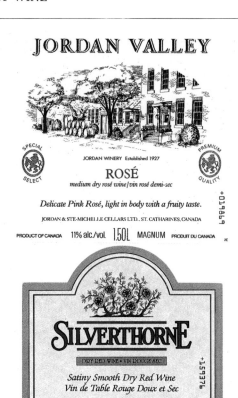

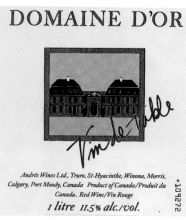

later worked in the Burgundy vineyards. Like Inniskillin, Bosc began in a barn but has now built a well-equipped modern winery. He too concentrates only on producing wines from vinifera and hybrid grapes. He has been particularly successful with Chardonnay from his own extensive vineyard holdings, and has made some outstanding wines with that grape.

More recently, a cottage winery has opened on Pelee Island, where 100 acres of vinifera vines have been planted. Ewald Rief, who supplied grapes to Inniskillin, has opened the fourth Niagara-on-the-Lake cottage winery, called Vineland Estate, and French Oak Vineyards at Beamsville has plans to construct a winery there.

On a larger scale, a group of Italian businessmen in Windsor opened a large winery, Collio Wines, at Harrow with a capacity of 250,000 gallons. But possibly the most significant indication for the future of Ontario wines was the establishment in 1985 of the Paul Masson Winery at Beamsville. Owned by the Canadian-based firm of Seagram, the Paul Masson name was chosen because of its reputation. The initial production bodes well for the future.

In the past decade, the Ontario wine industry has made great strides, but there are still no strict wine laws and the quality of wines depends entirely upon the integrity of the wine makers.

The other major Canadian wine-producing region is British Columbia. A much younger industry than Ontario's, its modern vineyards have been mainly planted with hybrid and vinifera varieties.

The British Columbia wine industry did not really start until the 1930s. The most significant firm to emerge was Calona Wines at Kelowna. Opened in 1932 and originally named Domestic Wines and By-Products Ltd., the winery survived the Depression through the sale of sacramental wines and, in fact, it was not until the 1950s that the business began to boom.

The initial idea behind the firm was to make wine from the surplus apple crop, which was prodigious. However, after only two years, the owners abandoned that course and began making wines with grapes brought from California. This is rather ironic, considering that Calona was located in the Okanagan Valley, which has since become

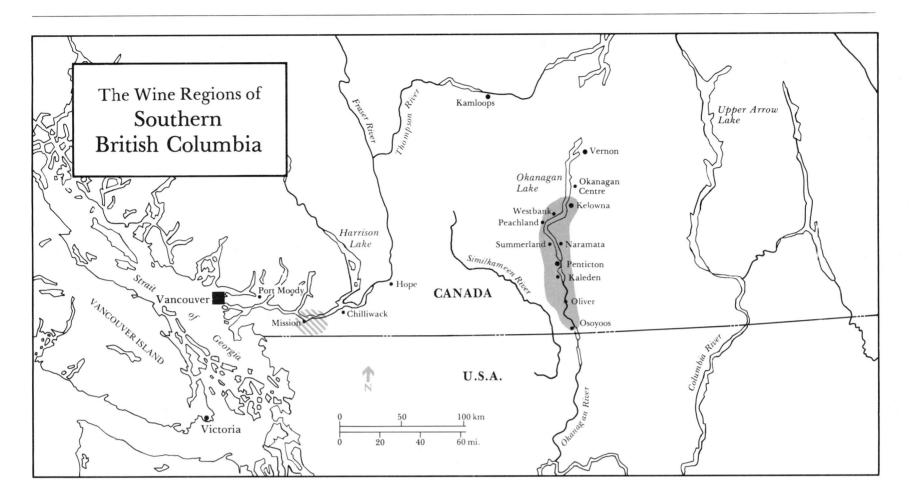

The Wine Regions of
**Southern
British Columbia**

one of the prime grape-growing districts in British Columbia.

The Calona example was soon followed by Victoria Wines and Growers' Wine Company, which were located on Vancouver Island. These wineries continued for a considerable time to make wines with California grapes, but began augmenting them with locally grown grapes, successfully creating the myth that they were actually producing domestic wines.

The wine industry in British Columbia remained fairly stagnant, and by 1960 there were less than 600 acres of vines. But in that year the provincial government passed a law requiring 25 per cent of the wines to be made with locally grown grapes. It was also stated, however, that by 1962 the requirement would be 50 per cent, and that this would rise to 65 per cent in 1965. It has now climbed to 80 per cent. The effect, however, was that farmers rushed to plant vines, and in four years the acreage had risen to more than 2,000 acres.

Another effect of the legislation was that new wineries began to emerge. Andrew Peller established Andrés Wines at Port Moody in 1961.

In 1967, a firm briefly called Southern Okanagan Wines. opened; today it is Casabello Wines of Penticton. In the same year Mission Hill Winery was built at Westbank overlooking Lake Okanagan.

Growers' Wines Cooperatives and Victoria Wineries merged and changed their name to Castle Wines. Originally owned by the Imperial Tobacco Company, Castle Wines was sold by Imperial in 1973 to Carling O'Keefe, and then became Ste-Michelle Wines in 1974, a subsidiary of Jordan and Ste-Michelle Cellars Ltd. Jordan has since moved the entire operation to the mainland and located at Surrey, south of Vancouver.

The latest large winery to locate in British Columbia is Brights, who built a facility at Oliver to make wine from grapes grown by the Osoyoos Indians in their Inkameep vineyards.

In 1979, the first cottage winery, Claremont, opened at Peachland and in the next few years other cottage wineries opened in the Okanagan Valley under the names of Sumac Ridge, Uniacke Cellars and Gray Monk.

Mission Hill went through a dark period when it was acquired by a construction magnate who

Overleaf: *Vineyard of Calona Wines sits amidst a typical British Columbia landscape — water, mountains and evergreens.*

Autumn colors provide a study in contrast in the Okanagan Valley.

Fermentation vats at Calona Wines, Kelowna, British Columbia.

renamed it Uncle Ben's Gourmet Winery, but that business failed. The winery has now been reorganized, and its original name has been restored.

The infant British Columbia wine business has already produced some very pleasant wines from hybrid and vinifera grapes. Okanagan Riesling, Johannisberg Riesling, Gewürztraminer, Chenin Blanc and Chardonnay are responsible for the best white wines, while the reds are mostly made with Maréchal Foch and De Chaunac grapes. Efforts are now going ahead to establish Pinor Noir and Cabernet Sauvignon vines.

A great deal of wine produced in British Columbia is still made with grapes brought from California, Oregon and Washington, but as the acreage of local vineyards increases, the province's wines may finally truly become local wines.

There are wineries located in several other Canadian provinces, but they mainly make wines from imported grapes, grape juice or concentrates.

One astonishing exception is Grand Pré Wines at Grand Pré, Nova Scotia, where Roger Dial grows vines in the Annapolis Valley. Although it is a tiny operation, it is particularly interesting because Dial has obtained some Russian Amurensis vines which are doing well in the Maritime climate. The Michurnitz and Severnyi are two red varieties that do very well. Altogether he has planted 60 hybrid and vinifera varieties and is looking ahead to making wines from Chardonnay, Riesling and Gewürztraminer grapes once his vines mature.

MEXICO

THIS COUNTRY has the distinction of being the first in the New World where the vine was planted. This occurred barely twenty-five years after the first voyage of Columbus. Cortez, obviously a wine lover, ordered every Spanish grant holder to plant ten vines for every Indian living on the land for five successive years. His scheme did not succeed.

It was not until the late seventeenth century, when missions were established at Loreto in Baja, California, that wine began to be produced regularly in Mexico.

Today, the vine is grown in the border states of Baja California, Chihuahua and Coahuila, and further south around the towns of Aguascalientes and Querétaro. The town of Paras, on the hills west of Monterey, is the leading vineyard center.

Red wines are produced from Cabernet Sauvignon, Cabernet Franc, Pinot Noir, Grenache, Mission, Gamay and Carignan grapes, while whites are made with such varieties as Sémillon, Johannisberg Riesling, Pinot Blanc, Chenin Blanc, Palomino and Rosa de Peru.

Mexican wines were rather undistinguished for a long time, tending to be high in alcohol and short on flavor. In recent years, however, several firms have drawn on assistance from California wine makers and technology. This has led to the production of a much higher standard of wines, the best of which are extremely pleasant drinking. The wines made with the Johannisberg Riesling grape, in particular, can be very attractive. Considerable progress has been made towards the production of lighter red wines, with those using the Gamay currently being most pleasant.

As the climate in Mexico is generally too hot for the production of top-quality grapes, it is unlikely that the country will ever produce great wines, but the evidence is there to show that they can turn out very acceptable everyday wines. A small amount of Mexican wine is exported, mainly to the United States and Canada.

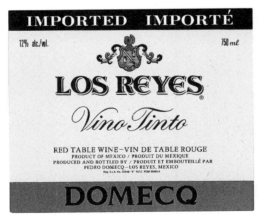

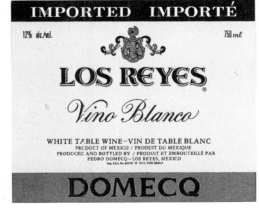

South America

THERE ARE a number of South American countries that produce wine. Their combined total output constitutes about one-tenth of the world's wine, but only three countries — Argentina, Chile and Brazil — are substantial producers; of these, Argentina and Chile are significant exporters. Brazil, however, has recently begun to address export markets seriously, particularly those in North America.

ARGENTINA

FOR MANY YEARS, Argentina was by far the largest wine producer in South America, and was responsible for more than half of all the wine grown on the sub-continent.

There are three principal wine regions in Argentina: Mendoza, San Juan and Rio Negro. Of these, Mendoza is the most important.

The vine was introduced into Argentina by the Spaniards, but it is only in the last one hundred years that serious cultivation has been undertaken.

Mendoza lies close to the Chilean border at about the same latitude as Santiago. Located in the foothills of the Andes, it was a huge, arid desert that had little plant life except where the rivers, fed by the melting Andean snows, meandered across its expanse.

It was not the Argentinians, however, who changed the face of Mendoza. Towards the end of the nineteenth century a large number of Italian immigrants arrived in the country. It was they who toiled on the land and used the rivers to irrigate it.

Initially, they concentrated on producing grains, vegetables and fruit; but it was not very long before they began experimenting with grapes. Given their Italian heritage, that is not too surprising.

In the Mendoza region and the San Juan region immediately to its north, many table and raisin grapes are grown, but the wine grapes are European noble varieties. Red wines are made with Cabernet Sauvignon, Malbec, Pinot Noir, Gamay, Barbera and Sangiovese, while white wines are made from Chardonnay, Sauvignon, Sémillon, Riesling, Muscadelle, and several Muscats and Palomino for Sherry-type wines and brandies. One legacy of the Spaniard missionaries is a considerable acreage of the native Criolla Grande grape, which is related to the Mission grape found in California.

To the south of Mendoza, the vineyards of Rio Negro produce the country's best white and sparkling wines. The region is at the equivalent southern hemisphere latitude as Champagne and some of the German wine regions, and this circumstance is reflected in the quality of the sparkling wines.

Argentina's Instituto Nacional de Vitivinicultura keeps a strict control on the massive wine in-

Tasting best reservas. Wine making in South America was practiced by Spanish colonials, but the modern industry has developed only in the last century.

Opposite: Entrance gate to Viña Concha y Toro's main cellar in Pirque, Chile.

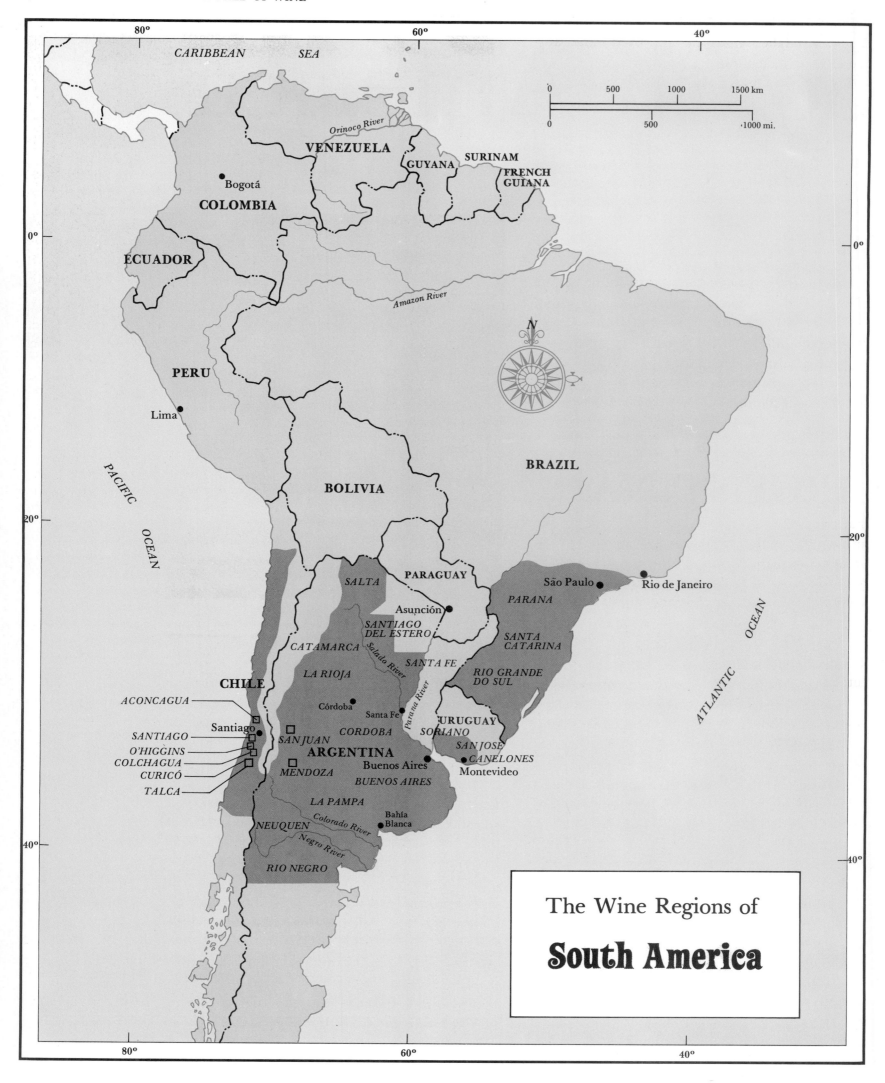

CARIBBEAN   SEA

Orinoco River

VENEZUELA

GUYANA   SURINAM

FRENCH
GUIANA

• Bogotá

COLOMBIA

0°

ECUADOR

Amazon River

N

PERU

PACIFIC

• Lima

BRAZIL

OCEAN

BOLIVIA

20°

PARAGUAY

SALTA   São Paulo •   • Rio de Janeiro

PARANA

Asunción •

*SANTIAGO
DEL ESTERO*   *SANTA
CATARINA*

CATAMARCA   *Salado River*   *SANTA FE*

LA RIOJA   *RIO GRANDE
DO SUL*

CHILE

ACONCAGUA   Córdoba •   URUGUAY
CORDOBA   *SORIANO*

SANTIAGO   Santiago •   Santa Fe •

SAN JUAN   *SAN JOSE*

O'HIGGINS   ARGENTINA   *CANELONES*

COLCHAGUA   Buenos Aires •   Montevideo •

CURICÓ   *MENDOZA*

TALCA   *BUENOS AIRES*

LA PAMPA

Colorado River   Bahía
Blanca •

NEUQUEN   *Negro River*

RIO NEGRO

ATLANTIC

OCEAN

0   500   1000   1500 km

0   500   1000 mi.

The Wine Regions of

South America

80°   60°   40°

dustry. All labels must be approved, and any claims to a vintage must be authenticated.

The largest part of Argentina's wines are of good, sound quality, but none of them is truly great. The vast majority of the wine produced is consumed locally — Argentinians regard wine as part of their diet — but the small quantities that are exported tend to be the country's premium wines.

CHILE

T HE VINE arrived in Chile along with the Spanish colonists in the early part of the sixteenth century, but it was not until the middle of the nineteenth century that the modernization of the country's vineyards was begun.

The truth about the coming of the vine to Chile has been lost in the dim early history of the country. There is some conjecture regarding the source of the earliest vines. Some theories contend that they were native to the land, but that seems unlikely. It has also been suggested that vines were brought from the Canary Islands or Spain, two possibilities with considerable credibility. By far the most far-fetched proposition suggests that vines were raised from the seeds of raisins, a favorite food of the Conquistadors. More likely, however, is that Catholic missionaries to Chile brought cuttings of vines with them.

Credit for being the first person to cultivate the vine goes to Don Francisco Aguirre, who planted vineyards in the region of Copiapo, some 500 miles north of Santiago. The first harvest from these vines was gathered in 1551.

It is also known that the modern Chilean wine industry began in 1851 when Don Silvestre Ochagavia enlisted the services of a French viticulturalist, M. Bertrand. He brought the first cuttings of the classic European vines with him and thus began laying the foundation of the Chilean wine industry, which today produces the best of South America's wines.

The Chilean vineyards are located in the foothills of the Andes between Copiapo and Concepcion, a distance of some 870 miles. There are four principal wine-producing regions.

Vines flower in a vineyard in Longué, Chile.

Vines held aloft by stakes sometimes resemble fruit trees.

The North-Central District covers the provinces of Atacama and Coquimbo. There is very little rain, especially in the northern part of the district, and cultivation of the vine is restricted to areas where artificial irrigation is possible. The majority of the vineyards are located on the slopes of valleys, with those in the valley of the Elqui River being held in the highest regard. The predominant grapes in the district are several varieties of Moscatel. Much of the wine is distilled to make a favorite Chilean liquor, Pisco, unique in that it is the only

Overleaf: Panoramic view of Cachapoal Vineyard in the Rapel Valley, Chile.

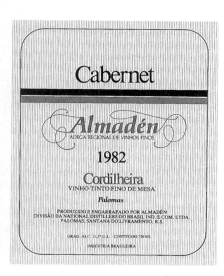

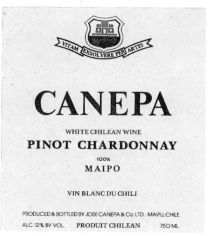

denomination that is protected under Chilean law.

The Central Valley is the heart of Chile's wine industry and extends through the provinces of Aconcagua, Valparaiso, Santiago, O'Higgins, Colchagua, Curicó and Talca. The red wine varieties are almost entirely Cabernet Sauvignon, Cabernet Franc, Côt Rouge, Merlot and Verdot, while the white varieties are Sémillon, Sauvignon, Chardonnay and Riesling. The area of the Aconcagua Valley produces almost 80 per cent of the country's grapes for export, but there are virtually no wine-producing vineyards left in the district. Within the irrigated area, the wines of the Maipo River Valley and the sector of Lontué Molina are considered the best. The unirrigated vineyards of the district are on the coastal hills between the Maule River in the north and the latitude of the city of Viña del Mar in the south. The rainfall in the area is just enough to allow the vine to be cultivated on "dry" land.

The South Central Valley extends from the Maule River in the north and the Bió-Bió in the south. The northern part of this district is really an extension of the Central Valley, but the main grape variety is the País, which produces some of Chile's poorest red wines. White wines are another matter, as the district grows Sauvignon and Sémillon grapes of good quality, which in turn yield excellent wines. Again, this region has an area of unirrigated vineyards on the coastal hills. The País also dominates there for red wines, but their quality is far higher than that of the irrigated vineyards. White wines of very good quality are also made with the Sauvignon, Riesling and Moscatel grapes.

The Southern District, located to the south of the city of Concepcion and stretching as far as the Cautin River, is barely suited to the vine. The quality of the wines has always been erratic, and the district is gradually phasing out its vineyards.

The actual making of wine follows European tradition exactly, almost to the point where it is more European than the Europeans are today. Primary fermentation is carried out in large open vats, and the wine is then racked into small casks to continue its progress. White wines are usually bottled after twelve to eighteen months, while reds are generally aged for thirty months prior to bottling.

Only premium wines are actually bottled, both

for the home market and for export. The majority of domestic sales are simple Tinto or Blanco wines which are sold through grocery stores in wicker-covered demijohns containing between five and ten liters of wine. It is, in fact, a rather formalized version of the situation in Italy, where people take their demijohns to the local winery to be filled.

Chile has strict wine laws which are enforced by the Internal Revenue Department. Everything from the planting of the vines to their care and the wine-making process is all strictly controlled.

At one time, alcoholism was a serious problem for Chile. To overcome this, laws were passed limiting domestic sales to 60 liters per capita. The result of this is that Chile is constantly seeking new and expanded markets for the balance of its wines, which are readily accepted in considerable quantities in European markets. North America has been comparatively slow to import large quantities of Chilean wines — a pity, as they are of very high quality. Varietal characteristics are preserved in the premium wines, which are of a quality and stature to rival the best that Europe has to offer.

In many respects the heavier reds bear a resemblance to the best wines of Spain's Rioja region, but the whites have a delicacy and finesse that is not matched by the whites of Spain.

As far as the wine lover is concerned, Chilean wines are undoubtedly amongst the best values for money that can be found anywhere.

Picking Cabernet Sauvignon grapes at Pirque Vineyard in the Maipo Valley, Chile.

The wine industries of Argentina, Brazil and Chile are now as modern as any in the world. Above: Stainless-steel fermentation tanks in Brazil. Below: A mechanized bottling line.

BRAZIL

As with most South American countries, it was colonists who introduced the vine. In the case of Brazil, the Portuguese brought vines from the Azores in the mid-sixteenth century and established the first vineyards in what is now the interior state of São Paulo.

Coffee and sugar, however, became the country's main exports, and the wine industry was perceived to be of minor importance.

It was an influx of thousands of Italian immigrants, beginning around 1870, that caused the development of the southern region of Rio Grande do Sul. These immigrants planted their vineyards around the communities of Garibaldi, Bento Gonçalves and Caxias do Sul, which today are Brazil's major wine-producing centers.

Finally, around 1960 the Brazilian government began to take a serious approach to the wine industry, and established a public school at Bento Gonçalves for the training of oenologists and other wine specialists. They also opened a research center for the purpose of determining the best grape varieties for the production of quality wines.

This activity led in turn to considerable expansion of the vineyards in the communities already mentioned and also in the area of Flores de Cunha.

In the mid-1970s a number of multinationals began to establish themselves in Brazil. Among them were Hueblein, Möet et Chandon, Cinzano and Martini and Rossi. One of their major influences was to switch the majority of vines back to the proven European varieties instead of the American varieties, which constituted almost ninety per cent of the vines at that time.

The main red varieties now in production include Cabernet Sauvignon, Merlot, Gamay, Bonarda, Barbera and Nebbiolo. The most significant white varieties are Trebbiano, Riesling, Saint-Emilion, Sauvignon, Moscato and Niagara.

A full range of red, white, rosé and sparkling wines is now being produced in Brazil. The best in each category is comparable to the best European wines made from the same varieties. With Möet et Chandon, Cinzano and Martini and Rossi involved, it is hardly surprising that considerable

Below: Distant mesa broods over Almadén vineyard in Palomas, Brazil.

emphasis has been placed on the production of sparkling wines. These include Champagne-style as well as others made in the style of Asti Spumante.

Until recent years, Brazil has made only a minor effort to enter the wine export market. This was partly due to the quality of the wines, but consumption on the home market also pretty well absorbed the total production. Vineyard expansion and upgrading of quality have changed those circumstances, and the Brazilians are now very actively pursuing exports, particularly in North America, and are gaining favorable attention there and in other markets. Where quality relates to price, Brazilian wines represent extremely good value.

URUGUAY

A COMPARATIVE NEWCOMER to the wine scene, Uruguay's vineyards were established around 1890. The main wine regions of San José, Canelones, Florida, Soriano, Maldonado and Paysanou are all located around the capital city of Montevideo.

The main red grape varieties are Cabernet Sauvignon, Cabernet Franc, Barbera, Nebbiolo and Vidiella, while white wines are made from the Sémillon, Pinot Blanc and Isabella grapes.

Uruguayan wines, which tend to be high in alcohol, are rarely exported.

PERU

THE VINE has been established in Peru since the sixteenth century. The majority of vines grown are all of the classic Vitis vinifera family.

The vineyards are located around the capital, Lima, and to the south of that city at Ica, Arequipa and Moquegua. The majority of the wines are white and are relatively neutral in that they are dry with little bouquet.

Most Peruvian wines are consumed within the country and are only occasionally found outside its boundaries.

COLOMBIA

THE VINEYARD area of Colombia is small and covers only about 400 acres. These are planted with Vitis vinifera vines from which red, white and rosé wines are produced.

A number of wines are also made based on such tropical fruits as bananas. The wines made from the grape tend to be strong and sweet.

In common with many of South America's small countries, the wines of Colombia rarely venture beyond its own borders.

BOLIVIA

A LANDLOCKED country, Bolivia's vineyards are largely planted in Vitis vinifera vines brought from Peru. Centered around the capital of La Paz, the wines produced are rather undistinguished and are mostly consumed in the home market.

VENEZUELA

LOCATED ON THE north coast of South America, Venezuela has a small wine industry centered around the capital of Caracas. The vines are almost all of the Vitis vinifera group. The wines produced are not outstanding, and again, are seldom seen beyond their homeland.

Above: *Brazil's vineyards produce some 55 million gallons of wine annually.* Below: Vitis vinifera *varieties were introduced into Brazil following World War I. Among the red grapes, the Bonardo variety succeeds best, but Barbera, Cabernet Sauvignon, Nebbiolo and others are also grown.*

Australia and New Zealand

THE FIRST VINES arrived in Australia along with the first settlers. Captain Arthur Phillip arrived in New South Wales in 1788 with eleven small ships and just over 1,000 men, women and children, including convicts and freemen. His primary assignment was to establish a British penal colony in New South Wales, but there were grapevine cuttings and grape seeds amongst the cargo. Why the leader of a British expedition would have thought of bringing vines with him remains a mystery, but irrespective of his reasons, every wine lover should be grateful to him because he gave birth to one of the best New World wine industries.

Phillip went on the become the first Governor and also the country's first vigneron. He planted his vines roughly where the Botanical Gardens are now located in Sydney. Although he did not remain long in Australia, ill-health causing him to return to England in 1792, his contribution to the beginnings of the Australian wine industry cannot be denied.

NEW SOUTH WALES

MANY PIONEERS made significant contributions to the encouragement and expansion of vineyards. The first truly significant area to be opened up was the Hunter Valley which, even today, remains one of Australia's better regions.

Generally referred to as the Lower Hunter to differentiate it from the area to the northwest near Musswellbrook, it has a small output, accounting for only about one per cent of the national production, but the Hunter Valley has long enjoyed a good reputation. The persistence of one man, Murray Tyrrell, finally resulted in the emergence of some excellent Chardonnays. The area also produces some very fine wines with the Pinot Noir and a wide range of grapes including Shiraz, Grenache, Cabernet Sauvignon, Verdelho, Trebbiano, and Sémillon. Sémillon is also called Hunter River Riesling.

One of the valley's wine producers is also one of the country's largest. Lindemans began in the Hunter Valley when Henry John Lindemans, who was a British surgeon, moved to Australia in 1840 and established his first vineyard at Cawarra in 1843. A disastrous fire wiped out his first winery in 1851, and Lindemans went to work as a surgeon and miner in the Victorian gold fields. His fortunes replenished, he returned to Cawarra, rebuilt his winery and expanded the vineyards. In 1870 he opened a head office in Sydney. He also expanded his operation by purchasing properties in the Murray River area at Corowa. When Lindemans died in 1881, the management of the firm was taken over by his son Charles, who continued to expand the business. The pattern of expansion by takeovers continued, and the firm's holdings spread throughout New South Wales and South Australia. Then in 1971 they themselves were taken over by the Phillip Morris tobacco company. The firm is still in a constant state of expansion.

Two other giant firms, Penfolds and McWilliam's, have had holdings in the Hunter Valley since 1904 and 1932 respectively, but both companies began their operations in other districts.

A relative newcomer to the Hunter Valley is Hungerford Hill Vineyards, founded in 1967. In preparing the ground, they introduced a water-injection system, a technique now used widely in

Opposite: Wyndham Estate Wines, New South Wales.

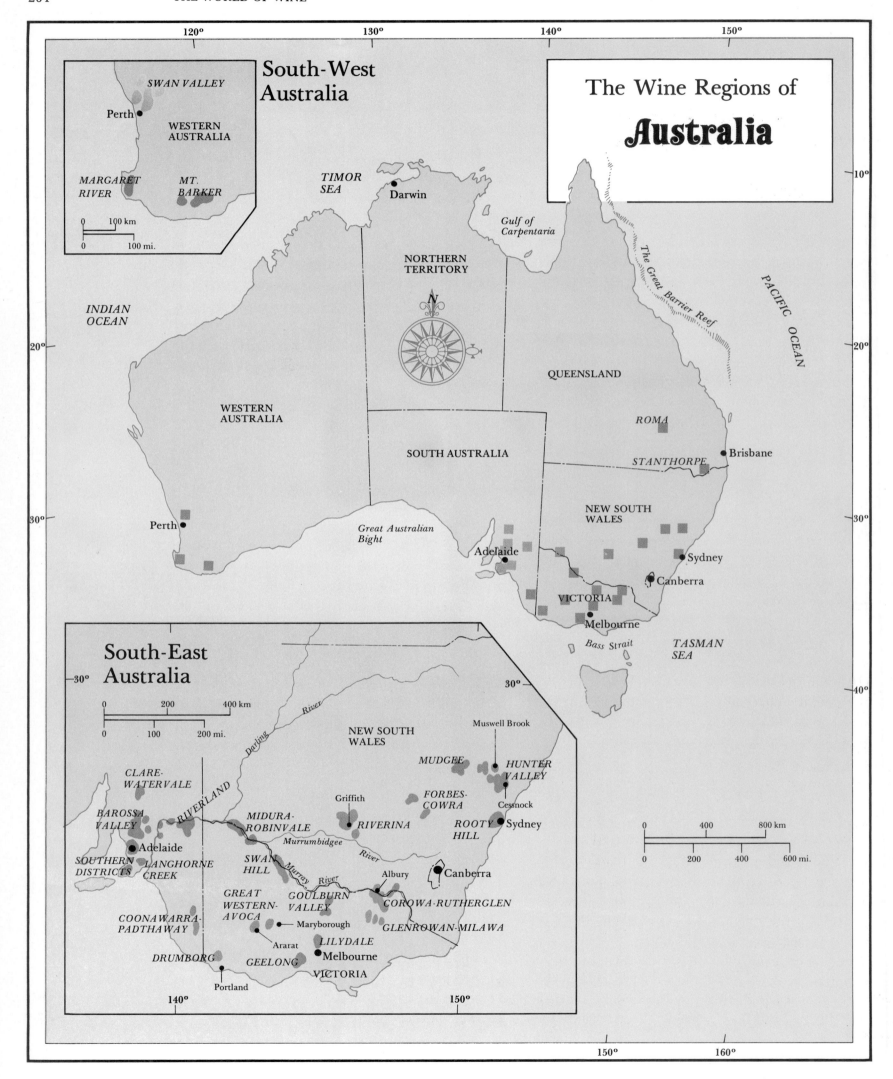

South-West Australia

SWAN VALLEY

Perth

WESTERN
AUSTRALIA

MARGARET
RIVER

MT.
BARKER

0   100 km

0   100 mi.

The Wine Regions of
Australia

TIMOR
SEA

Darwin

Gulf of
Carpentaria

The Great Barrier Reef

PACIFIC OCEAN

INDIAN
OCEAN

N

NORTHERN
TERRITORY

WESTERN
AUSTRALIA

QUEENSLAND

ROMA

SOUTH AUSTRALIA

STANTHORPE

Brisbane

NEW SOUTH
WALES

Perth

Great Australian
Bight

Adelaide

Sydney

Canberra

VICTORIA

Melbourne

TASMAN
SEA

Bass Strait

South-East
Australia

30°

0   200   400 km

0   100   200 mi.

Darling River

NEW SOUTH
WALES

Muswell Brook

CLARE-
WATERVALE

RIVERLAND

MUDGEE

HUNTER
VALLEY

Griffith

FORBES-
COWRA

BAROSSA
VALLEY

MIDURA-
ROBINVALE

Cessnock

RIVERINA

ROOTY
HILL

Sydney

Adelaide

Murrumbidgee

Murray River

SOUTHERN
DISTRICTS

LANGHORNE
CREEK

SWAN
HILL

Albury

Canberra

GREAT
WESTERN-
AVOCA

GOULBURN
VALLEY

COROWA-RUTHERGLEN

COONAWARRA-
PADTHAWAY

Maryborough

GLENROWAN-MILAWA

DRUMBORG

Ararat

LILYDALE

Melbourne

GEELONG

VICTORIA

Portland

0   400   800 km

0   200   400   600 mi.

140°

150°

120°   130°   140°   150°

150°   160°

10°

20°

30°

40°

Lindemans Hunter River Winery and facilities, Pokolbin, New South Wales.

the region. They have also installed a dam with a 110 million gallon capacity that can be used in case of drought. The company has a total of 1,000 acres, most of which is now planted with such grapes as Shiraz, Cabernet Sauvignon and Sémillon. They too have expanded beyond the valley and now have a winery at Buronga near the New South Wales border, and in South Australia, where they acquired Reynella Wines.

The Griffith area in the southwest of the state is also known as the Murrumbidgee Irrigation Area, but the wine growers prefer it to be called Riverina. The area is huge and produces about 75 per cent of the state's wine. The development of the area began only after 1906, when the New South Wales government authorized construction of a dam on the Murrumbidgee River. When the waters are released, they flow for 240 miles along the old river bed before being diverted into the irrigation canals on which the area depends for its fertility.

The first firm to arrive in the area was McWilliam's, who had first planted vines at Corowa on the Murray River. Almost before the main canal was completed, McWilliam's bought two 50-acre parcels of land in 1912 and planted them with vines. In 1917 McWilliam's built their first winery at Hanwood, and three years later constructed a second one near Griffith. Later a distillery and sparkling wine cellar were added.

Initially, the common perception was that good wines could not be produced in an irrigated area, and some of the early wine-making efforts tended to confirm that belief. But through the efforts of McWilliam's, that image is changing rapidly. The grape yields are very high, the berries tend to be very plump, and the wines are usually light. But the wine makers in the area have adopted the most

One of McWilliam's vineyards in the Riverina area of New South Wales.

awakening of interest in the production of table wines. So far it appears that the Victoria part of the region holds the greatest promise.

The Upper Hunter area, centered around Muswellbrook, presented quite a puzzle for many years. Many of the wineries seemed to be trying to imitate their more famous neighbors in the Hunter Valley, but in recent years they have struck an individuality, particularly with white wines made with the Chardonnay, Rhine Riesling and Gewürztraminer. These wines are, in fact, superior to any wines produced in the lower Hunter.

SOUTH AUSTRALIA

IF ONE REGARDS New South Wales as the birthplace of Australian wines, then South Australia must be considered the place where they came of age. Many of Australia's large wine firms, such as Penfolds, Hardy's, Hamilton's and Seppelt can trace their beginnings back to this region.

The state was established in 1836, and the main town of Adelaide was located on the banks of the River Torrens. The earliest vineyards were located near the town, but urban expansion long ago erased all trace of them, and, today, the area named Adelaide Metropolitan is now a mere token of its former glory, with only a handful of vines still remaining. Wineries located in the district have had to rely on grapes from other districts to maintain their operations for some years now.

To the south of Adelaide, in an area referred to variously as the Adelaide Plains, Southern Districts and Southern Vales, there is a very healthy wine-producing region. Until about ten years ago, the area was seen mainly as a source of big, full-bodied red wines and excellent Port-style wines, but its white wines are now beginning to gain recognition too. The Rhine Rieslings, including late-picked Rieslings, have been particularly noteworthy. Considerable new plantings have taken place in the past few years with Chardonnay, Pinot Noir and Merlot being introduced, while additional Cabernet Sauvignon vines have been established.

modern and sophisticated techniques and are now producing some excellent wines from classic grape varieties.

Penfolds is another major winery that began in the Griffith area in 1913 by planting cuttings of vines from their other Australian vineyards. The third large firm to locate in the area is Wynn, who began their operations near Yenda in 1959.

Mudgee, on the same latitude as the Hunter Valley, was subjected to considerable ridicule because of the clumsy heaviness of its red wines, but that perception began to change in the 1970s when there was an influx of new wine makers who brought in new ideas and techniques. In particular, the wines of Huntington Estate, Botobolar Vineyards and Montrose are notable.

Forbes/Cowra, in the central west of New South Wales, is a comparatively new area, but it is showing well. Of its white wines, the Chardonnays are particularly attractive, as are the Sauvignon Blancs. The area has also been planted with Rhine Riesling and Gewürztraminer for whites and Cabernet Sauvignon, Pinot Noir and Shiraz for reds. However, only the Chardonnay and Sauvignon Blanc have shown really well to date.

Corowa-Rutherglen is divided by the Murray River: part of the region lies in New South Wales and part in Victoria. The area has been best known for fortified wines, but there has been an

The district, which is centered around the village of McLaren Vale, now has almost fifty wineries, including two of particular historical interest, Thomas Hardy and Reynella.

John Reynell arrived in South Australia in 1838 and established a mixed farm which included some vines that he had brought from South Africa. In 1845, he bought additional vines from John Macarthur in New South Wales and expanded his vineyards. In the same year he also dug the Cave Cellar, which is now the oldest underground cellar still in use in the entire country. On his father's death, Walter Reynell took over and continued to expand the business. The line of heredity was broken because of deaths in the two World Wars, and the firm came under the direction of Ian Thomas, a grandson of Walter's sister. The firm was then taken over by Hungerford Hill in 1970. Reynella has extensive plantings of Cabernet Sauvignon which are used to produce a single wine in good years. In other years, these grapes are used in blends with Shiraz and Grenache to make generic red wines.

Thomas Hardy came to the Adelaide area first in 1850, but soon took off for the Victoria gold fields, returning to Adelaide in 1853. He bought a property on the River Torrens which he called Bankside and, having cleared the land, began planting vines. Hardy expanded rapidly and in 1859 sent two hogsheads of wine to England — the largest amount of Australian wine exported to that time. In 1876 he purchased the bankrupt Tintara vineyard at McLaren Vale. Hardy recovered his investment almost at once through the sale of Tintara's existing wine stock. By the time of his death in 1912, Hardy had built an extensive business which was passed on to his only living son Robert, who continued to expand the firm by opening wineries in other areas. Now under the leadership of the fourth generation of Hardys, the firm continues to expand and produce the quality of wines that have kept their business growing for over 100 years.

The Barossa Valley, which was pioneered by German immigrants, is probably the best known Australian wine district. The hot, arid conditions found on the valley floor are often reflected in the intense, almost burnt flavor of the wines, although modern techniques and some very determined producers are causing a change in that situation.

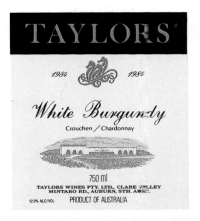

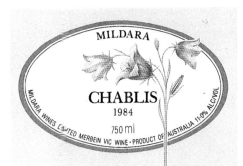

Aerial view of Lindemans Padthaway wine growing region. Lindemans own 600 hectares of vineyards, the largest single vineyard owned by any one company in Australia.

Although it has never had a reputation as a premium wine district like the Hunter Valley or Coonawarra, the Barossa Valley has produced some very good wines, particularly with the Rhine Riesling.

Created out of the necessity for economic survival during the Depression, the Barossa Cooperative Winery came into existence in 1931 when it was formed by a group of growers, and was named the South Australian Grape Growers Cooperative. The chief market they developed was Britain, but the Second World War cut off that trade. The cooperative survived mainly by selling their wines in bulk to other producers. In 1966, the company adopted its present name, but eight years prior to that, they made one of the most telling changes when they developed their own label, Kaiser-Stuhl, which quickly gained public acceptance and acclaim. Beginning in 1958 also, the cooperative decided to market wines from individual estates, allowing many of the organization's 450 growers to retain a certain individuality to their wines, while retaining the advantage of marketing it under an already well-known name. Perhaps one of the most commendable aspects of the entire operation is that so many people have managed to function for so long in a truly cooperative venture.

Other notable wineries of long standing in the valley include Leo Buring, Orlando, Yalumba, Seppelt, Hamilton's, Hardy's and Penfolds.

Clare-Watervale, which is South Australia's most northerly wine district, lies almost directly north of Adelaide. The district has experienced a considerable image change in the past decade and a half. Prior to that time, the district's wines were purchased mainly by wineries from outside the area who wanted the deep, flavored wines for blending. But the district is now emerging as a premium wine producer in its own right. Much of the credit for this goes to the Stanley Wine Company and wine maker Tim Knappstein. Although the firm is now owned by H.J. Heinz (of 57 varieties fame), Knappstein is the grandson of one of the four men who founded the winery in 1894.

Lindemans Rouge Homme and vineyards, Coonawarra, South Australia.

When Heinz took over in 1971, Knappstein was retained. He began producing red and white wines of considerable distinction that were highly successful at wine shows. Knappstein now operates his own Enterprise Winery at Clare, and continues to make wines of a very high standard.

Coonawarra-Padthaway is a tiny district in the southeast corner of South Australia. It has earned a gigantic reputation for producing some of the finest wines in the country, many of which can stand in the same company as the best wines from anywhere in the world. Coonawarra was the first part of the district to be developed. The countryside is very flat but has red and black limestone-based soil and a high underground water table that provides excellent growing conditions for the vines. Being as far south as it is, Coonawarra's climate is quite cool, thus allowing the grapes to ripen slowly. The harvest at Coonawarra often does not begin until April, whereas picking begins in the Barossa Valley around mid-February. The area is not without

hazards, however; frost is a very real danger, and can cause substantial losses. Likewise, in very cool years the grapes do not ripen fully, and the wines are of a lower quality. The vintage year is really significant on Coonawarra wines. The three classic grapes making the district's best wines are the Cabernet Sauvignon, the Chardonnay and Rhine Riesling.

The district has really come into prominence because of the Wynn family of Victoria who took over an existing vineyard in 1951 and began working to improve the business. The Cabernet Sauvignon from Wynn's Coonawarra Estate attracted a lot of favorable attention. Several major wine-making firms have now located in the area, and in the search for more land have moved slightly north to the plant at Padthaway. Hardy's, Lindemans, Seppelt, Penfolds, Mildara and Hungerford Hill have all joined Wynn's in the district, which also has a number of smaller growers.

Langhorne Creek is a small district to the south

of Adelaide. It took its place in the sun during the 1960s and 1970s when Wolf Blass of the Barossa Valley used some of the district's wines in his highly acclaimed cellar blends. The two wineries located there, Bleasdale and Metala, grow Cabernet Sauvignon, Malbec, Shiraz and Verdelho. The area's main strength is its red wines, which are dry and full-flavored.

Riverland, to the northeast of Adelaide, is the biggest single wine-producing area in Australia, and accounts for almost 40 per cent of the country's grape production. The main thrust of the district has been directed toward the jug wine and bag-in-a-box trade, but some efforts have been made to upgrade the image of the area's wines. They have had some success with their Cabernet Sauvigon and Cabernet Sauvignon blends in the reds and with Rhine Riesling, Chenin Blanc, Sauvignon Blanc and Chardonnay for whites. The majority of their wines, however, will most likely continue to serve their traditional markets.

WESTERN AUSTRALIA

THE WINE industry in Western Australia has undergone some considerable expansion in recent years, and the technology used at the wineries has been significantly upgraded.

The longest-established district in the area is Swan Valley near Perth. Its wines have been greatly refined. More premium vines have been introduced, and wine-making practices have also been modernized. The reds, in particular, have retained their former great depth of fruit, but they now have greater finesse. The Shiraz is especially rich in character. Their Chenin Blanc and Verdelho whites have also shown impressively.

Margaret River and Mount Barker are two relatively new areas that have been planted with premium grape varieties. Their Cabernet Sauvignon and Rhine Riesling wines have been compared to California's for their depth of fruit and intensity of flavor. Both districts are still in comparatively early stages of development, but their progress to date is very promising.

Even more recently the South-West Coastal district and an area of the Darling Range have been planted, but it is too early to make any assessment of their potential.

QUEENSLAND

THE CLIMATE in this state is not particularly suitable for viticulture and as a result, very little wine is made there. In fact, there is only one family that has pursued wine making there for more than a hundred years. Samuel Basset cleared land near Roma in 1863 and established a vineyard which he eventually expanded to cover over 400 acres. He travelled all over Queensland selling his wines, which were made from Riesling, Solverino, Syrian, Portugal, Red, White and Black Muscats, Hermitage and Mataro. None of the wines are particularly distinguished.

There is a group of about 30 wine makers clustered around Stanhope to the southwest of Brisbane; however, they are mostly people of Italian descent who make wine in their own traditional ways for their own consumption as well as that of friends and neighbors.

VICTORIA

THE AREA of Rutherglen and North East has a high reputation for fortified wines more so than table wines. A considerable effort has been made to try to change that situation, but the district continues to do best with its fortified wines, which can be very good indeed.

To the south of Rutherglen in the twinned district of Glenrowan-Milawa the story is completely different. Glenrowan reds, made with such varieties as Cabernet Sauvignon, have a great depth of character and style, while the wines of Milawa have good varietal character without the heavier weight

Above: *Hardy's old winery building at Houghton, in the Swan Valley, just west of Western Australia's capital city, Perth. The Houghton property was begun in 1836, and is now the largest producer in the state.*

Below: *Aerial view of Lindemans Karadoc Winery, Mildura, north-western Victoria, the largest winery in Australia.*

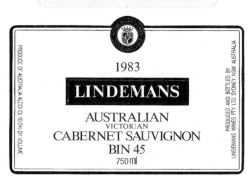

of their neighbor's wines. Glenrowan has not placed much emphasis on whites, but Milawa has done some impressive things with Chardonnay, Sémillon and Chenin Blanc.

Château Tahbilk was for many years the only winery in Goulburn Valley, but now it has the company of almost ten other wineries. Established in 1860, Tahbilk has been thoroughly modernized in recent years and is beginning to show what can really be done in the area with such grapes as Cabernet Sauvignon and Shiraz, which have been its strength in the past. The two largest newcomers, Mitchelton and Tisdall's, have produced some very creditable reds, but they have also done well with whites, especially the Rhine Riesling, which has made some extremely attractive wines.

The Yarra Valley, to the northeast of Melbourne, is an old area that is making a comeback. It was an important district until the latter part of the nineteenth century, when phylloxera wiped out the vineyards. It is now home for a number of boutique wineries who are using only premium grapes. To date several of the reds made with Cabernet Sauvignon, Shiraz and Pinot Noir exhibit excellent fruit and considerable complexity. Chardonnay and Rhine Riesling grapes are also showing very good varietal style.

Swan Valley, located on the Murray River, depends heavily on irrigation to produce a good crop. The area is primarily in the bulk wine business, although a number of wineries have produced some perfectly pleasant premium varietals, but they cannot achieve the weight or style that is possible in more favored districts.

Mildura is another River Murray irrigated district that built its reputation on fortified wines and brandies. In recent years, however, a greater emphasis has been placed on the production of white table wines for the bulk wine trade; some of the big wineries from other areas are finding these everyday wines very useful in meeting the demand for white wines. One of the district's best-known firms is Mildara, which continues to have a very good reputation for its Sherry-type wines.

Geelong and Districts, to the east of Melbourne, is another region that is going through a revival, although it has been going longer than Yarra. Like Yarra, however it is the domain of boutique wineries. The classic viniferas are grown for both red and white wines, both of which are showing excellent style and varietal character. The weather can, however, play havoc with the vines, so that there can be a considerable variation in quality from vintage to vintage.

Great Western became singularly linked with Seppelt, by far the district's biggest winery, because of the success of the firm's sparkling wines, sold under the Great Western label. The district's other main winery is Bests, a small operation that has placed its emphasis on the production of premium red wines in particular. Being in an arid area, they have had more than their share of setbacks, but in more recent years they have also had their share of successes.

Avoca, to the northwest of Great Western, has the considerable advantage of being a frost-free district. It has been developed over the past twenty years, with the first arrival being Château Remy, set up in cooperation with Remy Martin of France. The initial idea was to produce brandy, and 200 acres of vines were planted. Three-quarters of the vines were White Hermitage, and the balance were Doradillo. In practice, however, as a shift in consumer preference was perceived, half of the wine produced was used as the basis for sparkling wines.

Since that time several smaller vineyards have been established, and some very elegant red and white wines are being produced with premium grapes. .

TASMANIA

I T IS ONLY in the past twenty years that there has been renewed interest in establishing wineries on the island state of Tasmania. A significant point to be borne in mind about Tasmania is that it is so far south of the equator that its temperatures are lower than those of most European vineyards and, consequently, the ripening of the grapes is also slower. Nevertheless, the classic Cabernet Sauvignon and Pinot Noir for reds and Rhine Riesling and Chardonnay for whites are prospering. One of the pioneers, Claudio Alcorso, who carried out his main planting at his Moorilla Estate near Hobart in 1966, produced a Pinot Noir

in 1975 that augurs well for the future of Tasmania. There are several small vineyards of between five and ten acres being planted, and it is confidently anticipated that some outstanding wines will be produced.

NEW ZEALAND

T HE WINE INDUSTRY of New Zealand has a rather checkered history. The first vines were planted by a missionary in the early nineteenth century. There was a modest growth until around 1908, when Prohibitionist activity upset the market completely, and many vineyards were ripped out and replaced with other crops.

The grape growers petitioned the government for greater support and limits on imports. The First World War, however, threw the industry into another hiatus because of lack of labor and a continuing Prohibitionist force.

Conversely, the Second World War gave the industry an enormous boost. Vines, not always the most suitable for wine making, were planted with a vengeance, and dozens of small operators began producing wines to slake the thirst of the home market and that of American servicemen. But quantity did not equal quality. In 1946 evidence presented to a Royal Commission stated that in most wine-producing countries, many New Zealand wines would be considered unfit for human consumption. Needless to say, the Royal Commission, in common with most such bodies around the world, took no action.

Peculiarly, the introduction of even more severe import restrictions proved to be the salvation of the industry. Many Australian firms had been exporting a considerable amount of wine to New Zealand, and observing that their market was vanishing, they bought into existing vineyards. Such large operations as Penfolds, Seppelt and McWilliam's established themselves in New Zealand bases. But the greatest benefit of this move was that they also introduced modern techniques in the vineyards as well as the wineries. On

this foundation of imported talent a considerable portion of the country's present wine industry has been built. This is not to impute that there were no people making good wines previously, but the change of direction did discourage the incompetent from continuing.

The vineyards are planted with a combination of the classic vinifera varieties, including those for the production of fortified wines, and French-American hybrids. The total area now under vines is in excess of 3,000 acres.

There are seven wine-growing regions in the country, with six of those being on the North Island. The Northland district is, as one might expect, the most northerly region, and is located around Warkworth. Moving south, the next region is Auckland, which is the largest of the country's districts.

Waikato, located between Auckland and Hamilton, is the next district. Gisborne and Hawkes Bay are two regions that occupy land on the island's east coastal areas, while Manawatu-Wellington is on the southwest tip of the North Island. The South Island's only wine region is located around Nelson at the northern part of the island.

New Zealand is now producing some very good wines and the quality, along with the quantity, have finally earned the country a sound international reputation.

Opposite New Zealand vineyard seems to stretch into an endless, golden horizon.

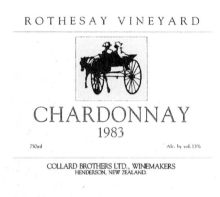

INDEX

Cave champenoise, France.

BIBLIOGRAPHY

Amiel, Roger et al. *Les Grands Vins de Bordeaux*. Bordeaux: Dussaut, 1978.

Bespaloff, Alexis. *The Fireside Book of Wine*. New York: Simon and Schuster, 1977.

Camarena, José Ferrer et al. *Anuario del Vino Español*. Valencia: SUCRO, S.A., 1984.

Debuigne, Doctor Gérard. *Larousse Dictionary of Wines of the World*. New York: Larousse and Co. Inc., 1976.

Evans, Len. *Australia and New Zealand Complete Book of Wine*. Dee High West, NSW: Paul Hamlyn, 1973.

German Wine Atlas and Vineyard Register. Mainz: Stabilisierungsfond für Wein, 1977.

Jamieson, Ian. *The Mitchell Beazley Pocket Guide to German Wines*. London: Mitchell Beazley, 1984

Penning-Rowsell, Edmund. *The Wines of Bordeaux*. New York: Stein and Day, 1972.

Poupon, Pierre and Forgeot, Pierre. *The Wines of Burgundy*. Paris: Presses Universitaires de France, 1979.

Quimme, Peter. *American Wine*. New York: Signet Books, 1980.

Ray, Cyril. *The New Book of Italian Wines*. London: Sidgwick & Jackson, 1982.

Torres, Miguel A. *The Wines and Vineyards of Spain*. Barcelona: Blume, 1982.

PHOTOGRAPHIC CREDITS

Almadén National Distillers, São Paulo 16–17, 24, 258, 259, 261

Barnes Wines Ltd., St. Catharines 242, 243

British Information Services 210

Calona Wines Ltd., Kelowna 22–23, 246–247, 248

Jose Canepa y Cia. Ltda., Santiago 253 *below*

Chris Bennion 237

Commercial Office of Spain, Toronto 1, 5, 6, 168, 169, 172, 173, 174, 180–181

Kennon Cooke 151, 154, 155, 160, 163

Deinhard & Co., Koblenz 124

Galilee Wines, Toronto 197, 198

German Wine Information Service, Toronto 120, 122, 125, 126, 129, 132, 133, 135, 137, 138, 140

Greek Exports Promotion Organization, Athens 194

Hardy's Australian Wines 19, 271 *above*

Hungarovin, Budapest 187, 188, 189

Inniskillin Wines, Niagara-on-the-Lake 240

Koöperatieve Wijnbouwers Vereniging, S.A. 200, 201, 202, 204, 205

Lindeman (Holdings) Ltd., N.S.W. 265, 268, 269, 271 *below*

D. McCormack 41, 46, 47, 58, 59, 60, 73, 76, 87, 90, 92, 136

McWilliam's Wines Pty. Ltd., N.S.W. 266

Miller Services 71 (*Prazak*) 142 (*Messerschmidt*), 148 (*Cignovic*), 152 (*Camerique*), 157 (*Lattes*), 158–159, 161 (*Straiton*), 166 (*Otto*)

Montana Wines Ltd., N.Z. 274

Portuguese Government Trade Office, Toronto 8, 15, 25, 176, 178, 179, 180–181

St. George's English Wines, E. Sussex 209

B. Seppelt & Sons Ltd., S. Australia 7, 270, 271

Sopexa Canada Ltd., Toronto cover 12, 20, 21, 26, 28, 32, 33, 36, 37, 39, 42–43, 48, 51, 52–53, 54, 56, 57, 64, 65, 68, 69, 70, 74, 77, 78, 79, 81, 82, 83, 88–89, 92, 93, 95, 97 (*Promo Champagne, France*), 98–99 (*Promo Champagne, France*), 101, 103, 104–105, 107, 108, 109, 110, 112, 114, 115, 117, 118, 276 (*Promo Champagne, France*)

Taylor Wine Company, Inc. 212, 230, 231, 232, 233

Trade Representation of the USSR in Canada, 193

Viña Concha y Toro, S.A., Santiago 14, 250, 251, 254–255, 257

Viña San Pedro, S.A., Santiago 253 *above*

Wine Institute, San Francisco 11, 216, 217, 220–221, 222, 223, 224, 225, 227, 228, 229

Wine Institute, Vienna 184, 186–187

Wootton Vineyards, Somerset 206

Wyndham Estate Wines, N.S.W. 262